Lust,
for life

For Jean

With my very best Wishes

James D. Hadfield-Hyde

Lust,
for life

Diaries, journals and confessions of an epicurean

James Hadfield-Hyde

Bernini Publishing

First published in the United Kingdom in 2012 by
Bernini Publishing

ISBN 978–0–9572770–0–7

Produced by
The Choir Press, Gloucester

Contents

Contents

Contents

Contents

Author's note: For those unfamiliar with the British system of
honours, the BEM is the British Empire Medal. A CBE is Commander
of the Order of the British Empire; OBE an Officer of the Order of
the British Empire; and MBE a Member of the Order of the British
Empire.

Acknowledgements

To my dear friend, Ruth Waterfield, who has had to put up with me over the past ten months of writing, and whose invaluable contribution to the editorial content is so greatly appreciated. Mike and Lynn Healing have endured my barrage of questions, due to my lack of computer literacy, and have helped me with both words and photography. I sincerely thank them all for their patience and encouragement.

Dedication

I dedicate this book to my two uncles, James and Patrick, who gave their young lives for our country shortly before I began mine.

In the beginning

I'm sure most of us can remember our very first major event of life, whether it be falling out of the pram or coming face to face with the family pet. Mine was standing with my back to the fire and watching my mother and father in ferocious verbal conflict. I can clearly remember the distress of it and hearing my mother say, "Now look what you've done, you've made the baby cry." It was 1951, I was two. My father walked out and I was to have an almost passive relationship with him for the rest of my life. If ever there were two people destined for incompatibility, it was my mother and father. I suppose you have to look at the time and the circumstances.

My father had nothing to be ashamed of; he was handsome and tanned, a cross between Errol Flynn and Clarke Gable. He was a truly superb pianist with a propensity toward jazz, women, and the Big Band sound. I remember years later attending a jam session with him, Syd Lawrence and his other friend Bob Turner of the BBC Northern Dance Orchestra. Syd Lawrence asked my father to do recordings with him but he was totally disinterested. During his time in the forces he met Louis Armstrong, who was entertaining the American troops. Louis offered him a job in America as one of his pianists after he was demobbed, but when the time came he couldn't be bothered. My mother deplored his lack of ambition. His other great talent was art and for some time he worked as a poster designer, painter and sign writer. He had returned to England from India after being stationed there up until 1947. War had left a profusion of eligible young women and a shortage of young men.

On the day my father was due to go to war he was cruelly told by his mother that he was not her son. His real mother, Sylvia, had died in childbirth giving birth to him; she also had been an accomplished pianist and a beauty queen. His birth name was Anthony Kenneth Curran. I remember him telling me that he felt such overwhelming despair, as he boarded the troopship that day, that he hoped he would be killed in action. When my mother and he got together she was determined to reunite him with his real family but as was his trait he was not overly enthused. Unbeknown to him she made contact with his older brother, Tredennis, or Den as he was known. He owned a poultry and fish business in Manchester. My mother said she was amazed at the visual similarity between the brothers and that Den's wife Alice was the most beautiful young woman she had ever seen. Den and Alice went on to have five equally beautiful daughters – Mo, Suzie, Ruth, Val and Jane – but my uncle Den always wanted a son. Den spent the war years flying Lancaster and Wellington bombers; by the time he was made an officer he had received the DFM (Distinguished Flying Medal) for acts of extreme bravery under heavy enemy fire.

My grandfather, Edward Curran, had died only a year before the meeting between his two sons. In the earliest years of the twentieth century Edward had a penchant for the arts and acting. He was part of a touring dance group along with his then friend, Charlie Chaplin, called "Eight Lancashire Lads", not that they were all from Lancashire; Charlie was a London boy. My great-aunt remembered when Charlie would occasionally stay with them at their house in Manchester and he and my grandfather would entertain the family and practise their tap-dancing on the stone hearth in front of the fire. Their other mutual friend was Stan Laurel. In those early days before Hollywood conquered the world's film industry, there were numerous small motion picture companies being set up in England and Europe, one of which was the Manchester Film Company. Edward Curran appeared in silent movies of the time and I often wondered why he didn't go to America with Charlie and Stan when he had the opportunity. It was only many years later that I found out the reason. My grandfather was starring as Jack Shepherd in a silent film called *Jack Shepherd the Prison Breaker* and during filming he had to ride a horse and be thrown into a pond. After numerous takes, he got a fever and nearly died from pneumonia. By the time he recovered, Charlie and Stan had gone to California. Edward decided he no longer wanted to have anything to do with the film industry and the rest is down to history.

As a small boy, my uncle Tredennis remembered going to the cinema with my grandfather. When the film began, he jumped up on the seat and shouted out loud, "Look, that's my daddy, that's my daddy!" As the years rolled by they all continued to keep in touch and when Stan Laurel and Oliver Hardy came to Britain on tour they called to see Edward. My aunt Dorothy remembers as a little girl sitting on "the fat one's knee" in their front parlour. By this time Edward Curran was long established with his poultry and fish business on Alexandra Road between Whalley Range and Moss Side. He had married again to a woman called Molly, an alcoholic, and they had three daughters. Edward died in 1948 leaving £26,000 in the bank and a thriving business. His hard-working son, Tredennis, was forced to buy his father's business, where he had worked from being a small boy, from the "wicked stepmother". She took the money and the three girls to Australia, but not before destroying Edward's collection of reel copies of his films, theatre posters and photographs of Charlie, Stan, him and the Lancashire Lads. I can't help feeling anger at such a deed, not only from a family interest point of view, but as a small but important contribution to Manchester's social history.

My mother came from a long line of farmers. They were Irish, Catholic and prolific. My grandfather, Patrick Hughes, had two farms and eight children; three boys and five girls. They leased out their farms in 1937 before moving over to make a new life in England. Not many years after arriving, the two eldest boys gave their lives for King and Country in the Second World War. James was a gunner, guarding a Polish ship called *Lwow* and lost his life at the bombing of Bari Harbour in Italy on December 2nd 1943. Patrick junior was a soldier and was hit by a mortar bomb while taking some German prisoners back to camp on March 2nd 1945. Both he and the prisoners lost their lives. The names of James and Patrick can be seen on the cenotaph outside the Town Hall at Sale in Cheshire (now part of Greater Manchester).

The remaining children in order of age were Mary, Margaret (my mother), Betty, Andolores, John and Philomena. Sale in those days was highly gentrified with some of the grandest real estate outside of London. The intrusion of an Irish family into the town was not met with rapturous applause by the local snobbery. Nonetheless, the family purchased a six-bedroom house called "Willoughby" on a private unadopted road. It was far too vulgar to have numbers attached to the property there. Objection was such that two old spinsters who lived opposite, and were distant cousins of the King, got a petition together to prevent such contamination, and so for good measure my grandfather purchased the other six-bedroom house next door as well; he realised the potential of the rental market and that property could give you income and capital appreciation. I remember as a boy my grandfather saying to me, "Property makes you rich while you sleep in your bed: buy lots of it." Those wise words have since stood three further generations of his offspring in good stead; all have become millionaires.

While continuing to build a substantial property portfolio, the family still received income from the tenant farmers on their farms in Ireland which they didn't sell until 1951. In addition to that, periodically my grandfather would go over to America to make further monies and send it back to my grandmother. She was the engine of the establishment, a wise and rotund strict disciplinarian of a woman. My mother, who was named after her, inherited her appreciation of the value of money and her acute business acumen.

Each of my grandfather's children received a house as a wedding present, and some received more. Mary, for example, believing she would never marry and remain an old maid as my grandmother once said, received three: one called "Lillybank" and two cottages. My grandfather wanted to buy her two shops on King Street in Knutsford but she didn't want them. She did however eventually get married at the grand old age of twenty-eight, to Bill Flatley. From the start he was riddled with jealousy and insecurity at the family wealth, and the fact that she was financially independent from him. After suffering incessant bickering she secretly gave the cottages away to her brother, John. When Bill found out he was mortified. He made poor Mary's life even more of a hell after that. All of the sisters and John went on to marry, prosper enormously and multiply. Throughout history all families endure a concatenation of undulating fortune; my mother's family was on the up!

After my father's exit from the marital home, Mother and I returned to Willoughby where I enjoyed the very earliest years of my life with her, my grandparents, John and the sisters. At kindergarten I received extra tuition for my reading from Miss Nelson. I adored her; although only young she had snow-white hair tied neatly in a bun at the back. She had been engaged to a Spitfire pilot who had been shot down and she remained "Miss" for the rest of her life. There at St. Joseph's I met my first love – I was five and she was six. Her name was Celeste Shosi: she was an American girl with long dark hair and the most beautiful olive skin. When she smiled her two front teeth were missing, which I found incredibly attractive at the time. On the staircase to an upper classroom I kissed her full on the lips and she vowed never to tell anyone. She was the first woman to betray me, the first of many. At playtime the playground resounded to the chants of "James kissed Celeste Shosi, James kissed Celeste Shosi." I was horrified. I was never to go through that stage that most boys go through of hating girls, I loved them from day one.

1957–1958

Big School • Winning my spurs • Alton traditions

The time came, at the age of seven, when I was to attend Big School! The key to upward mobility in England is undoubtedly boarding school and although I was oblivious of the fact, that is exactly what my mother had in mind for me. I was to be, quite rightly, schooled as an English gentleman.

The glorious thing about the English class system is that the nobility and upper classes have never been shy about marrying into the lower classes, providing there is sufficient pecuniary advantage and that the money is one or two generations old.

My big day was nigh. My uncle John, my mother and I took the steam train and arrived at the sleepy village of Alton in North Staffordshire. I distinctly remember being enveloped in smoke as the train chugged away under the bridge and on down the Churnet Valley. As the air cleared, I stood on the platform holding my mother's hand and I got my first glimpse of what was going to mould my life entirely – Alton Castle. Perched high on the cliff edge was this great Germanic grey stone monstrosity. Built in the early nineteenth century by the Talbots, Earls of Shrewsbury who commissioned Pugin to build it in the Rhineland style, it resembled Colditz. The road leading up to the castle seemed almost vertical and we stopped at regular intervals for John to catch his breath as he struggled with my suitcase. My mother had commandeered it from my grandparents. Covered in Cunard stickers, it was a testament to their many trips across to New York by ship.

The uniform was similar to that of Eton, with very large highly starched collars and black bow ties. Junior boys were subjected to wearing short trousers. All things in the school had remained completely unchanged from mid-Victorian times, including some of the staff, which included nuns, layman masters and the occasional priest.

Upon our arrival and after formal introductions, a boy called Potts was assigned to show me to my dorm and give me a set of rules. The first one was that no boy was ever referred to by his first name. Single last names, double-barrelled names or nicknames were acceptable. For example Hawksworth was Hawkeye and Dowker-Parker remained so. I went through my entire school years there without ever knowing the first names of even my closest of friends.

I returned to the main entrance to the castle where my mother and John were waiting to say goodbye. As I watched them walk away across the moat bridge, it was the loneliest moment of my life, then or since, but I refused to let them see me cry. With my hand raised I saw my mother turn and smile; a final wave and they were gone. I know my mother loved and adored me but this was now the time for her to fulfil a lifelong dream of her own, to make a new life for herself in America. She eventually arrived in New York in May of 1958. She tells me that she always intended to send for me the minute she got established, but life doesn't always go to plan, and it would be two years before I saw her again.

The following morning I was introduced to my first harsh lesson in boarding school discipline. I was put into Piggy Pugh's dorm. He was fat and ugly with a sadistic streak and looked incredibly like Billy Bunter. He was also the school Head Boy. Having never slept in a room with seven other people before I found the stuffiness and over-bearing smell of sweaty socks and feet intolerable. I remember getting out of bed and heading over to the huge cast-iron-framed Gothic window in a vain attempt to open it. From beneath the sheets of the bed nearest to the window came Pugh's aristocratic voice, "And what the bloody hell do you think you're doing, new boy?" No sooner had he spoken when in walked a member of staff, a nun, whose name escapes me. "This new boy went to open the window without permission," said Pugh. The nun then proceeded to slap me about the head and face, and I remember my ear was red and throbbing. No act in the dormitory was permitted without the permission of the Dorm Prefect. Prefects had the power to administer discipline in the form of punishment by beating with a slipper, with a maximum sentence of six of the best. For even the smallest of misdemeanours you could find yourself being called over accompanied by your own slipper. Crying at night of homesickness and disturbing other boys' sleep was usually two strokes. A badly made bed or unfolded clothes, four strokes. Answering the Prefect back or refusing an order, definitely six strokes.

Later that day, I was down in the locker room with a few other new boys when a group of older ones came in. One of them grabbed me by the neck and put his knee in my back, forcing me to the ground where he then proceeded to twist my already sore ear. This was great sport to the bigger boys and they all laughed and cheered. When he eventually let me go I jumped up, pulled at his Eton collar, the stud popped and his bow tie flew across the room. I then bit him on the wrist and kicked him several times on the shin. I think he was so utterly shocked at my ferocious retaliatory action that he retreated, "allegretto". I had expected him and his chums to give me the beating of my life but they all shuffled off muttering things like "Aggressive little bastard." I was from Celtic stock and no toffee-nosed chinless wonder was going to get the better of me, no matter how big he was. At that moment I had won the admiration of my peers and the respect of my elders; I had won my spurs!

That one piece of action was to set a precedent for things to come. It guaranteed that I would never be singled out to be a Fag. Fagging was a long-standing tradition throughout the entire English public school system. Junior boys were chosen to be the personal butler/manservant/slave to the Prefects and some of the older boys. If you were picked, like any slave, there was no escape. On occasion, as in ancient Rome, you could win your freedom. Scoring all the goals at a junior interschool match might do it. You were usually only a Fag for a year or so because by the time the older boys were eligible to have their own Fags they left not long afterwards. Then everyone moved up and there was a whole new fresh bunch of unsuspecting rookies billeted in.

In those days Alton Castle was run in the true Dickensian manner of traditional English boarding schools with all the rituals, rules and regulations. Throughout the castle the bare wooden floors were polished once a week by our two resident housemaids – "Katie Crackpot" and "Mary the Maid". Katie and Mary had the combined IQ of an ostrich and were tortured mercilessly by the boys. Tins filled with marbles balanced precariously on top of a door ajar would bring great mirth to a group of boys hiding further down the corridor and out of reach of Katie's broom handle. The clatter of the tin and the cursing and swearing of Katie as she slipped and slid on the marbles never failed to amuse us and she fell for it every time. Another one was to knock a small hole in the bottom of Mary's metal mop bucket. Through it all we all loved them dearly and I believe they were both there until the day they died.

Twice weekly, on Wednesdays and Saturdays, the Tuck Shop was opened, where we were allowed to purchase one shilling's worth (5p in decimal currency) of sweets. There was a comprehensive selection in the shop, including halfpenny chews, liquorice and gobstoppers but chewing gum or bubblegum were strictly forbidden. That had to be smuggled in at the beginning of term or on a parent's visiting day. If you didn't share that with the Dorm Prefect then that could warrant as much as four strokes. No money was exchanged as the Tuck Shop allowance had been pre-paid by our parents. Sweets were used as currency amongst the younger boys for comics and collectable cards, but the older boys had their own system of bartering for cigarettes and porno books.

Smoking was always conducted at the top of the unfinished tower of the castle, but that was strictly out of bounds to younger boys. When you were allowed into the inner sanctum of the unfinished tower you knew you had made it to the seat of power.

Most of the dorms had their own removable floorboard which even Katie or Mary knew nothing of, or so we believed. All kinds of contraband was stored there and you had to keep a sharp eye out for marauding raiders from other dorms.

Uniform dress code was extremely strict at Alton, especially when travelling at the beginning of term or the end. As we were often told, "Remember boys, you are ambassadors for your school, behave as such." Many boys, myself included, would get the steam train. In my case I would board at Alton, change at Macclesfield or Stoke and terminate at London Road (now called Piccadilly Station). Trains had small individual compartments with two long facing seats, and above them were sepia-coloured photographs in brass frames of national places of interest: Torquay, the Lake District and the like. Just below the ceiling were long brass-rail luggage racks with string netting rather like a hammock. These were wonderful to climb up into and lie in during the journey, smoking our cigarettes and discussing the highlights of the term. At each station it was imperative that all of us would hang out of the window in order to deter potential intruding passengers.

1959

Hyde's Army • The loss of a friend • Mary • Parental visits

It was September 1959, our first day back after the long summer holiday. Lowe arrived at school sporting a new hairstyle, Brylcreemed at the sides with a stubble brush cut on the top and what was known as a DA neck, which stood for Duck's Arse. These were the days of the Teddy Boys and skiffle groups. He wore his full school uniform with Eton collar and bow tie accompanied by bright pink fluorescent socks and winkle picker shoes. His feet hardly touched school property when he was frogmarched to the school Head. The barber in the village was summoned to the castle immediately and Lowe returned to the ranks with short-back-and-sides, regulation socks and black brogues.

On rare occasions, a serious act of school criminality warranted a public flogging on the stage at morning assembly. I distinctly remember one such occasion happening to me. A boy called Mantel and myself were resident in "Pink Dorm", which was up on the battlements of the castle, and usually out of limits for a staff inspection. We were in the midst of a major pillow fight. At the very second that Mantel's pillow ripped open, and duck-down feathers flew everywhere, in walked "Battleaxe Burke", our Latin teacher; we were instantly condemned to the maximum sentence.

The following morning, and with foresight, I placed a copy of the *Beano* comic down the inside of my underpants. The flogging was with a bamboo yard-stick. Bent over, and facing the school, I received my beating without a wince, while all the time smiling at my audience. By the fifth stroke, the bamboo stick began to split.

Poor Mantel was less prepared, and his yelping at every stroke did him no favours in the eyes of our peers. Later that day Mantel spent time in the toilets trying to get bamboo splinters out of his own backside. Today's wimpish society would be horrified at such brutality, but we just accepted it as character-building, part of the process of producing "military officer material".

I had not been too many years at Alton before I had taken complete control of the school. I did this by forming what was known as Hyde's Army. I had excelled in the boxing ring and had gathered a following of fans. I realised that by recruiting several of the other toughest and best sportsmen it would be simple to create a major following and it worked. My friend, Fuller, had formed a rival army but it wasn't too long before his men defected or were defeated. Fuller became my chief officer along with Mitchell, Fletcher and Hawkeye. My new status gave me two additional perks, my own Fag in the form of a boy called Hampshire, and total control of the smoking area in the unfinished tower. Our Sports Master, Mr. Owen, firmly believed that I would be one of the nation's great military leaders and Fuller and I were extremely keen to go on to Sandhurst Military College. At Alton we regularly had officers from Sandhurst coming to show us films and give talks to encourage enrolment. For many years later, Sister Philomena and Sister Carmel would remind me of how amazing Hyde's Army was. They also thought I would be a Churchillian leader but the only similarity between me and the great man is that we both loved art and were rubbish at Latin! As I've said before, life doesn't always go to plan.

We were playing football one day – in those days the playing field was some distance from the castle at farmer Weeldon's field overlooking the valley – when my chum Scottie complained of a pain in his back and decided to go and sit by the touchline for a few minutes. The following term Scottie didn't come back to school, then one day the Headmistress, Mother Malachy, came into our class. She had obviously been crying, Scottie had died. We abandoned lessons and the entire school filed into Chapel for prayers. It was beyond my comprehension that a close friend could die and I would never see him again. Dr. Scott requested that some of the boys from the choir come and sing at his son's funeral. As a member of the choir and a close friend I was one of the chosen few.

I remember a coach, a charabanc, or chara as we used to call them, arrived to take us up to Oldham in Lancashire. With no pomposity intended, at that time of my life I had never seen an industrial town before, and it was indeed grim. It seemed so utterly depressing as we drove through the town to the church, with row after row of terraced properties and cobbled streets. There was not a tree, not a flower, not a blade of grass, and no bird-song to hear. Thick dark grey smoke bellowed from every chimney as far as the eye could see and there was poverty, poverty everywhere.

I was blindly unaware that only two generations before me, some of my own ancestors were such people as these. Charlie Chaplin, Stan

Laurel and my grandfather were all born in such circumstances in the 1880s and 90s.

We were the subject of great curiosity upon our arrival, all looking like a young Mr. Pip or Tom Brown with our very peculiar way of speaking. The church was packed and it appeared as if the whole town had turned out. Dr. Scott was obviously a highly respected man. That day, never God's finest celestial choir nor an angel in heaven could have sung with more clarity, sweetness of voice or sincere feeling than that privileged group of boys. With tears streaming down our faces and surrounded outside by those "dark satanic mills" we sang "Jerusalem". As I write, it is over fifty years since that day but in my mind's eye, it was yesterday.

Back at the castle I had fallen for an unreciprocated love; her name was Mary. We had by this time changed our football field to Byatt's field over at the other side of the village, which meant that we returned via the village High Street. Mary was the daughter of the landlord of the White Hart Inn. She was the most beautiful creature I had ever seen. I would find any excuse to linger just to catch a glimpse of her. My bootlaces would always come undone on High Street or some of my studs would be missing and you would have to remove your boot and hobble back. In those days football boots were similar to brown army boots. We would have to buy a bag of studs which were a halfpenny each. Each little stud was made of layered leather and had three small nails. You would literally nail them to the sole of your boot. They only lasted a few weeks or they would just fall off, a ridiculous idea really. My infatuation with Mary was long- lasting and all-consuming but it got me nowhere.

The boys at Alton were only allowed one parental visit per term, but there were the occasional school events such as plays, concerts and garden parties which would include parents. In my case, with the absence of my father and the fact that my mother lived three thousand miles away, the Dowker-Parkers would sometimes most kindly include me in the visit to their son. I do however remember two occasions vividly. Mother and I would write to each other regularly, and much to my excitement she was going to be in England in time for the school garden party and teas on the castle lawn. It was a glorious sunny day and the parents and families rolled up, some with their chauffeurs. It was all white Panama hats and genteel conversation. I can't for the life of me remember why my grandfather was unable to drive her, but my mother got the steam train as far as Stoke. At that point the railway workers went on strike. In utter desperation to get there on time she wandered into a lorry driver's transport café to plead for a lift. There she met the driver of a large gravel lorry who was making a drop at Cheadle about five miles or so from Alton. On hearing her plight he detoured to the village and kindly offered to drop her in the castle grounds, but the embarrassment of that was too much for her. I was so thrilled to see her and she looked so wonderful. She arrived just in time for the cucumber sandwiches to be served. I never knew how she got home but to me on that day, it didn't matter.

I will never forget the one and only time my father came to the castle. I was in the school library one afternoon (which alarmingly contained an English copy of *Mein Kampf*, by Adolf Hitler), when a boy said there was a soldier down in the dry moat wanting to see me. I dismissed it as yet another practical joke but started to take it seriously when further boys confirmed it was true. As I descended the steep steps to the dry moat, there before me was indeed a soldier in full battle dress with leaves and branches sticking out of his helmet. It was my father.

I think that after the war he missed the camaraderie of military life and so joined the Territorial Army. His battalion had been doing manoeuvres in the hills near to the castle and he thought he would pop over and say hello. I was granted permission to go and take tea with him in Byatt's Café on the High Street. What a bizarre sight we must have been, me looking like Lord Ponsonby-Farquar-Smythe and him looking like he'd not known the war was over.

As yet another term drew to a close we all looked forward to the long summer holiday. Fletcher, whose father owned tea plantations in Ceylon, Donague, whose father had some company in Iraq or Persia and Law's family who had business interests in Borneo, were each getting ready for their long journey to see their parents. Each time boys would return from far-flung parts of the Empire, they would bring artefacts and tell wonderful tales. One boy brought a genuine shrunken head from Papua New Guinea. In those days there were still head hunters in those parts and we all examined it with great interest. I remember it had the lips sewn together with long hanging pieces of string. He knowledgeably explained how they did it by peeling the skin off the skull and filling the skin bag with hot sand to shrink it but retain the features. We were all terribly impressed. We thought we would try it by killing a rabbit and doing the same. We did manage to kill a rabbit and skin it, but we forgot to salt it and it quickly rotted in my sports locker, so the shrunken rabbit-head idea soon faded.

1960–63

New York • Final days at Alton • A new life
• High School • The gazelle

One summer, my mother, who I had not seen in over a year, asked me to fly out and join her in New York. It was to be my great adventure and I was so looking forward to seeing her again. In those days before package tours, long-distance travel was the reserve of the wealthy few. Most people had their holidays in local resorts like Blackpool or Scarborough and the idea of a young boy travelling alone to New York was almost unheard of. The morning of my great adventure arrived. My grandfather, who had recently treated himself to a brand new Vauxhall Victor De Luxe with leather seats, central column gear change plus radio, was ready to take me to the airport. He had always driven a 1938 Morris 8 which I believe he purchased from new. It was all so thrilling. A few minutes before leaving, my grandmother called me to one side.

With all the diplomatic skills of a charging rhinoceros she told me my parents were divorced and my mother had married a black man in America, which was totally untrue. I showed no emotion and walked to my grandfather's car. If you had ripped my stomach open with a chainsaw it wouldn't have hurt as much. Silly as it seems, I had no idea that my parents weren't together. I was always casually informed that my father was a businessman working in London. I don't know why I didn't add up that if that were so, why would my mother be in America? As a child you just blindly accept things. It didn't seem unnatural not to see your parents as most boys' parents were all over the world.

I boarded the brand new BOAC Boeing 707 and I got a window seat. I spent much of the journey crying as discreetly as possible while pretending to look out of the window. The elderly couple next to me slept for much of the journey. The plane got within sight of New York, but we were informed that we were unable to land due to bad weather. We circled for another hour in turbulent conditions, and it all got too much for me and I was violently sick.

I was greeted by my mother and Dr. Karuna Maitra, a tall, distinguished and charismatic man from one of the noblest families in India.

The second I saw him I recognised him. As a student at Manchester University he had been a tenant of ours. This was not the vision created by my grandmother but she obviously disapproved of my mother's relationship with him to be so vitriolic. The reason that I knew him was because I remember him bringing me a toy gun for my third birthday; you don't forget these things. Karuna was kind and charming and all was forgiven. It was a super holiday. After seeing the sights of New York and making a recording of myself at the top of the Empire State Building, we drove on to the town of Peekskill to meet up with relatives. There my cousin Frank took me up the Hudson River in his wonderful boat and we stopped off at West Point Military Academy. That was of great interest to me. I remember talking to soldiers and staff who were amazed at my knowledge of military history. Mother and I then flew on to Chicago to stay with my grandmother's brother, John. We were then subjected to the longest and most tedious journey I can remember to his farm in southern Illinois. Great-uncle John had accidentally killed his first wife in a road accident. He had been devastated by her death and in the small town of Newton he donated a sold gold tabernacle on the altar of the church and erected a large memorial statue in the grounds to her. Mother and I returned to Pittsford, New York and after a visit to Niagara Falls and a trip into Canada I returned to Alton with great tales of my own.

I returned to continue my education at Alton for another couple of years but the lure and excitement of America began to pull at my heartstrings. The prospect of Sandhurst and life as a military man began to fade. Eventually the long-awaited letter arrived. It was my mother asking me to come and live with her and Karuna: by return of post, the answer was 'Yes!'

Willoughby and life with my grandparents had been my only base and I would always feel a security in returning there. In growing up I had periodically gone over during school holidays to work and play on family-owned farms in Ireland. Although my grandfather had disposed of his own two farms there were still about another four farms in the family possession. I have so many wonderful memories of those times, but now a new life beckoned.

My mother and Karuna by this time had left New York and moved to Chelmsford in Massachusetts. 17 Shepherd Lane was a typical timber-framed American-style ranch house. It stood on a slight hill with the driveway sweeping around the side where the car would disappear into the garage in the basement; middle-class American

My paternal grandmother,
Sylvia Curran (neé Howsam)
in 1916.

My maternal grandparents
in 1919, Patrick and
Margaret Hughes.

top: My mother and father, 1948.

below: My father just after leaving my mother, seated on his Norton, 1951. Note the white silk scarf!

left: I arrive, 1949.

LETTING OF LAND

And Sale of Stock, Crop and Motor Car.

AUGHNAGON

We are instructed by Mr. Patrick Hughes to let by

PUBLIC AUCTION

ON THE LANDS

On Wednesday, 17th Feb., 1937

All his two farms in the above townland, for Cropping, Cutting and Grazing for the ensuing season.

Also to sell 2 Milch Cows, 3 Calves, useful Mare and Horse, both good workers; 3 Goats, 9 doz. laying fowl, Hay, Straw, Corn Seed, Potatoes in Pits and a Morris Saloon Motor Car in PMO.

Terms; Cash and Auction Fees at Sale.

WHELAN & LAMBE, Auctioneers, Newry

My grandfather leases his farms and sells his remaining livestock, 1937.

Alton Castle, 1957.

Early days at Alton. Junior
boys wore short trousers.
Note the dreaded Eton collar
and bow tie!

Mother begins her new life in America, May 1958.

Hyde's Army. Regimental drill improved considerably after this photo was taken.

At one of the family-owned farms in Ireland. My first kill!

suburbia. There were fields and woodlands to explore; it all looked good.

My enrolment at the High School was a serious culture shock. Firstly I had never been in the company of so many stunningly beautiful fully formed girls before, with breasts the size of grapefruits. Secondly, I had never encountered such a total disregard for discipline or a complete lack of respect for teachers and staff. This sloppy, slovenly informality was totally alien to me. Nobody ever stood to attention when a teacher or guest entered the room. Boys would sit during the entire lesson with their feet on the desk and call the teacher "Bob". There was no uniform and everyone without exception chewed gum. I hadn't come to a different country, I had landed on a different planet.

I enjoyed great popularity and novelty value to the girls of Chelmsford who found my accent irresistible. I was perpetually hearing reference to, "Oh my Gawd, he's so cute." At the time I was flattered. I was physically considerably less mature than virtually all the American boys in my class. I was at that stage in a young chap's life where you check each morning in the bathroom to see whether another hair has sprouted on your chin or moustache. My classmates were all six feet tall and over, with full beards and hairy chests and they all weighed over 200lbs of muscle. I was five feet five inches, weighing in at eight stone (112lbs) when wet. The difference really manifested itself in the shower room after games. These fellows had equipment which was the size of two Spanish onions and a cucumber. Mine looked like two grapes and a chipolata. My weight and size went completely against me on the American football field but as luck would have it they had only just introduced soccer into the school sports curriculum. That's where I came into my own. At Alton in my last year, although I'd never made it to Head Boy, I had managed to make captain of both the football and cricket teams which was quite a rare accomplishment. I was in my element and these great hairy Neanderthals didn't know what had hit them. I was little, fast and had total mastery of the ball. I scored time after time, much to the rapturous joy of the Chelmsford girls and the cheerleaders. The Games Master had not quite got his head round the rules of the game, he'd never even heard of a throw-in, and so I became his advisor and soccer mentor.

At the other end of Shepherd Lane lived a girl sent by God to torment me. She looked and walked with the beauty and grace of a gazelle grazing. Her doe eyes never met mine, no matter how hard I tried to catch a glimpse or a smile. Every time I saw her sitting on the fence outside her house she was always holding court with several of the Spanish onion and cucumber brigade. She looked seventeen but I was reliably informed by my dear friend Leo LaVoie, who lived a few doors away, that she was actually only thirteen. She was magnificent. Months passed during which, like a cat staring at a jug of fresh cream, I was allowed no closer. I eventually dismissed the idea of ever holding her in my arms as an unfulfilled fantasy, a dream not to be, so I availed myself to date Janice Henry instead. As the term drew to a close, exams were over and before the long summer break the words on everybody's lips were "Who are you going to take to the High School Prom?" I am now light years away from Eton collars and midnight feasts in the Norman-built kitchens of the castle. Part of the recreational curriculum at this school was barn-dancing, can you believe that? I consulted my chum Leo as to the protocol and he patiently spent the afternoon teaching me the very latest thing, The Twist. "They're bound to play it at the Prom, everyone is doing it," he advised. It was *Grease* and *Saturday Night Fever* and I was living it for real! Janice Henry informed me she was going to go with the lead scorer of the basketball team. He was six feet five and had his own car; big bloody deal!

I decided to ask Pam, a sweet rounded girl who had been born in England. Thanks to Leo, I followed the tradition by finding out the colour of her dress and with the assistance of my mother went to the florist to buy the appropriate corsage. I'll never forget the cascade of lemon flowers and white orchids. The night arrived and I was all suited up and ready to go. I was greeted at the door by Pam, who screamed and ran into the kitchen to show her mother the corsage which matched her dress so perfectly. The evening rang out with "Swing your partners and do-si-do" and then sure enough Chubby Checker and "Let's Twist Again Like we did Last Summer". Pam was returned intact to her doting parents and after a goodnight kiss all duties and obligations were complete. Sweet though she was, neither she nor it was really my cup of tea.

The summer began and my mother decided that rather than waste my time in the woods hunting and generally messing about, I should find gainful employment. I got a job as paper boy working for the *Boston Globe*. I think that without doubt I was the worst paper boy in the entire history of their employ. My casual approach to both delivering their newspapers and collecting their money was completely novel to them.

It was on such a night when I decided to go and collect some of the paper money that my life was to take another turn and change forever. I had walked the length and breadth of Chelmsford that evening and was returning down Shepherd Lane to do the last few houses. It was 7p.m. I arrived at the house of the "gazelle".

The door was opened by her ten-year-old little sister. "Please may I speak to your Mother or Father, I've come for the paper money?" said I. "My sister fancies you," came the reply. A shout came from one of the bedrooms to tell her to shut up but the little one continued to tease her. Just then the gazelle appeared at the door – she was utterly, staggeringly beautiful. "I'm sorry, but my mother and father have gone out to dinner. My dad's in the army and we leave for Germany tomorrow. Dad's been posted there for three years," she said. Mozart could never have produced such gentle melody as the sound of her voice to me at that moment. Her sister persisted in tormenting her and in girlish anger she pushed the little one into a bedroom, holding tight onto the door handle. Then in a second she ran toward the front door, caught hold of my hand, and at full speed led me up the steep hill behind the house and into the orchard below the main road. We hid in the grass beneath the trees watching and listening to her little sister calling for us. The street light filtered through the trees and the grass was still warm from the day-long sun. We lay for a while watching the comings and goings of the inhabitants of Shepherd Lane.

Till my dying day, I will never forget the feel of her full moist lips at the very second of that first gentle kiss. I remember touching her face and hair with all the tenderness with which one would instinctively touch a gazelle. She quietly assisted me in undoing her blouse; her breasts were full, rounded and firm. They were strawberries and cream and I was in paradise. I kissed every inch of her flawless body and as we lay naked together, she seduced me with all the understanding and experience of a woman of thirty, while allowing me to think that I was the seducer.

"Oh my God, look at the time, it's 11.30p.m.! My mother will bloody well kill me. She will probably have already called the police," said I, breaking the serenity of the moment as we dozed in each other's arms. Kissing her goodbye at her doorway was the most agonising event of my life. I wanted to devour her and adore her forever.

I ran as fast as I had ever done but when our house came in sight, my pace changed to a canter then a skip and finally a dance. I thought, "I've become a man tonight! Sod the bloody paper money!"

When I arrived, the house was in darkness. There was a note on the kitchen table. It read, "Hi son, gone out for dinner with John and Molly, will probably be a bit late, meal prepared for you in the fridge, Love Mum xx." It couldn't get any better!

"Oh thank you God, thank you, it was wonderful."

The following morning my gazelle and her family left for Germany. I cried in my bed that night, I so longed to hold her and love her again and I didn't even know her name.

By now she is probably running a Whore House in Frankfurt with her souteneur, but whoever you are and wherever you may be, with the whisper of my last dying breath, I shall love you and thank you for that first precious magical night.

When not preoccupied with girls, Leo and I spent much of our out-of-school time hunting in the woods with Fisher. Fisher was a craggy-faced old trapper who spent his life living off the land and hunting wild mink, musk rats, otter and deer. He had no source of income save for selling pelts to the furrier. He was Daniel Boone and Davy Crockett and the twentieth century had passed him by. I learnt a lot from Fisher, about survival mostly. There was an abundance of deer and pheasant in the woods and we would often join him for dinner at the camp fire, eating what had been killed and drinking pine-needle tea. He was the last of the true frontiersmen, the sort of man that every schoolboy only dreams of meeting, a wonderful character.

One day Leo and I were hunting alone, hoping to get a deer, when in a clearing in the woods I was confronted by a skunk. I'd never met one before and they were quite a bit bigger than I had imagined. Leo was behind me and we slowly backed off, but Mr. Skunk was having none of it, he was up for confrontation. Every time we backed, he moved forward and then the tail went up. We darted out of the way of the first jet spray. The smell was so pungent that Leo and I began to gag and vomit. That was it! I raised my hunting bow and the first arrow went clean through Mr. Skunk's body, sticking out the other side. But Mr. Skunk seemed unperturbed and unfazed by the fact that he had an arrow sticking out of him and continued with his attack. Leo fired and missed, I fired again and missed but my third shot went through his shoulder and heart. We lost four arrows that day. We were told that if you get sprayed you just have to burn your clothes. Fisher said tomato juice can get rid of it but we weren't going to put it to the test.

Life was very comfortable and I was happy. Mother had a black maid at that time called Alberta. There's not much to say about Alberta save for the fact that she thought that we were so rich that it wasn't necessary to do any washing. Each week my mother would go to the dustbins to retrieve all our socks and underclothes.

I was in my bedroom one day with the door closed when I heard my stepfather and mother whispering in the kitchen. Curiosity got the better of me and without so much as a sound I held the handle tight and opened the door to an eighth of an inch, just enough to press my ear to the crack. My mother was going to have a baby, and how were they going to tell me?

The news was broken with the least amount of trauma and it didn't seem long before the arrival was imminent. It was March and the snow had been particularly heavy. As I arose and got ready for school I heard a joyous sound: the siren from the fire station! That meant that the school was snowed in and it was too dangerous to get the school bus out. Mother had gone to hospital in Lowell and Karuna was told to return home as there was nothing he could do. In those days men weren't allowed to be present at births. Then came the call, wonderful news: "Well, Dr. Maitra, you have a fine healthy baby girl. Congratulations."

Karuna was overjoyed, his first-born, and I was so genuinely thrilled for him.

He and I decided to celebrate before going to the hospital and open a bottle of Champagne from the fridge. Unbeknown to us the bottle was so charged that it exploded in his hand and he was left with a severe gash. We gingerly drove to the hospital with his hand wrapped in a bandage which he hid from mother in order not to upset her. My new little half sister was the ugliest thing I had ever seen. She was covered in black hair and I noted that she had a far fuller beard than my own. Mother and Karuna were blissfully happy with their little bundle of joy and with each other and I was happy for them.

Mother had a new little family now and in my own heart I felt I didn't belong there anymore. It was nobody's fault, it's just the way it was.

At no time did Karuna make me feel I was anything less than his real son. He was always generous and firm, as any father should be. He had one of the most brilliant academic minds on earth. He got his Bachelors degree at the University of Bengal, his Masters at Manchester and his Doctorate at Princeton where he became an acquaintance of Albert Einstein. He was professor of Columbia University in New York and at the time of my sister's birth was working on the top secret American space project. Although not born in the United States, President Kennedy gave him maximum national security clearance. He was a brilliant sitarist and had shared a flat with Ravi Shankar in New York. He taught me to appreciate the genius and complexity of classical Indian music.

I, on the other hand, came from a long line of farmers with no academic leanings whatsoever and he and I were living in two different mental solar systems.

The strain began to show. Karuna and my mother rarely argued, but if they did it was always about me. If I were to stay I would be a wedge in the happiness of their marriage and I was old enough to understand that I couldn't do that. Where could I go?

I didn't really cherish the idea of returning to the full-time dominance of my grandmother at Willoughby. Perhaps I could try my father?

I wrote to him and his return letter said I was welcome.

1964–69

Living with my father • Family sadness and happiness • My first jobs • Yvonne • Two near-death experiences • Toronto adventures • Early business ventures • Chrissie

I had no idea of my father's circumstances but I was about to experience yet another culture shock. He was on his third wife by this time and was totally skint. He was living in an attic flat in a dingy converted Victorian house in Chorlton-Cum-Hardy with his wife and two grown-up girls, who were hers from a previous marriage. From the second I arrived I knew I most certainly didn't belong there either. Their kindness toward me helped blot out the reality of my new circumstances. They all smoked and it wasn't long before I joined in the habit. I toyed with the idea of returning to Willoughby but decided I would try and stick it out for as long as possible. I briefly enrolled in a local school, but thankfully I didn't have to stay long as I was sixteen and I couldn't wait to get out and become completely independent. In my predicament, sadly, I felt it was pointless even contemplating further education.

One evening the doorbell went and I ran down the stairs to answer it. It was Phil, my mother's youngest sister, and her fiancé Peter. For a couple of horrible seconds I remember feeling ashamed that they would find me living in such a dreadful place. A tenant had left a bicycle in the hallway. The walls of the ascending stairs were scraped, revealing bare plaster where endless amounts of furniture had been moved up and down the stairs. It was utterly ghastly.

I loved my aunt Phil and when I was very young at Willoughby she had been like an older sister to me. As she stood at the door she looked pale and her eyes were all red.

"Your grandfather has been killed," she said, and we both burst into tears and hugged each other. He had been inspecting some work being done to the roof of a block of flats, recently purchased by my aunt Andolores and her husband Brian Leigh, when the ladder slipped and my grandfather fell and hit his head on the concrete below. He died in Stockport Infirmary of a brain haemorrhage. My mother flew over immediately; it was January.

By March there was a wedding in the family, Phil and Peter, and a very grand affair it was. I was a groomsman and looked terribly Ascotesque in my top hat and tails and took the job most seriously. Phil was upset that her beloved father was not there to give the bride away. Mother was unable to return so soon after their father's funeral and in addition she was pregnant again, with my half brother, Paul.

From childhood I was always groomed to assume that I would be a gentleman; all former Alton boys were army officers, clergymen, barristers, gentleman farmers and the like. My stepfather had promised that if I got into university in America he would give me a trip to anywhere in the world of my choosing, but I'd thrown my education away. I felt at this point of my life that I'd failed before I'd started. I was at the bottom of the heap, living in a shit flat with my father and no prospects. Whatever happened to that leader of men? The boy that took control of the school? I had got to dust myself off, take stock. This world doesn't owe me or anyone else a living, so bloody well get on with it!

I trawled the newspapers for a job. I thought perhaps I should do something arty and I went for an interview for a job as window dresser with Dolcis shoes, Manchester. The manager was terribly impressed by my slightly mellowed public schoolboy accent. Although I had been in America I never adopted an American drawl, but my accent had become less clipped and a little more easy on the ear. I was there for five days when the manager called me into his broom-cupboard of an office. "Your services are no longer required, you're fired!" And just when I thought I was doing rather well!

There was a great deal of unemployment at that time and work of any kind was hard to find. So if I was going to start at the bottom and work my way up I'd better start now.

I got a job loading steel sheets onto lorries at George O. James Ltd., Trafford Park. The pay was four pounds ten shillings and six pence a week (£4.52½).

I had earned £5 at Dolcis. After a few weeks my hands were sliced by the narrow gauge sheets and oil had impregnated them. They became as thick as elephant skin.

One day while sitting outside eating our sandwiches the senior foreman joined us. He turned to me and said, "What the hell brings a chap like you to come and work here?"

Without thinking, I replied, "Poverty, sir." He roared with laughter but I was ashamed of myself for such pomposity. I liked my workmates, they were good chaps and many a good time was had.

After my grandfather's death I assumed responsibility for all of my grandmother's properties and each evening I would walk the two miles across Chorlton meadows to Sale. I would arrange for plumbers and builders, interview new tenantry and deal with the paperwork, then walk the two miles back, at midnight.

Weekends involved parties, debauchery and sex, lots and lots of sex. This was the beginning of the age of "free love". Throughout mankind's history, women were always restricted by religious and moral restraint and a lack of safe birth control. Now at this time the Pill was suddenly invented and they had a million years of repressed sexual liberation to catch up on. I was a rooster in a hen house. Then along came Yvonne Kane. Yvonne was Brigitte Bardot with dark hair. As I settled into a stable relationship, we engaged in more outdoor pursuits of hiking, climbing and pot-holing – and sex while we were doing all three. We would get the train to Chinley or Hayfield and hike up to Kinder on the moors. We even had sex up there, in a freezing snow blizzard. I adored the freedom of the outdoors; it was the nearest thing in England to my times with Leo and Fisher. My roots have always been with the land; I've never been a city boy.

This also was the time of the "brain drain" and as always the Labour government was making a total mess of the economy. Under Harold Wilson excessive taxes were causing the professionals and high earners to leave the country in their thousands. Coupled with that, countries like Canada and Australia were desperate for additional labour. Australia was offering a new life and passage for £10. I always remember the headline in one of the newspapers saying "Will the last person leaving Britain please turn off the lights" (a headline so good that it was later to be reused in a more political context).

My father and his wife Ivy decided they might like to try Canada for a few years and Ivy's two girls, Yvonne and Avel, had got married by this time. I thought to myself, "That might be interesting and a new adventure", plus, Toronto was not too far from Boston where I could pop over to see my mother.

We were to sail out of Liverpool on April 6th on the first voyage after the long winter, on the *Empress of England*, one of Cunard's luxury Liverpool to Montreal liners.

The weekend before my departure my chum Steve Appleton (nicknamed Appy) and myself decided to have one last hike and camp up on the moors near the caves at Chinley. The tent was erected in a reasonably sheltered spot and although still under age we decided to walk the two miles to the nearest road and chance our luck at a pub. We were welcomed and politely asked to remove our boots at the door. An inviting coal and log fire, several pints of local brew and a few games of darts with the locals all added up to a very enjoyable evening. By the time I reached the road from the front door it hit me like a thunderbolt: I was out of my brains. Appy was in no better condition and how we staggered and crawled our way back to that tent is a mystery to me. We fell into a drunken sleep and at 3a.m. I was awakened to feel every inch of my body soaking wet and driving sleet beating against my face. The tent had been completely ripped out of the ground. It was almost impossible to stand against the ferocious winds and up on the moors the night is totally black. Salvaging only our bag we stumbled our way to a pot-hole we had discovered earlier. The hole was just big enough to squeeze into and it dropped vertically thirty feet down like a chimney where it opened up into a cavernous room at the bottom. A steady stream of water followed us down, and not only were we soaked but we were completely caked in mud.

Our bag contained candles and a cigarette lighter and the candle-light revealed that we were in a collapsed mine tunnel. Two rusted narrow gauge railway lines disappeared into a wall of rubble and the hole we climbed down must have been some sort of air vent to the surface. We were in serious trouble: nobody knew where we were and hypothermia was setting in very rapidly. Within minutes as we huddled on the floor we began to shake uncontrollably. Although still shaking, Appy suddenly fell asleep. I dragged him up from the floor; we must keep awake, we must keep moving. We sang songs, danced, jumped up and down; minutes seemed like hours. Every hour or so I would climb all the way up the vent to the top believing it was daylight, only to find blackness. After the longest and worst night of my life, we both survived. I have never enjoyed a breakfast from a transport café as much as that morning, along with a pint of tea in a cracked mug.

I got home only to read in the newspaper that Britain had been hit by the worst storms in sixty years.

That evening I went to say my *au revoir* to Yvonne, as I had no intention of staying in Canada long term. I made love to her twice on her sitting-room floor while her parents watched television in the next room (I liked to live dangerously) then again up against the front door as her parents got ready for bed.

The following day Ivy's son-in-law, Peter Dawson, drove us to Liverpool Docks. There seemed to be thousands of people milling around. Everywhere people cried and hugged their loved ones who were staying behind. People threw coloured streamers from the ship and shouted last messages to those on the dockside. I, on the other hand, stood in silence, observing it all. I felt I was dying at this point because a dreadful fever had come over me following my camping escapade. I spent the first three days at sea in my bunk. My father and Ivy had their own cabin but I had to share with three other men in a four-bunk berth.

On the fourth day I felt better and after a stroll around the decks I was feeling decidedly peckish. Then came the captain's announce-ment that we were heading straight into a mid-Atlantic hurricane. We were to steer due north toward the Pole in order to try and avoid the brunt of it. Hurricanes usually start in the Caribbean, climb up the American eastern coast, go across to Iceland and fizzle out at Scotland. We couldn't be in a worse place. I thought, "Just my bloody luck. I escaped death last week and now I'm going to die in the freezing waters of the North Atlantic."

That night the hurricane struck. The crew lashed all the doors with thick ropes, the grand piano in the dining room was tied to a post and anything that moved was secured.

As the storm got under way, plates, cups and glasses flew everywhere. The waiters and crew tried their best but it was impossible to stand up. Looking at the portholes was like looking into a washing machine in mid-wash. People in their hundreds lay in the corridors clinging onto the brass rails. I saw literally dozens of people vomiting all at the same time, the walls and floors were covered in sick and the stench was unbearable. There was no air as all hatches were battened down tight. In everyone's mind there was the constant fear we were going to sink.

The captain tried to keep us informed with regular announcements. We heard that an Italian fishing vessel was very close and had sent a Mayday. She had lost members of her crew overboard but there was nothing we could do. Obviously the captain's biggest additional fear was a mid-ocean collision.

By luncheon of the following day it seemed as if the worst was over, but I was wrong. What follows a mid-Atlantic hurricane is a terrifying giant swell. Great mountains of water standing higher than the funnel of the ship suddenly disappear into valleys. Half of the ship's bow seems to stand proud of the water only to embed itself into the oncoming mountain. No less than one third of the ship submerges itself under the sea before reappearing on top of the next mountain. That was far more terrifying than the fullness of the storm. Passengers were still locked in and the ship's crew did their utmost to clean the place up but they were on a losing battle. You may think that I am exaggerating for dramatic effect but you have to remember, this wasn't just a bad storm at sea; this was a full-blown hurricane!

The following day we found calm waters. We were just south of Greenland near Newfoundland but our next problem was giant floating icebergs. It is the time of the year when they break free and start to float down the Canadian coast. I saw about half a dozen but I thanked God when we safely entered the mouth of the St. Lawrence.

A cutter ship had broken the ice for us as we entered the river and the doors were opened. Everyone flooded out onto the decks. The sun shone and the air was crisp and clean. We took such deep breaths that the chilled air would hurt your lungs. There were more prayers thanking God that day than he could possibly cope with.

We cruised at a leisurely pace past the Heights of Abraham and Quebec and on to Montreal.

In Toronto we were met by some friend of my father's and almost immediately we moved into a very smart apartment with its own private beach next to Lake Ontario – Shoreline Towers, Lakeshore Boulevard, Mimico; things were looking up!

Days later I took a Greyhound bus to Boston to visit mother for a week or so. By then they had a very grand Colonial house in Wayland Hills.

Upon my return to Toronto I got a job working for an advertising agency called BBDO – Batten, Barton, Durstein and Osborne. I was a trainee writer on the very handsome salary of $55 per week.

I made friends and chummed up with Ken Kendal who came from Stretford. His real name was Arthur but he thought Ken sounded more cool.

Ken and I had the run of the town! The whole world was suddenly being swept along on a tide of Beatlemania. The music of Liverpool and Manchester pop groups could be heard in the remotest parts of the globe. Ken and I could, without telling lies, say we were Merseysiders as the river Mersey divided Stretford in Lancashire and Sale in Cheshire. Our pathetic impersonation of a Liverpool accent proved invaluable in the "Canadian Girl Pant Dropping Department". Our hunting was done in the Night Owl Club in the week and at weekends we would take the ferry over to Toronto Island. There is a whole book in itself of tales of our success rate but I'll leave that for another day.

I got a new job working on Bloor Street, next to the Canadian Broadcasting Corporation, at Medallion Films as an assistant film editor: salary, $75 per week.

Each evening I would get the street car (the Toronto tram system) home. On several evenings I would arrive at the front door of the apartments at the same time as a very smart business executive in his mid-forties. After the usual pleasantries he told me he was going on a business trip to Manchester, and as he had never been there before I really must come over to his apartment for a drink. Over the next few days it became embarrassing as he constantly reminded me of his invitation, and in the end I reluctantly agreed. The door to his apartment was opened by the prettiest boy I had ever seen. He looked like Brit Eckland when she was nineteen; another boy was in the kitchen. I was given a drink which I pretended to sip. I had the horrible feeling that they might have spiked it. The pretty boy told me that Robert was visiting some friend in another flat and would be back shortly. Half an hour passed when the door of the bedroom opened and out came another boy followed by Robert still in the process of dressing himself. Everybody sat down and all eyes were focused on me. I thought, "Oh no, I'm in trouble here!" After a few minutes of chat Robert came straight to the point. "We are having a little party at the weekend, some of the city councillors, a couple of judges and a few of the city's richest grandees will be here. James, I really want you to come and if you co-operate I will pay you $400 for the night." I began to shake with fear and he could see my discomfort. After promising not to mention it to anyone they allowed me to leave. You would never in a million years believe he was a rentboy pimp.

The following night, I was returning from the Night Owl and catching the late street car home; it was around 2.30a.m. It only went as far as Queen Street and then you had to get a connecting tram to Lakeshore. The streets were deserted but a scruffy man appeared from nowhere. He started to go into graphic detail about all the things he wanted to do to me but he made the near-fatal mistake of taking it one step further – he caught me by the arm. I hit him with a right hook that Mike Tyson would have been proud of and he crumpled to the ground. Just to make sure he didn't get up, I kicked him in the ribs once and took off like the wind to the next tram stop half a mile away. I felt dreadful about it but I'd had quite enough of homosexual advances for one week.

I was fed up with Canada by now. I'd been here a year and I longed to see Yvonne again and to walk the Pennine Hills. If the truth be known, Ivy was glad to see the back of me and finally have my father all to herself. I had a healthy bank account by then, and before leaving I took another trip to Boston to see Mother. Upon my return to England I resumed my duties of running all of my grandmother's properties and she would have liked me to move back to Willoughby. There were numerous houses of our own I could have lived in but I needed total and singular independence. I got my own rented flat elsewhere.

The night I returned, I went to see Yvonne. Her parents were away and I made love to her up against the front door. We devoured each other with such animal savagery we didn't even make it to the nearest room.

I was back! Just like old times.

The employment situation had slightly improved in Britain and I got a job, firstly as a writer for Great Universal Stores and shortly afterwards as the Assistant Advertising Manager of Marshall Ward which was a subsidiary company of Great Universal. This time the salary was £11 10 shillings, not the sort of money I was used to but for my age, pretty good. The older men in the warehouse were on £7 a week. My boss, the Advertising Manager, was earning £23 and within a few weeks my wages had increased to £13, and I was still only eighteen.

George Best was given a modelling contract by Great Universal to have his own clothes section in the catalogue. They paid him £20,000. He had recently opened the George Best Boutique with a partner called Malcolm Mooney, firstly at Washway Road in Sale and then at Bridge Street in Manchester. At the time, though it is hard to believe now, I looked very similar to George. Half the time George wouldn't turn up at the studio for the photo-shoots and so all the back shots and side shots were of me and not George. He only had to do front face shots, but he was so unreliable they didn't renew his contract. In the catalogue you couldn't tell the difference between us. He and I became friends at that point and we would sometimes meet up at the Grapes Pub in central Manchester along with his other pals: Selwyn Demmy, who owned Gus Demmy betting shops, Rodney Marsh, Mike Summerbee, Malcolm Mooney and occasionally Mike Parkinson (now Sir Michael Parkinson) who read the news on Granada Television. I couldn't keep up with George; he had an alarming capacity for alcohol and as he rocketed into superstardom our friendship waned. Over the years we would bump into each other at social events and it was always nice to see him. (Early in the evening and sober!)

Marshall Ward in those pre-union days was rather like the civil service. One knew exactly the rank of an individual by his surroundings. Bob, my boss, had a very large desk with two phones and a large comfortable chair with arms. I had a slightly smaller desk with one phone and a comfortable chair with arms. Joe, our assistant, had a small tatty desk, no phone and a thoroughly uncomfortable chair with no arms.

In the morning Bob was saluted by the commissionaire; I signed his book; Joe and the workers clocked in. We used the executive lift; the workers used the goods lift.

Working for other people was only a temporary means to an end as far as I was concerned. If I was to return to the gentlemanly classes then I would have to do it via my own enterprise. What better time to start than now?

There were 400 women working at Marshall Ward and there had to be a way of cashing in on that little captive market. I decided I would do a weekly raffle. Every woman in the place smoked and those that didn't had husbands who did. We'd start there.

The top prize would be 100 cigarettes. I entered 400 jumbled numbers in a book, thus preventing anyone from working out the arithmetic. There would be lesser prizes of 10 and 20 packs. Before long I had every woman without fail purchasing a ticket each Wednesday. The draw was on Friday. Each woman paid one shilling and I made sure the 100 cigarette prize was won by a different floor each week. The women were elated. I was grossing £20 and making a net profit of £17 10 shillings. Added to my salary of £13, this made my take-home pay £30 10 shillings. That was £7 10 shillings more than my boss was earning!

At the same time I set up another business in the office called Brassart Productions. I had been on a visit to Alton, and while there took some brass rubbings from the tombs of the Earls of Shrewsbury just for the hell of it and brought them into the office. Women started to ask if they could buy them. This posed the question, how could I mass-produce them? Years before at Pittsford, New York, we visited an author friend of my stepfather's called Wyatt Brunnett. I had greatly admired a sixteenth-century Chinese wallhanging he had over his fireplace. That's how they could be done! I'd silkscreen them onto hessian and make them into wallhangings!

My rented flat in Chorlton was turned into a silk-screening factory. The other tenants and the landlord couldn't figure out where the smell of paraffin was coming from. A whole range of colours and sizes appeared on the walls of the office, the largest being five feet tall: price £2 10 shillings; production cost 3/6d. They sold like hot cakes! Bob my boss was totally bemused by me; I wonder why?

The job of Assistant Advertising Manager was a simple one. Bob and I would receive a massive annual appropriation to spend as seen fit. We checked the success rate of the previous year's advertising and followed the same basic formula. Much of our time was spent in blissful inebriation as the magazines and newspapers would wine and dine us with the utmost extravagance in order to get a piece of our money pie.

I was about to get my very first lesson in business. I approached a newly opened and ultra trendy shop in Manchester called Habitat, owned by a chap called Terence Conran. I brought a number of samples of my Brassart wallhangings in the hope of expanding into the bigger retail market. They were wildly enthused when they saw them and said they would probably give me an initial order for 5,000. I was staggered by the prospect. I could only produce about ten per night in my little flat and I didn't have the money to invest in a factory-sized facility. I had to be honest with them. Weeks later someone came into my office to congratulate me. They had seen them in the picture department of Boots in Manchester. I ran firstly to Boots and then on to Habitat. Yes, it was true, they had employed a large manufacturer to reproduce them. Not long afterwards my silkscreens were scrapped and taken to the tip; I couldn't compete.

On a brighter note, I was sitting at my desk when I was suddenly struck by a heavenly vision. Her name was Chrissie Kelly. I watched her breasts jostle beneath her sweater as she bounced by. She had the gait of a dancer. She was petite and had a slim hourglass figure to die for. Her clothes were very French and stylish and she had the face of an angel. I was smitten. In a desperate attempt to charm her, I took her to a new club called Tiffanys. I could never forget the place – it cost £3 each to get in and the drinks were £2. You could go through an entire week's wages in a couple of hours. I employed all my powers of charm and wooing tactics to win her heart. Eventually, and with much persuasion, she offered me that most precious of gifts, her virginity!

My relationship with Yvonne had gone beyond the point of no return and we had parted company the best of friends.

It was a late summer's day in 1969, and I was walking in Stretford when who should I bump into but Ken Kendal! It was lovely to see him. He had also become disillusioned with Canada and returned home, after me. We discussed old times and both agreed that the only thing we really missed about the place was a decent hamburger!

"In that case," I said, "we'll open our own place here in England serving genuine North American burgers. A minor problem was, Ken had no money. "Not a problem," said I, "I've got money and we'll open the place as equal partners!"

In those days the only thing similar in Britain was a Wimpy burger, which at that time was only about the size and thickness of a jam pot lid. We were used to half pounders!

I made my appointment with Mr. Kemp, the managing director of Marshall Ward. When I walked in he said, "Ah! I'm glad you're here, I want to talk to you about this raffle you're doing. Where exactly does the money go?"

"Before I answer that question, Mr. Kemp, I've got something to say to you. I've decided I no longer want to be part of this ridiculous charade of climbing the corporate ladder, and I'm utterly bored with being in the company of all those sycophantic nodding dogs who slobber and whimper outside your office door. Ta Ta."

Poor Mr. Kemp, he was such a nice old man and he was completely dumbstruck. Nobody had ever spoken to him like that, especially someone so young.

1970-72

I turn 21 • The Chuckwagon • A roadtrip with my stepfather

On May 13th 1970 I was twenty-one and Mother flew over for my birthday.

My aunt Andolores and Brian put on a fabulous black-tie party for me at their house, for which I am eternally grateful. They had always been so kind to me. My mother and father danced together at my request and for my benefit only. These little things are important to children from broken homes.

Ken and I rented our first shop on Manchester Road, Altrincham, and the doors opened on October 26th of that year. The company was called THE CHUCKWAGON Charcoal Grill Co., and within minutes of opening, a beautiful Rolls-Royce Silver Cloud parked outside. Two T-Bone steaks was our first order from a man called Jim Parry. The second customer was Bob Greaves, a TV presenter on Granada Television and before the night was over, the pop group Herman's Hermits came in. Funnily enough, all three would become lifelong friends.

We had previously looked at a shop two doors away but it had been empty for years. The back of the shop had been completely vandalised with the rear door removed and the windows broken. One night after closing, Ken and I were sitting in the back room drinking lots of wine and discussing our business strategy when Ken said, "There's a cabinet in the vandalised shop; we could use that as extra storage." It was around 2.30a.m. No sooner had we started to carry the thing back into our rear yard when a young police officer came round. It was his first week on duty. The police had only just been given individual walkie talkies; prior to this police officers only had whistles. He panicked and called for backup and within seconds the shop was surrounded with police cars. You would have thought we were Al Capone's mob. Ken and I were handcuffed and carted off to Altrincham police station. We were charged and thrown in a cell for the night. The thing was, we knew all the police in Altrincham except this young one. Whenever a police officer came into the shop we would always give them their meal for free. We felt utterly betrayed by them.

My prison cell had been recently whitewashed and so with the grease and dirt from the bottom of my shoes I wrote a beautiful large sign on the wall:

EAT AT THE CHUCKWAGON, THE FOOD'S BETTER!

In the morning the hatch in the cell door opened and a mug of tea and beans on toast on a tin plate was passed through. At 10a.m. we were handcuffed again and led up a narrow staircase which opened out into the dock of the court. The magistrate, realising that we weren't Al Capone, fined us £5. The following day the headline in the local newspaper read: "Café owners raid shop!" I was horrified! There was a long procession of my grandmother's tenants saying how disgraceful it was that her grandson was a criminal. I had to think fast. I immediately got two mug-shot photographs of Ken and myself. I placed an advert in the local paper of a large WANTED poster. The advert read: "WANTED, for serving the best hamburgers in town!" My grandmother, who never read the local rag, thought the whole thing had been a joke. A week later two police officers came in and as usual walked out without paying. I leaped over the counter and shouted at them, "You two haven't paid." They sheepishly returned to pay their bill to the cheering and booing of the rest of the customers. Revenge was sweet, but we had paid the larger price.

For the next week or so the shop was packed. I realised the power of infamy and publicity – we were the talk of the town.

The Chuckwagon would never have functioned properly without

the assistance of a young boy called Paul Docx. He was amazing, and the minute he finished school each day he would head straight for the shop to see how he could help. I am eternally grateful to him and his sister Monnie, for their friendship and loyalty in those early days.

I have never worked as hard as I did in the days of the Chuckwagon. More than four hours sleep a night was rare. For a while we had no transport and would leave at 6a.m. for Smithfield Market to bring big boxes of chickens back on the bus, having only closed at 2a.m. We had youth and ambition on our side. Chrissie and I were still very much in love. She was wonderful and stuck by me through it all. She worked in an advertising agency in the day and helped in the shop at night, even moving to a flat on Willowtree Road in Hale in order to be close to me. In May of 1971 we decided to have a weekend break for my birthday. We checked into "The Bull" on the High Street at Alton as Mr. and Mrs. Ridiculous as it seems now, in those days, hoteliers would refuse you lodgings if they thought that you weren't married. The whole adventure seemed so terribly risqué and exciting. With a rusty nail, I carved our names on Cromwell's Rock and as I write, over forty years later, they can still be seen there as a lasting testament to our love.

Ken and I had opened another shop by this time, on Withington Road in Whalley Range. We had eight staff and as things were going so well we treated ourselves to two new cars. Ken got an MGC hardtop with a three-litre engine and I got a red convertible MGB Roadster with wire wheels. I thought I was the bee's knees. In addition I had bought two family-owned houses from an uncle and was busy buying a third. I was twenty-two years old.

As time went on Ken had got a new girlfriend and things began to sour. I tried to convince him that we could expand the business to a chain of retail outlets and in addition we should invest in building a company-owned property portfolio. But I'm afraid he was being influenced elsewhere. We sold Whalley Range and plans were being made for me to buy his shareholding.

Meanwhile my mother and stepfather had moved to a new and magnificent home in Santa Barbara, California, overlooking the town and the Pacific Ocean. My stepfather had a space contract to complete in New Jersey and was then driving all the way to California, a total of over three thousand miles. He asked me if I would like to join him and share the driving; I jumped at the chance. Chrissie was going to keep an eye on things for me in my absence.

I flew to New York and Karuna had arranged for a helicopter to take me to his place in New Jersey. The following day our journey began. We decided to take the northern route through Pennsylvania and on to Chicago rather than the southern route via Route 66. We stopped off at honky-tonk towns and drank jugs of beer in Laramie and Cheyenne with the cowboys. It was a wonderful trip and after staying in Salt Lake City and the casinos of Reno we finally arrived at the Pacific Ocean and San Francisco. I will never forget visiting a restaurant there. After wandering the streets we decided to dine Turkish! The restaurant was dark and not terribly busy, save for a few tables of businessmen. No sooner had we started our meal when the silence was broken by a three-piece Turkish band and a belly- dancer with the biggest pair of breasts I'd ever seen. These great mountainous jellies with a matching pair of buttocks wobbled their way from table to table, much to the delight of the businessmen. Before long, $5 and $10 bills were being pushed into her pants. Karuna and I continued to eat and I could see him inwardly praying for her not to come near. She approached him from the back! I will never forget his expression. The piece of Steffado on his fork remained motionless six inches from his mouth, his entire head became enveloped by these giant mammary glands: only his nose could be seen from between them. I had to pinch myself to stop myself from laughing, but thought better of it. Karuna was a very prudish and dignified man. She got no money and went to the next table. Our forks were raised again and in silence we continued eating. It was never mentioned again.

Upon my return, Ken and his girlfriend went immediately on holiday to Africa. Chrissie informed me that in my absence Ken had shown little interest in the business. His mind was obviously made up. What was deeply disturbing is that I returned to a mountain of debt. There were serious discrepancies in the books, the wages weren't correct and monies had been removed from our account. Our suppliers were refusing to give us credit. I went to our joint friend and solicitor, Ben Halpern. He drew up an agreement whereby Ken would sign his entire shareholding over to me for nothing. I met Ken a year later in the street. He profusely apologised and said that I had always been good to him. I said, "Ken, don't worry about it. It's over and all in the past. You wanted your liberty and I wanted to continue the business, we both got what we wanted." We vowed we would renew our friendship but sadly I never saw him again.

After that, my first port of call was the landlord and I persuaded him to sell the property to me.

1973-75

California and Las Vegas • A proposal, of sorts • Cold feet
• Pat Phoenix • California again

In 1973 Chrissie and I went to California. My mother was privy to my intentions. I bought a solitaire diamond ring, not too large to be vulgar and not too small to be stingy. Chrissie and I took the Greyhound bus from Los Angeles to Las Vegas and checked in to a small motel called "The Palm Tree" on Las Vegas Strip. In those days Las Vegas bore little resemblance to how it is today. Great expanses of desert lay in between each of the large casinos. Ones such as the Flamingo and the Sands were too expensive for us so we had to settle for the Palm Tree Motel. Chrissie had never seen a light fingers machine in the bed before, and for 25 cents it would gently vibrate you to sleep. As we lay getting 50 cents' worth, Chrissie let out the most blood curdling scream. Perched on my collar and about to crawl up on to my neck was a massive locust. All hell let loose, with lots of shouting and jumping up and down on the bed. The floor beneath the bed was littered with the corpses of dozens of them along with upturned carcasses of cockroaches. The following day we walked the length and breadth of Las Vegas, visiting every casino all the way up to Fremont Street.

On the third night I arranged dinner on Cleopatra's Barge in Caesar's Palace. The lights were subdued, the ambience was perfect and the band played romantic music. Everything was just right and as I placed the box with the ring in it in her hand and watched the glee in her beautiful face, those words of ultimate commitment just couldn't blurt out. So emotionally charged was the moment that we just spent the rest of the evening kissing each other in between each mouthful of food. At no time were the words "Will you marry me? / Yes I will" ever actually uttered. Irrespective, we were both euphoric with happiness at the prospect of being together for ever.

We returned to England and I continued to run the business. We lived together in Chrissie's flat in Hale and made the long-drawn-out plans with meticulous detail for our marriage. As the moment drew ever closer and the Banns were posted on the Church, my feet grew colder. I couldn't understand it. Here was a woman I loved and adored. Everything seemed so right and yet something deep within my subconscious kept saying "Don't do it!"

The marriage was called off and understandably I was persona non grata with a lot of people. I was a cad, a bounder of the lowest order. Engagement presents had to be returned and her wedding dress remained in its box. I just couldn't understand myself. Perhaps a psychologist could explain! Maybe it's a defence mechanism, an inbuilt fear of rejection or failure. A cleverer person than I would know.

I had become acquainted with a wonderful actress called Pat Phoenix. Ken and I had met her in the early days of the Chuckwagon. Pat played the role of Elsie Tanner in *Coronation Street*. She lived in a lovely, but unlisted Georgian house on Glebelands Road in Sale. At the time she was with a Shakespearean actor called Alan Browning.

Pat was a star of the Jane Russell/Mae West ilk. She just loved being a star and lived the part for her public. She and Alan bought a little pub in Chinley called "The Navigation", which became the centre for some truly great parties. The first time Ken and I went there, the party started with everyone being given loaded soda siphons. Straight away an almighty soda battle began and that was before the real drinking started. I went to several 'Do's' at Pat's pub. Sadly Alan died and Pat was distraught and sold her house in Sale for development. She had a lovely original Georgian fireplace surround with magnificent Corinthian columns in the sitting room of that house. I had admired it and before the bulldozers arrived, Pat said I could have it. I told her I felt guilty taking it for nothing but she kept insisting. In the end she took £5 just to shut me up. I still have it to this day. When Pat took up with Tony Booth I didn't see her after that. I only met him once and I couldn't see what she saw in him. I thought he was rude and uncouth. He married Pat on her deathbed and ended up being the father-in-law of the worst Prime Minister in my living memory: Tony Blair.

Chrissie went to Bahrain, probably to be as far away from me as possible, and worked for the airlines there. But then I got a call from her. Her mother was desperately ill and she was flying home immediately. Chrissie and I went to the hospital and were led into a private room by a doctor. It was the worst possible news; she had weeks to live. It was decided that she would be better dying in her own home. I helped nurse Chrissie's mother every day for the next six weeks until her parting breath. She had been a beautiful woman and "the apple hadn't fallen far from the tree" in Chrissie.

I'd become lethargic to the prospect of expanding the Charcoal Grill Company alone by this time and managed to sell both the business and the shop. It was time to move on.

Across the Atlantic, Mother was busy building their own property empire. Karuna continued to work as a scientist. Now that the space race no longer existed between Russia and America he was somehow involved with advancing military projects. Like her own mother before her, Mother was the engine of their marriage. She bought two modern blocks of flats in downtown Santa Barbara, some houses in Lompoc and was building a further twenty-eight apartments in Ventura. She had also recently purchased an office block in Oklahoma which was rented to the government. As I was at a loose end she asked me to come over and paint the Santa Barbara apartments. At a more than a leisurely pace it took me six months, for which I was paid handsomely. Chrissie came over to California where we agreed we were unable to turn the clock back. She returned to France (where she had once been an au pair) and met a Frenchman called Fredrick, married and lived happily ever after. I'm delighted to say that both Fredrick and Chrissie have continued to remain my friends and it seems that she has forgiven me, I hope.

1976-79

Antiques • Sue • Morocco • The Powder House • Loss of a loved one

I returned to England in September of 1976 and started work on one of my cottages in Sale, with the intent of making it a bachelor pad for myself. Our tenant of almost forty years had died, leaving the place available for me. At about the same time I had been asked by my Uncle John in Canada if I would join him in his import/export business, mainly dealing with antiques. This was a subject of which I had a reasonably comprehensive knowledge and I was to be his UK buyer.

After a couple of weeks back in the UK it became almost a prerequisite that each morning I would wander down into Sale town centre for my newspaper and breakfast at Kents. It was on such a morning that I spotted the sweetest-looking little blonde with the most glorious smile. The following morning I enquired of the lady members of staff whether they knew anything about her. "Oh yes," came the reply, "she expressed considerable interest in you!" That was enough for me and I went straight to her office and asked her to take luncheon with me. She accepted. Those were the embryonic moments of an exciting, turbulent, never boring relationship.

Although she looked eighteen and a junior member of staff, she was actually in her twenties and owned the company: Staff Selection, Employment Agency.

She was a Lancashire lass with a very sharp mind and a razor wit, called Sue Hodgson. Once it was established that we were in a relationship I arrived at her flat with my own double mattress to replace her single one. The first time we made love it was done with such urgency that I forgot to remove my cowboy boots. As I got up, a shilling (5p) fell from my pocket. Sue laughingly, said "Is that payment for services rendered?" I then paid her a shilling every time we made love. In three months we had £18 in our jar. (I shall leave you for a moment to do the maths.)

We went to a garden centre and bought a beautiful Jerusalem Palm for her flat with the money. It died a few weeks later of a lack of sunlight and I stopped paying her after that.

Sue and I lived a spontaneous and almost jet-set life. Most things were done at the drop of a hat. For example; one day we said, "Let's go to Morocco tomorrow and stay in a mud hut." So that's exactly what we did. I got dysentery and nearly died. I remember thinking, "I really don't want to die here in Africa." As I was recovering we made our way to Tangier and got the boat to Gibraltar for some decent food and clean drinking water before returning to Morocco.

We decided to trek up into the High Atlas mountains to seek new adventures. Perched precariously on the side of a mountain was a village. Each house was made of mud and sticks with a flat roof and it would be a rare thing for these people to see northern Europeans. We'd met an Australian girl on our travels who asked us if she could tag along. As we got close to the village we were greeted by a young boy who invited us to meet his mother. He was extremely proud of the fact that his was the only house in the village which had two floors. We were made to feel welcome and made ourselves understood via a mixture of French and pidgin English. It was primitive in the extreme with no furniture of any kind. In the corner of the room was a mud oven with a charcoal fire beneath it. Live rabbits were incarcerated in a hole in the wall where they could view their relatives being prepared for the pot.

As we left the house, I gave his mother some money which she eagerly accepted but then we suddenly found ourselves confronted by all the men of the village. We didn't understand a single word they said but one thing was for sure, it wasn't cordial.

The oldest of the men started shouting and the rest joined in with the chorus. Several started to pick up handfuls of rocks, which they proceeded to throw at us. We retreated as fast as our legs would take us out of the village, followed by a marauding posse of men out for our blood. Had we found ourselves in a cul de sac, they would most definitely have killed us.

It wasn't until we got a local bus to Asilah that we met a young Dutchman and he explained the reason. Sue and the Australian girl were wearing shorts! He had experienced his own trauma while trekking through the country. He was on a bus near Rabat when someone put a knife to his throat and he was thrown off it, headfirst. Then there is the other side of the coin. Sue and I were again taking a local bus through desert villages somewhere near Marrakesh. We stopped at a small Arab town and for the life of me I couldn't tell you where. The driver disappeared for what seemed like eternity. The bus was empty, save for the two of us who sat on the front seat next to the open door. Within a few minutes I was face to face with the most pitiful sight. There standing before me at the foot of the door was a little boy of no more than five. I doubt if he had ever come into contact with soap and water and his clothes were nothing more than rags. Attached to him by holding on to his shoulder was an old woman. Her skin was blackened by dirt and the desert sun, but what was most shocking was that her eyes had been removed. He was her eyes and wherever he went, she went. As I sat there, cold and arrogant, my belief was, if you give to one beggar you will be swamped by them. The driver returned and started the bus, but as he was about to drive off he got off again. He emptied the change from his pocket and gave it to them.

I was devastated. That Arab bus driver was little better off than they were. In that one minute of time, with all my devout Catholic upbringing, it took an impoverished Muslim man to teach me more about humility and compassion than all the priests, bishops and popes did in twenty years. I wept with shame as the bus drove off into the desert. In a biblical land I had witnessed the genuine good Samaritan. I vowed I would be a better person and I have so often thought of that little trio of people.

Back at home, the cottage I was renovating had been completed by this time and Sue and I moved in. She complained incessantly that the place was cold. I had knocked the internal walls out to make it all open plan with a free-standing staircase in the centre. I was busy with the antiques business, sending John a forty-foot container almost every month. I bought horse-drawn carriages, churches full of pews, house clearances, clocks, you name it, I bought it. I nearly bought a tank once but I thought that was probably pushing it too far. I did arrive at Sue's office once wearing a Nazi uniform. I bought that from an old chap who took it from a German prisoner. Sue loved the unpredictability of what she might come home to. It was quite simply the greatest fun.

When I wasn't rushing round the country on my buying sprees I would be out exercising the horses at my friend's livery stables. Once or twice a week I would ride out with the mounted police along the river bank. My dear chum, Norman Lloyd, who owned the livery, was also a great antiques collector and when he and I weren't buying horses he was with me at the antiques auctions. He was a great chap. In his younger days he had been a fairground fighter. I remember them as a boy. A boxing ring would accompany the fairground from town to town. The resident fighter would challenge any man in the town. If you beat him you won £5. No one ever did as they would sew lead weights into the sleeve part of the opponent's gloves. By round three they couldn't keep their arms up. Norman would get a knockout every time.

Sue and I lived in the fast lane. We travelled regularly and even took her mother on a tour of the Holy Land, but that is a story in itself. There was hardly a weekend when we weren't entertaining, drinking and partying. Our close friends, Ruth, Don, Robin and Peter almost became like family. Ruth was very pretty and incredibly posh, Don was highly intelligent, pipe-smoking and ponderous, Robin was a former officer in the Grenadier Guards and Peter was an alcoholic.

We were staying at my aunt's summer house near Porthmadog (Portmadoc) when in casual conversation my aunt mentioned that the headland peninsula and the Powder House were up for sale. The house was alone at the edge of the sea and was surrounded by the golf course on three sides with its own beach to the front. The entire family, Sue and I walked over to have a look. It was love at first sight; breathtaking. From the sitting room it looked across the estuary to Harlech Castle and the open sea. The view to the right from the bedroom was all the way down Black Rock Sands to Criccieth Castle and to the left was Portmeirion. You would struggle to find such natural beauty anywhere else in the British Isles.

I got in touch with the owner, Mr. Cooper, who was from Dorset. He was headmaster of a public school and like so many academics he hadn't an ounce of common sense. The house was in the most appalling state of disrepair. On our tour of the property, Mrs. Cooper continually told us things like, "Of course, we bought these curtains from Libertys and that chair came from Harrods." The fact that the curtains had been a banquet for both mice and moths and the chair had a broken leg seemed to pass her by.

After much negotiation and after assisting him in reducing his potential Capital Gains Tax, I managed to buy it jointly with Sue. The house and land had an illustrious history. It was called Ynys Cyngar, meaning the island of Cyngar. Cyngar was one of the early Welsh saints, in or around the fifth century. He was an abbot and confessor and in the Middle Ages this little peninsula was an island. He lived there as a Hermit and people would row out to him to confess their sins. The only drinking water, St. Cyngar's Well, comes from a fresh- water spring which is just at the side of the Powder House and runs down on to the beach. St. Cyngar was said to be the son of Prince Geraint who fell at Longborth and the brother of Cador, Duke of Cornwall.

It is believed Lloyd George did much of his courting of Margaret Owen down by the Powder House. Other people of note include Lawrence of Arabia who was brought up a couple of miles away at Tremadoc and the philosopher, Lord Bertrand Russell.

The first day we took possession of the place, we had an enormous bonfire on the beach of all the contents. There wasn't even anything worth sticking into a container in the hope that a Canadian would buy it, that's how bad it was.

In what the Coopers loosely called the Boat House, hanging on a peg was an army greatcoat and tin helmet, never touched since the soldiers guarding the coast had left it there in 1945. The coat was in a state of semi-fossilisation but we kept the helmet. The only other thing undamaged was a beautiful Victorian cranberry glass wall lamp. Everything else went.

I started work immediately and my eternal gratitude goes to my

Uncle John who came over from Canada, leaving that end of the antiques business in the hands of Cliff, his business partner.

John and I worked continuously every weekend in creating an architectural fantasy, and the physical work in such a magnificent setting was such a pleasurable experience.

Periodically I would employ the services of Jim, who was head of the gypsies in Porthmadog, to do bits of building work. He was a wonderful character. The gypsy camp was behind the town and the locals weren't at ease with the gypsies, but you couldn't find a more decent person than Jim. Porthmadog Council were trying to get them out of their caravans and force them into council flats. I told him that he could take as many rabbits as he wanted from my land and so rabbit stew was always on his home menu. Sometimes the sea around the house would boil with mackerel and you could almost scoop them out with your hand. We would get maybe a dozen of them, and I would gut them and open them up on the barbecue. Jim would eat them, heads, bones and all. He wasted nothing.

Jim and his wife and family invited me to dinner at the camp. Yes! Rabbit stew from my own rabbits. I arrived and ploughed my way through the abandoned cars in various stages of being dismantled. Piebald horses were everywhere, trucks, Land Rovers and Alsatian dogs, lots of them, and children all over the place, running free among the caravans. Jim's home was a modest caravan with a home extension built on the side. This was made out of bits of corrugated iron, any wood they could find and a window which was part of a car door, allowing you to wind the window up or down at will. The ceiling was wood with black bin liners nailed to it. In the corner was a pot-belly stove, which Jim found on a tip. The chimney was made from different types of pipes, some cast iron and some terracotta.

Amidst all this, the makeshift table had a beautiful handmade lace tablecloth on it. The one thing gypsies don't skimp on is their crockery, and there were Royal Doulton cups, saucers and plates and the glasses were Edinburgh crystal. They had done it all for me and I was deeply touched. You couldn't have more courteous hosts or enjoyed better company. Jim told me that a year or so before, Sir Clough Williams-Ellis and Lady Ellis had popped in for dinner.

My grandmother, who had played such an important part in my life, died during Christmas week of 1979. We buried her on Christmas Eve. For some time she had told me she was going to die soon, but I always dismissed it, telling her not to talk like that. She assured me by saying, "My children are all grown up and my grandchildren are growing up, it's time I went." If there is such a thing as a perfect death then my grandmother had it.

By then she lived alone at Willoughby, but every day one or two of my aunts would call to do any chores that needed doing. She had bought Christmas presents for every single member of the family, including seventeen grandchildren, friends and some of the tenants. The day before she died my Aunt Betty came early to start wrapping and labelling all the gifts. That night, with the task complete, Betty left her seated in her favourite chair in the sitting room. Early the following morning my Aunt Phil arrived to make her breakfast. My grandmother had passed away peacefully in the night, never stirring from her chair but surrounded by boxes and bows; a parting gift for everyone. She died as she had lived, a fountain of generosity.

On the morning of December 24th my grandmother's body was brought into the sitting room at Willoughby in order to "lie in state". It was a miserable day in every sense of the word. Relatives, friends and tenants came from far and wide to pay their respects and express their sympathy. The expressionless wax-like corpse had little resemblance to the sparkly-eyed Granny I had been with a few days before. I remember my mother gasping as the coffin lid was opened by the undertaker.

Within minutes the room was filled with a chilled air the like of which I have never experienced before. I could feel the cold go right through to my bones and yet the rest of the house was warm. After a few minutes of reverend silence, the undertaker quietly called my mother to one side. I was privy to this conversation. He said. "Don't be alarmed if in a few hours your mother gets her rosy cheeks back, only we've been having a few problems with our fridges." Granny was frozen solid!

1980

A new business • Lord of Alderley

In or around 1980 the pound became very strong against the dollar, which had a devastating effect on our antiques export business. As we were buying our stock in dollars it was no longer viable. Many of the dealers were going out of business. When times were booming some dealers had remortgaged their homes, with disastrous consequences. We weren't in that situation but business-wise I was at a loose end.

I placed an advert in the *Manchester Evening News* declaring that I would back any business with potential. I knew right from the start that I would be inundated with lunatics and crackpots and I certainly wasn't disappointed. Of all the crazy schemes which were put to me, only one small business based in Oldham was of interest. It was a mould-making business run by a chap called Ernie Bland. Ernie was a very grubby individual with an equally grubby and overweight wife. Although still only in their twenties they looked twice their age. It seemed as if they had lived their entire life on a diet of chips, peas and puddings. His wife would sit watching him for most of the day, and her bulk would remain fairly motionless except when Ernie would demand, "Put brew on, cock." Ernie was a wealth of malapropisms. We were discussing education one day when Ernie declared, "I were never very epidemic at school." Although I jest at his expense, he was a brilliant craftsman and I liked him a lot. He manufactured moulds for plasterwork and precast concrete in the form of cornices, ceiling roses, garden urns and statues. I think it was the artistic side of me that drew me to it rather than the money: big mistake!

The premises he was working from were chaotic and unsuitable. Before long, I found myself totally engrossed in the business, ploughing money into new machinery and tools. I even bought a small factory in Oldham and moved the whole operation into it. Ernie couldn't believe his luck; he'd struck gold. His standard of workmanship was very high but I persuaded him that our moulds would be far better being mass-produced in plastic rather than laboriously and individually made in fibreglass. I consulted my old chum, Jim Parry, who owned a plastics company manufacturing plastic buckets. He advised me that in our case, vacuum forming was the answer rather than injection moulding. I bought a vacuum forming machine. The masters were made and everything was going according to plan. Not only did we start to make the moulds and supply them to precast concrete companies but we even started manufacturing the end product and supplying the garden centres.

One day I received a call from a friend in London, asking me to call into a company in Oldham which specialised in manufacturing steel moulds; Lyson Steel Moulds Ltd.

When I arrived, the director and a group of men were pondering over a problem of how to create patterns in wet-cast concrete moulds for fence panels. Previously, patterns could only be reproduced from a fibreglass mould. Their steel trays produced plain panels only. Immediately the idea hit me. I could produce a thin patterned liner to fit perfectly into their trays; that way they could interchange any number of patterns in the same tray. I foolishly suggested that we work in harmony. Lyson, Ernie and myself went to a patent agent in Manchester and registered the patent in all three names.

We set about manufacturing and it was enthusiastically received by the industry.

We expanded the range of moulds to create decorative wet-cast paving. To this day, as I travel the country, I see the patterns that Ernie and I created, at people's homes, on pavements and in shopping centres throughout the land.

Prior to this, and through my relationship with the Richards family at Gawsworth near Macclesfield, I was catapulted into the lower ranks of the nobility. I was to become Lord of Alderley. I believe it was Grandma who initiated that I should receive the title and all manorial rights. All noble titles in Britain are known in law as incorporeal hereditaments; property without body. It is something which is of value, can be inherited, but you can't see it, smell it, or touch it. The title had travelled through recorded history, starting in the late twelfth century with Robert de Montalt, then the Orrebys, de Arderne, de Wever, Fittons of Gawsworth, Tattons of Wythenshawe, Stanleys, Richards and now me.

I wrote to Lord Sudeley who suggested I get in touch with Robert Smith, who was the Chairman of the Manorial Society; an unofficial governing body of feudal lords. At this stage I was totally unaware that I was about to become public property and fair game for constant intrusion into my daily life by the media.

From this time onwards "the slings and arrows of outrageous fortune" were to fly in my direction, thick and fast.

1981-82

A family crisis • The parting of the ways • A new company
• Planning the Domesday celebration

It was 1981. My stepfather, who was well documented as being one of the greatest rocket research scientists in the world, went for an operation for an aneurism and came out with brain damage. I flew to California to be at Mother's side and spent every day and every night for a month trying to talk him out of a deep coma. We succeeded, and although he never fully recovered he did have a quality of life. For the next twelve years Mother washed him, dressed him, fed him and loved him. No man on earth had a more loyal, devoted and caring wife than he. In addition to that she controlled all the properties, ran the household and sorted out my brother, who was going through that rebellious stage that so many young men go through. Against all odds she took on the might and power of the American medical world and won. They paid her a very substantial settlement, five minutes before walking into court.

On the home front the atmosphere was becoming strained with Ernie and me. His artistic temperament overruled his sense of business. He would start as many as six jobs without completing any of them. Much as I tried to impress upon him the importance of getting orders out and keeping customers happy, it made little difference. In the end it all became too much. I had always paid him a good salary and had bought him a company car. We had two full-time reps on the road bringing in the orders but something had to give. Ernie could see his umbilical cord being severed and it turned nasty. I could no longer keep ploughing money into something when he wasn't keeping his side of the bargain. I paid him a lump sum and waved him goodbye.

Sue and I also began to drift apart. She took less interest in going to the Powder House at weekends and more interest in her passion for ballroom dancing. Sue is one of those people who goes into things with a full-on commitment. Hats off to her, she ended up with just about every gold medal for dancing that you can get. I couldn't get enthused, as you may remember from my barn-dancing days at High School in America. Sue purchased a flat at Brooklands and she and I moved into it for a while; I sold the cottage. On a business flight to London she met someone else and for a time we went through an emotional yoyo while she decided – him or me. One night when she didn't come home, I'd had enough. I drove to his house in Bramhall near Stockport. He answered the door in nothing more than his dressing gown; it was around 1.30a.m. I hit him square on the jaw, knocking him down his hallway and after a few pleas of shock and dismay, I let him go. He wiped the blood from his face and offered me a gin and tonic. After several more gin and tonics, I discovered the poor man had previously not known of my existence. His relationship with Sue was to be a short-lived one. In actual fact, on the night that he got his jaw rearranged she was nowhere near him as she'd gone to Chester.

That marked the denouement to our relationship and six months later Sue married a gentle and shy man called Nick Waterfield.

I carried on with the business but relied heavily on my personal assistant, Patricia Platts-Judd. Patricia was the third wife of one of my dearest friends, Peter Platts-Judd.

Peter was the grandson of a marchioness and he had all the social graces of an aristocrat but not a pot to pee in. He had been successful and was a great craftsman. He was one of the queen's jewellers at Garrards for a time, before setting up his own jewellery business in Dublin. There he met Patricia and fell in lust and in love. He was forty and she was eighteen. Patricia was loyal and incredibly hard- working and Peter was the laziest man on earth but charming with it. Peter got divorced and he and Pat came to England and moved into a rented shop in Stockport where they set up an antiques business. Pat went out to work ,while Peter loosely looked after the shop, but he was utterly incorrigible. I remember one time when they were down to their last five pounds; all they had for a week's groceries. Pat left him in charge of the shopping. When she got home he had bought two tins of baked beans and a fine bottle of Claret at £4. He just couldn't help himself, he was an aristocrat!

When Sue and I were together we were invited to their wedding at Stockport Register Office. We arrived, all dolled up and dressed to the nines and were politely shown into a waiting room. After several minutes Sue and I whispered to each other how incredibly scruffy the other guests were. It took another few minutes to realise that we were in the Social Security Benefits Office, next door.

After the ceremony the wedding car arrived. It was Peter and Pat's old Volvo estate car, loaded with furniture with a wardrobe tied to the roof. They were a wonderful couple. Pat stuck with Peter through thick and thin and many years later, Pat, Sue and myself were at Peter's bedside when he died. I still miss him.

With Ernie no longer on the business scene, I needed an injection of expertise, someone who knew the plastics industry and someone who knew about vacuum forming. I was not remotely interested in passive investors or sleeping partners, except my new little secretary called Adele. Pat had found the daily journey from Stockport to Oldham too much and sadly left my employ. Adele was seventeen when she came to work for me. She was chirpy, fun, intelligent, pretty and utterly nubile. Every morning she brought sunshine into a grey Oldham day. She hadn't typed too many letters when I had her in my arms. I thoroughly enjoyed making love to Adele. She had few inhibitions. She had her whole life ahead of her and she was going to live every minute of it. Again, I advertised for working partners and sieved through great armies of unsuitables. Barry Gray had been our sole supplier of plastic sheeting right from day one and he had been most helpful in overcoming technical problems. His weekly visits to my office were always informative, chatty and fun. As our supplier and over time, he got to know us very well and on one such visit he asked me if I would consider him as a possible investor/partner. He seemed perfect: he had been in the plastics industry since he left school at fifteen and he was now forty. We found another investor in the form of Bill Sherrington. Bill had a mechanical and vacuum forming background and there was nothing he didn't know about machinery. Like Blue Peter, if you gave him a washing up bottle, a toilet roll and a piece of string he could make a vacuum forming machine out of it. The success of the firm seemed inevitable.

On the advice of my accountant it was decided to form a new company. I would exchange the existing company for shares and Gray and Sherrington would invest money in exchange for the same, thus saving a Capital Gains Tax liability on my part. The structure of the shareholding would be: me, 39%, Gray, 39% and Sherrington 22%.

Thermovac Plastic Products Limited was the new company and it continued to trade from my factory (rent free). After a while we decided to take advantage of Mrs. Thatcher's new Enterprise Zone Scheme and move the whole operation to Trafford Park in Manchester. That allowed me to rent my little factory to an engineering company. The distance was easier for me but Gray had to travel each day from Leeds.

In my lordly capacity I was asked to attend a meeting in the House of Lords. I arrived and after a few drinks in the Lords' Bar we all filed into one of the chambers. Present were the Earl of Cork, Viscount Masserine, Lord Montague, Lord Sudeley, Garter King of Arms Sir Colin Cole, a host of Members of Parliament, a variety of toffs and nobs and of course, Robert Smith, Chairman of the Manorial Society.

Her Majesty the Queen had approved the idea that a great celebration should take place in 1986, marking the 900th anniversary of the Domesday Book and royal administration of the country. After much debate, regional chairmen were proposed and seconded. Three guesses who was voted as Northern Regional Chairman? It would mean a great deal of work and at that time I didn't think too much about the possible personal cost. I was also involving myself in charity work. In the forming of Thermovac it was all agreed that leading up to and including 1986, my other duties would prevent me from being totally committed to the daily running of the business. This didn't seem to create a problem at first, but as time went on there was a major personality change in Gray. His resentment of me and my lifestyle became patently obvious. He hated it when calls would come into the office for me either from Members of Parliament or from people like Margaret, Duchess of Argyle, who had become a dear chum. His endearment of me was not enhanced when he unexpectedly walked into the office and caught me in a slightly compromising position with Adele. She really disliked him and so did the workers. Adele also found travelling such long distances to work and having to spend more time with Gray and less with me too much, and she gave notice. I was deeply saddened to see her go.

I was now in my thirties and I became aware of an overwhelming urge to have a family of my own. I was never destined to have a normal and conventional life and in retrospect I wouldn't have had it any other way. Some of us are happy to spend life on the merry-go-round, going round and round with only the slightest undulation. Some go on the bumper cars. I chose the roller coaster of life.

1983-84

Kelly • Good news and bad news

In October of 1983 I treated myself to a new Range Rover and was feeling rather good about myself. I was driving along Washway Road in Sale when I spotted the vision of a raven-haired gypsy girl with the most wonderful figure. I had to take a second look and drove around the block to pass her again. I couldn't believe it. It was one of Bill Kelly's girls, all grown up! Bill Kelly had done work for several members of the family as a plumber. She spotted me and beckoned me over. I was a moth to a flame.

Not being the sort of chap who is slow at coming forward, I asked her if she would like to spend the weekend with me at the Powder House. She flatly refused.

She told me she worked at a dance school as an instructor. I remember thinking at the time: "Oh no! Not another ballroom dancer."

I didn't hear from her for a few weeks but then I got a phone call asking me to attend her twenty-first birthday party, on November 21st. I was thirty-four.

Our romance ignited fairly quickly, after which she dispatched her previous boyfriend with the ruthless efficiency of a female praying mantis. I, as the conquering male, ignored his whimpering, albeit at my peril at a much later date. Love blossomed and my desire to have children was discussed at length.

Mother had purchased a flat at Brooklands as a pied-à-terre in England and as a temporary measure Kelly and I moved into it. She started training with British Airways as a stewardess. I had never met a woman so keen to improve herself as much as Kelly and I admired her for that. She even went to elocution lessons. My mother's family and many friends didn't approve of my relationship with her, although at this stage of things they were too polite to make a big issue of it.

In July 1984, Kelly phoned me from London; I was going to be a daddy. I had never before experienced a feeling of such overwhelming joy and elation as I did at that moment in my life. No child to be born on this planet was more wanted than this one, as far as I was concerned.

Mother was over from California at this time, but was staying at my aunt's house. I was so blinded by the absolute bliss of it all and I just couldn't wait to tell my mother and everyone else my wonderful news. Kelly remained in the sitting room with my aunt and uncle while I took Mother into the kitchen to explain why I was all aglow with a big smile on my face.

The explosion of the first atomic bomb was the equivalent to popping a blown-up crisp packet in comparison to the explosion that took place in that kitchen. I had never heard my mother scream before, not like that!

"You stupid fool. You have fallen for the oldest trick in the book. A girl like her would do anything to get a catch like you. Get her out of this house and out of my sight." I feebly tried to explain that I really wanted this child. "Then you're a bigger idiot than I took you for!" she screamed. I tried again to explain that this baby was planned, but it was no use. Kelly and I walked hand in hand back down the driveway.

It would be a year before I spoke to my mother again. It broke my heart and I'm sure hers also. Although I hadn't spent a great deal of physical time with my mother in my life, we had always been close. It was so sad, she just didn't understand how much it meant to me and how much I needed this in my life.

For the last three months of Kelly's pregnancy the doctor decided there was a serious possibility of her losing the baby. She needed to be admitted to hospital. I went every lunchtime and every evening. By the latter end of 1984, Kelly was becoming increasingly depressed at her confinement in hospital and I managed to persuade Mr. Cowie to let her home for Christmas and New Year. It was a wonderful time. I watched over her, cared for her and never let her out of my sight for a second. Her depression deepened and she started to interrogate me over my relationship with Adele. At one point she even told me she had found a lace garter belonging to Adele under the bed at Brooklands, which wasn't true.

1985

A new arrival • A (cold) weekend in the country
• Lewis Collins and the missed opportunities
• Reconciliation • More Domesday duties • Ravi Shankar
• Sculpture • Sebastian's christening • A coup!

January 29th 1985. The day began with my attendance at work. Barry Gray had become more alien and we had started to avoid each other. The atmosphere was becoming strained and thoroughly unpleasant. At 10.30a.m. I got a call from Park Hospital to tell me Kelly had gone into labour but I wasn't to come as this could go on until tomorrow.

At 11.30a.m. her waters broke; "Come immediately," they said. At break-neck speed I arrived at 11.50a.m. and remained by her side for the rest of the day. I was so impressed by the care and attention of the staff. They were all so kind. By 5p.m. the nurse told me I must go and eat something as she might need my full attention later. At 6.30p.m. the nurse and I wheeled Kelly into one of the theatres. I dressed in the appropriate surgical attire and we were ready to go! There were several babies being born at that time and they seemed to be short staffed. The nurse said to me, "You're not going to faint on me are you?" I assured her that I was a country boy and in my youth I had assisted in the birth of sheep, horses, pigs and cattle. How different was this going to be? "Not much," she said.

Kelly gave birth in silence and although in pain without a murmur. She was just wonderful. The cord was wrapped around my son's neck and the nurse held it while I cut it. The second he was born I was the first to hold him; I cried and he didn't.

Just at that moment a doctor arrived on the scene and he got me to weigh him and measure him; born 7.10 p.m. 8lb 8oz, 21 inches long.

He was brought over to Kelly who said, "Thank God he's not got red hair." Her grandmother had red hair and one of my grandmothers had also. Kelly fell asleep almost immediately. The doctor then started to become concerned as the baby began to lose body temperature very quickly. We took him to Intensive Care and I sat by his side until 1.30a.m. The nurse assured me he was fine and I was sent home. I phoned again at 3a.m. just to make sure.

My uncle, Brian Leigh, collected Sebastian, Kelly and me from the hospital in his Rolls-Royce and the first drink Sebastian had, apart from his Mother's milk, was pink Champagne. I hoped it would be a good omen of things to come for the rest of his life!

For the first time in my life I had someone who was totally mine. Someone I could give unconditional love to. To guide him through life and to share the joys of life. I would never abandon him in any way. I felt that I was the happiest and luckiest man alive.

A week later I was due in London for a meeting of the Domesday Committee.

I arrived at Robert Smith's house at Kennington only to be met with a blazing row between Robert and Michael Farrow over money. I didn't quite get the gist of it but I thought, "This doesn't bode well, the committee is only just beginning and we are already at war." I met Michael later for a few drinks at the Carlton Club before moving on to the House of Lords for our strategy meeting. All the time I was missing Kelly and my new little son, Sebastian. In the earlier stages of her pregnancy we were at the Powder House when we received a visit from Sebastian Chance. If I remember correctly, he was related to Sir Hugh and Lady Chance who had a place nearby. After he left, Kelly said, "If we have a boy, I'd like to call him Sebastian." I agreed, and Sebastian he became.

In early March, we set off for the Powder House to spend our first weekend there as a family. For some reason I had replaced the Range Rover with a Land Rover. Don't ask me why. By comparison, it was an uncomfortable and bone-shaking experience.

By the time we got over the hills past Chester and before getting to Ruthin, we were hit by a snow storm, the like of which I'd only experienced in Canada. The wipers couldn't clear it and the Land Rover struggled to plough through it. Inwardly I was becoming deeply concerned for our safety. My normal route from Ruthin to Porthmadog was over the highest moorland, via Ysbyty Ifan and on to Llan Ffestiniog. At two miles per hour we finally pulled into the Griffin Inn at Ruthin, where we were offered accommodation. Several Hot Toddies by a roaring coal fire made everything well again.

The following morning was the most glorious day imaginable. Crisp clean air and a cloudless sky. Our cautious journey over the moors was breathtakingly beautiful. The following day, Kelly, Sebastian and I played on the Powder House terrace. Life couldn't possibly get any better; it was just wonderful.

My duties, commitments and invitations were coming in daily. John Richards phoned to ask if I would join the royal party on Saturday at the Grand National with Princess Anne, but I was already obliged to attend the weekend at Merlin's (Lord Sudeley) ancestral pile, Toddington Hall.

I employed a nanny to help Kelly in looking after Sebastian. Kelly was desperate to return to working on the airlines but she breastfed him for the first six months. The nanny didn't last too long. Kelly came home one night to find he hadn't had his nappy changed all day and, quite rightly, she fired her.

I had ordered a little red sports car from the factory, a Panther convertible, but had to wait for three months as there was a waiting list. It was utterly unsuitable for a family but there was just enough room for Sebastian's travelling cot behind the two seats. Kelly loved it; Panthers are fun little cars.

I arrived at Toddington in it. The house was a truly magnificent pile, a sandstone building resembling a smaller version of the Houses of Parliament. It even had its own "Big Ben" tower. Merlin greeted me at the main entrance and I was shown up to my bedroom. Some of his guests were taking tea in one of the drawing rooms, including a rather loud American lady cousin of his from Virginia. One of Merlin's family had been one of the founders of Jamestown there.

At 7.30p.m. we were called to dinner. Dress was black ties and terribly formal. The meal was atrocious. Cold soup, cold plates, cold chicken, cold vegetables but at least the Claret was warm.

The following morning I awoke early and went down for breakfast. Cold egg, cold bacon, cold tea, cold hands, cold feet, cold rooms. After breakfast I took a stroll around the grounds and then went into the library where Merlin had arranged for a learned speaker to talk about the Domesday Book. He was an enormous frame of a man with the most debilitating speech impediment and a great bushy beard. The muffling effect of the beard along with the impediment of speech made it completely impossible to understand a single word he said. In addition to that he marched up and down in front of us, waving his arms in great sweeping gestures. I got a fit of the giggles. I tried so hard to control myself and look learned, nodding in the right places whenever his gaze met mine, but it became torturous.

The day continued with a further selection of utterly potty people.

That evening dinner was again black ties, only this time the food was joyfully hot. I drank far too much and retired at 3a.m.

The following morning I had the most dreadful headache. Jamie (Lord Neidpath) had invited us over to his family home, Stanway Hall, a few miles away for luncheon.

We arrived at Stanway village, a beautiful, quintessentially English country village, totally unspoilt. The thing that struck me was the heavily encrusted growths of lichen on all of the buildings, including the Manor House. The second was the presence of scallop shells. Every building was festooned with them: they were on finials, on pediments, on lead drainpipes, literally everywhere. Jamie's father, the Earl of March and Weymes, chatted to me for a while and then I was invited into the Great Hall. This was an enormous place and no attempt had been made to change its Elizabethan austerity.

It was so cold, I started to feel a similar feeling to the one I'd had the day my granny lay in her coffin.

Lady Neidpath was lying on the stone hearth next to the dying embers of a fire in the huge open fireplace. She was dressed in torn jeans and army boots and was sporting a high-standing, brightly coloured Mohican or cockatoo hairstyle. The furniture was mostly eighteenth- and pre-eighteenth-century and almost all of it was in a delightful state of decaying splendour. The upper drawing room had two of the most splendid Chippendale day beds in it. We were all just admiring them when there was an almighty scream from Merlin's American cousin. There was a dead bat on one of the tables. Jamie casually informed her that it had died and fallen from the ceiling two weeks before. The one thing I must say about this house is that it is totally lived in. Personal items are scattered everywhere and although I believe they do open to the public there is no attempt to cater for tourists. There is nothing pretentious about it or its occupants.

Over luncheon I engaged in conversation with an attractive and very stylish woman called Anne Maxwell. She was the daughter of Robert Maxwell, the newspaper magnate. Anne and I stayed together for the rest of the afternoon; she was amusing and very charming. The old Earl asked me if I would give him a lift back to Toddington but was less keen when he saw my little red convertible Panther. By the time we got back, there was another meal awaiting us. Anne joined myself and two of my friends, Rosamund de Tracy-Kelly, who is the most brilliant sculptress, and Gerald Rand, Lord of Lynford. I'd had enough by this time. The thought of shaving again in ice-cold water in the morning was more than I could cope with. I made my apologies and drove to Chalfont St. Peter to visit another chum of mine, Lewis Collins.

Lewis was going out with Kelly's best friend, Sheilah. He was an actor from Liverpool and had first starred on television in a show called *Cuckoo Waltz*, but at this time he was in a weekly TV show called *The Professionals*. Bodie and Doyle were the two characters and Lew was Bodie. Lew had started his working life as a ladies' hairdresser, working in the same shop as Mike McCartney (Sir Paul McCartney's brother), later of Scaffold fame. The comedian, Jimmy Tarbuck, also worked there. Lew had a number of claims to fame of his own. Firstly, he was an exceptional drummer and if I may say it, with considerably more talent than Ringo Starr.

Lew, Mike and Paul grew up together. In the transitional time when Paul's group was called The Quarrymen and then later The Beatles, Paul was looking for a new drummer. Mike suggested Lew should talk to Paul about joining the band. Lew replied, "Why the hell would I want to join your kid's band?" His second claim was many years later. Lew had starred in a film called *Who Dares Wins*. The film was given a private showing to Ronald Reagan in the White House and the President loved it. (The film bombed in the United States because of its content, where a British SAS unit rescued an American ambassador. The yanks couldn't cope with that storyline.) Cubby Broccoli's wife saw Lewis and was very keen to have him as the next James Bond. Lew would have been perfect as James Bond – he was handsome, suave and tough. But when it came to it, Lew had some disagreement with Cubby Broccoli himself and that was the end of that. To mess up on being a member of The Beatles and James Bond takes some doing. I can only relay these stories as told to me by Lewis himself.

I arrived at Lew's house, a beautiful half-timbered Elizabethan farmhouse with a cluster of outbuildings, set in three acres. After some tea and headache pills I started to feel better. I decided I would stay at the pub down the road. Lew had a huge Alsatian dog who had serious mental problems. One minute he wanted to play, then for no reason he wanted to eat your leg off. I'd be petrified if I wanted to go to the loo in the night with him wandering around the house. That evening Lew and Sheilah came to join me at the pub. I woke the next morning with yet another splitting head; it was April Fool's Day and didn't I feel the fool. I couldn't wait to get back to Cheshire to see Kelly and Sebastian; I loved and missed them so much.

The following weekend we loaded the Land Rover and Kelly, Sebastian and I headed off for the Powder House. Toward the evening my Uncle Brian and friends arrived with the guns to set up a clay

pigeon shoot from my headland. My performance was not outstand-
ing but I bagged sufficient clays in order for it not to be embarrassing.

The following day the artillery arrived again and this time they
brought the womenfolk with them. I was so proud of Kelly; she
bagged a high-flying clay with her very first shot, having never held a
shotgun before. She continued to do well. My performance was
utterly dreadful. I couldn't have hit an elephant's arse from ten feet
away with a barrel-load of buckshot. The shooting party left as
darkness fell and Kelly and I started a barbecue for ourselves. The
tides were high and the full moon hung over the hills behind Harlech
Castle. We settled down for the evening, the fire all aglow with the
sound of the sea lapping against the rocks just below the house.
Before retiring, I wrote my diary by the light of the oil lamp and Kelly
made hot wine toddies. We made love in front of the fire. Life was
good, very good indeed, as nearly every weekend, Kelly, Sebastian
and I headed for the Powder House.

At the beginning of May I received a call from my mother. I was
thrilled. She told me how much she had missed me and loved me.
She asked all about Sebastian and said she couldn't wait to see him.
She also said she had been in a terrible state over it all.

When I agreed to being on the Domesday Committee I had no idea
just how much work was involved.

At the risk of boring you, I will just give a synopsis. So far, I'm
involved in helping with the London exhibition which includes the
actual Domesday Book and dealing with Sir John Donaldson, Master
of the Rolls; getting Sir Ron Dearing to arrange the issue of postage
stamps for the year; helping the BBC to try and recreate a modern
Domesday Book involving children throughout the country; doing
endless numbers of radio, TV and press interviews; organising a
Northern Domesday Gala; organising a Northern Domesday charity
dinner; arranging with all the northern education authorities to bus
children to the exhibition in London; getting schools to do their own
exhibitions ... The list goes on and on and not a penny of expenses to
be seen. (I think the whole thing ended up costing me, over a few
years, a staggering forty thousand pounds! All for the good of the
nation.)

It is May 13th, my birthday. I have to attend another meeting today
in the House of Lords followed by a drinks party there. The drinks
begin to flow and there are the usual offerings of sausages on sticks
etc. Her Grace Margaret, Duchess of Argyle, arrives with her usual

escort, a flamboyant character who reminds me of Teezy Weezy, the 1950s Hollywood hairdresser. I don't remember him, but he remembered every word I said to him a year before. Margaret comes over to me for a chat and overall the little soirée goes rather well.

Around 8.30p.m. most people leave the Lords and we head over to the Carlton Club for dinner. I can no longer call it a "gentlemen's club" as Mrs. Thatcher has just been made the first lady member in a hundred and fifty years. Sir Colin is unable to join us and I take his place next to the Duchess. We have the most wonderful evening. Although I have met Margaret several times before I have never really got to know her properly. We get on like a house on fire and she promises to give me a copy of her book, *Forget Not*.

She has also agreed to come to my charity dinner in Manchester as my guest. She has invited me to a party at her penthouse suite. Over dinner she says, "James, you and I are old friends now, my name is Margaret, not Your Grace. I only hate it when that cheeky bugger Robert Smith calls me Margaret. I never gave him permission."

Back at the office, things are improving and it is becoming very busy, although my relationship with Gray is not any more cordial. The Duchess phones, much to the displeasure of Gray. She has a copy of her book for me, and at the party, she would like me to come earlier than her other guests in order to have a little private parley.

A week later I arrive at Grosvenor House. I am informed by reception that I may go straight up to the penthouse; Suite 148 is the London home of the Duchess. I am greeted by the beaming and welcoming smile of her butler, who takes my coat and politely asks, "Would Sir care for a sherry?" The sitting room is grand and in the most exquisite taste. The furnishing is classical; Louis XVI gilt and pastel colours abound. Above the Robert Adam fireplace hangs an enormous Venetian mirror. Pieces of jade and objets d'art are scattered throughout the place. A bronze bust of a much younger Duchess features most prominently next to a silver-framed and signed photograph of her friend, John Paul Getty.

The drawing room has front and rear terraces and the view over the park is remarkable. Margaret shows me onto her main terrace and explains with delight how she has recently had the walkway re-tiled: "It makes it so much easier for Alfonse."

Just then Alfonse arrives on the scene, treats me with suspicion, barks a few times, and then ignores me. Today he is wearing his diamond-encrusted party collar.

Her guests start to arrive and as expected, the Duchess has a very cosmopolitan group of friends. Lady Molly Buckley and the Argentinean Chargé d'Affaires, who is charming despite the fact we are at war with his country. He and I chat about everything except politics. Also Charmine de Silva, who apparently was painted by Picasso and hailed as the most beautiful woman in the world. When I first met Charmine, years ago, she was indeed stunning, but tonight she's looking a little past her sell-by date. There are Arab sheiks, art dealers, lords, barristers and some woman who owned Beirut before they razed it to the ground.

The actor, Anthony Andrews, arrives with his wife, but I find him slightly irritating as he is still in character as Sebastian in *Brideshead Revisited*. Also present are Margaret's son and daughter-in-law from her marriage to the American golfer, Sweeney. The butler serves Champagne all evening but I stick to Bucks Fizz as I want to keep a clear head. As the guests slowly filter away at around 9.30p.m. Margaret and I jump into a taxi and head for one of her favourite restaurants, "The Walton" on Walton Street, Covent Garden. The food at The Walton is truly magnificent and so is the price; I pay! Over dinner we gossip about every person we both know and she also tells me she is at war with the people who run the Bleakholt Animal Sanctuary in Rawtenstall, Lancashire, of which she is Patron. Margaret helped fund the thing in its early days. The following morning I opened the Daily Mail to see a headline: "Duchess Accuses Destroyers in Animal Sanctuary".

June 22nd 1985. I heard that Ravi Shankar was performing at the Albert Hall in Bolton and so I decided to introduce Kelly to the intricacies of classical Indian music. Upon our arrival, Ravi was informed that I was in the audience and as we were seated the manager came to tell us that "he will be delighted to see you in his dressing room after the performance".

The performance of the great man, accompanied by the master of the tabla, Alla Rahha, was everything I expected. I first began to enjoy the sitar as a boy, without understanding it, because it is without Western melody. It has a precise and scientific melodic structure and form. That master of violin, Sir Yehudi Menuhin, paid the most remarkable tribute to Ravi when he said, "Ravi Shankar has brought me a precious gift and through him I have added a new dimension to my experience of music. To me, his genius and humanity can only be compared to Mozart."

The show ended and Kelly and I were led up the stairs to the dressing room. A large number of the audience remained behind in order to catch a glimpse or get an autograph from their hero. Ravi welcomed me warmly, and firstly we both greeted each other in the traditional way of India, with joined hands as if in prayer, and then we hugged. He asked me about Karuna and my mother and I told him the sad news of my stepfather's condition. His eyes filled with tears. We chatted for a while and he promised to call on my mother and Karuna when he was next in Santa Barbara. We parted and in minutes he was mobbed by the crowd.

I bought Kelly a new Mini 1000. It was nice to see her so happy. I managed to sell the Panther. I'm afraid I had to return to a Range Rover; far more suitable for a family. Work seemed to be going in the right direction and my relationship with Barry Gray was improving. Sebastian spent each day charming everyone with his chuckles. We were very blessed indeed, he was such a happy little chap.

Around this time, Rosamund de Tracy-Kelly phoned to ask when she could do a bronze sculptured portrait of me. She had been asking me for years and much as it appealed to my vanity, I just hadn't had the time. In August I finally made it to Rosamund's. I had never seen her home before. The house is a very fine Georgian country mansion just near Oxford and built in that lovely yellow Cotswold stone. One enters the grounds from the far corner and the driveway sweeps quarter circle to the front door, passing some architecturally grand stables on the way. I was quite certain I was in the right place because as I entered the main hall, to the left of me was an enormous portrait of Rosamund's father. The walls of this lovely house are so filled with historic portraits, some of them very early indeed, that there is barely wall-space between them.

Rosamund was busy cleaning her studio in preparation for my arrival. I'm very honoured that she would go to so much trouble. Her studio is on the top floor of the stables, directly below the clock tower. She showed me around the grounds before we joined her parents for luncheon. This was served in the vast oak-panelled dining room. Someone looking remarkably like Richard III looked down at me disapprovingly as I slurped the hot soup and spilt it down the front of my shirt. Rosamund's father and I talked incessantly about antiques and art. At one point he tried to quiz me but there was nothing he possessed that I couldn't date within ten years!

We wasted no further time and Rosamund worked with me right

through until 9.30 at night. Some operatic society had requested to use their drawing room and it was decided that we should dine in the enormous Victorian kitchen. Rosamund's mother only drinks water and I was amused to see that she decants it into an old whisky bottle. The family name being de Tracy, naturally the wine was Chateau de Tracy from some relative who owns a vineyard in Normandy. They, along with Lord Sudeley who is also a Tracy, descend from one of the four knights who murdered Thomas Becket.

I slept well and we had an early start. This sitting still for hours is hard work. I was amazed at how quickly that lump of clay became as me. Rosamund would periodically keep measuring parts of my head and face with a calliper. Because time was limited she also took endless amounts of photographs in order to get a perfect detail after I'd gone.

Again she worked through until late but I took her to a little French restaurant for dinner instead of dining in the big house. By noon the following day we had gone as far as time permitted and I was due at Chalfont St. Peter to pick Kelly and Sebastian up at Lew's house. I arrived at about the same time as Kelly. She was deeply upset as someone had broken into her little Mini car. Lew's mad dog attacked me and so it was back to the Bull at Gerrard's Cross for us for the night. The following morning we drove straight to the Powder House only to find Ray Teret and his girlfriend sitting on the doorstep. Ray was one of the first disc jockeys on Radio Caroline before having several shows of his own on different radio stations and the occasional appearance on Top of the Pops. He was great friends with Sir Jimmy Savile and although, I think, Ray was considerably wittier and far cleverer than Jimmy, his style was very similar. The airwaves covering Britain just weren't big enough for two Jimmy Saviles.

We had a wonderful evening, and it was lovely to see them both but it had been a very long day for Kelly and me.

Saturday, September 14th 1985 was Sebastian's christening. I felt it only right and proper that he should be christened at St. Mary's Church in Nether Alderley. The weather was appalling – rain, sun and howling winds all at the same time. The service was wonderful and although Reverend Roberts and I have had our differences in the past, that day he pulled out all the stops.

During the service, after Sebastian had been accepted into the Christian faith, Reverend Roberts asked the congregation to sit quietly while he carried him around in his arms, talking to him and explaining all sorts of things about the church, as if he were an adult. It was hilariously funny. Lewis was his godfather which attracted a great deal of press interest, much to the bewilderment of Reverend Roberts. Sheilah was the godmother and a friend of Kelly's called Philip was the second godfather.

After the service my aunt Phil and uncle Peter put on a fabulous reception at White Hall which was their family home on Whitehall Road in Sale. Again the press were waiting for us. It was a memorable day and my only sadness was that my mother was unable to be there to share it with us.

I was entitled to a few days off from the office and so I took advantage of the time to work on the Powder House. While I was there, my totally loyal secretary, Alison, phoned me to tell me that Gray and Sherrington were plotting something in my absence; my *coup de grâce* was being planned! She said that Gray had been through my diary and expense sheets and ransacked my files and desk. I was utterly disgusted and deeply hurt. We were a long way from the Barry Gray whom I had become so fond of when he was a rep for Imari Plastics.

At this time of year, just before Christmas, the pre-cast concrete companies wind down and don't place their orders until the beginning of January. Our company was on the brink of sealing a massive contract with Barclays Bank for the manufacture of all of their exterior signs. Although the contract was not fully implemented at this date, we were in the process of working out a lot of technical problems regarding their specific Barclays blue colour.

Despite this, Gray and Sherrington called an Extraordinary General Meeting on the morning of my return to the office, Wednesday, November 20th 1985. In attendance was a firm of solicitors and our company accountant who sat silently throughout the entire meeting like a bloody great dummy.

At the meeting, their solicitor recommended that the shareholders vote for the company to be liquidated. My protests were ignored. Gray and Sherrington raised their hands. I was told to hand over the keys to the office and I walked away with nothing. I found out later from Companies House that they had set up another company in Leeds with almost the same name, six weeks before the Extraordinary General Meeting. At the Creditors Meeting only one turned up; *quelle surprise*! Their new company bought everything from the liquidator for pennies. I went to a corporate solicitor in Manchester for advice. He gave me a cup of tea and said, "James, you've been screwed" and as I walked out of his office five minutes later, he handed me a bill for £80. At that rate he was the biggest crook of all.

As I write, I have learnt in life that if you are kindly, honourable and moderately wealthy you are fair game for every gold-digging jackal there is. The super-rich are immune to it and the very poor are not worth pursuing. I was brought up to believe that honour, integrity, respect and a sense of duty are the basic hallmarks by which one should live one's life. But this is a predatory world and Barry Gray had not finished with me yet.

The Domesday celebration was looming and with my predicament it would have been easily justifiable for me to offer my resignation as Northern Chairman, but that would be a defeatist cowardly way and would mean letting a lot of people down.

1986

**Highjinks with Johnny • More time with the Duchess
• Domesday events • Royal Windsor Horse Show
• My Charity Domesday Dinner • Willaston Hall
• Market rights • A California wedding**

In January we held Sebastian's first birthday party, which was a wonderful diversion from the woes of the time. February came quickly and I was due to attend a reception given by the Mayor of Chelmsford. Rosamund called to say that she had completed my bronze portrait and would I call on her. With the liquidation of the company my Range Rover was also taken from me and I borrowed a little white sports car from a friend. The night before leaving Kelly insisted on making love for the entire night. I think she thought that if she tired me out I wouldn't think of getting up to any mischief. I was so fatigued I stopped at a lorry drivers' café and slept in the car for an hour. Upon arrival at Oxford, Rosamund led me by the hand to the foot of their grand staircase. Half way up on a plinth stood my portrait, directly beneath a ten-foot high painting of King George IV. I was very flattered indeed.

Rosamund insisted I stay the night and we dined with her parents. I was fed on locally shot pheasant and Chateau de Tracy. I awoke in the morning to find the little white sports car had disappeared under a foot of snow! The drive to London was a slow and dangerous one. There I met up with Robert, Sir Colin and Nirj Deva. I had a lot of time for Nirj, he was a likeable fellow. About this time he was made a Deputy Lord Lieutenant of London and was later to be the second Asian-born person to become a Member of Parliament. The journey to Chelmsford was a nightmare. Much of it consisted of Robert screaming his head off at Nirj over his driving, while Sir Colin and I sat quietly in the back keeping our heads down and pulling faces at each other. The mayor had gone to a great deal of trouble to put on a splendid reception for us and had invited all the county mayors.

The following morning Big Ben struck 6.45a.m. as I drove over Westminster Bridge. Although the weather had improved slightly the roads were still treacherous with black ice. It was the slowest drive back to Manchester I can remember. I couldn't wait to see Kelly and Sebastian again.

I had only just walked in when the phone rang. It was Johnny Briggs, the actor who played Mike Baldwin in *Coronation Street*. He warned me that the press might give me a call regarding an incident he and I had had several days earlier.

Johnny and I were drinking in the Film Exchange Club, a restaurant and bar on Quay Street in Manchester; the place was exclusive to showbiz and television people. Johnny and I got progressively more drunk and he challenged me to an arm-wrestling contest. As I am considerably taller than him and in order to make it more equal we both lay on the floor amidst the diners in the restaurant. Everyone seemed highly amused at our drunken revelry except the new owner of the place who kicked us out, shouting at us that we were both banned, never to return. We staggered down the road holding each other up when Johnny had a brainwave. He marched back in and pulled the photograph of himself off the wall. He and I stumbled out again carrying the picture with us. The following day the *Daily Mirror* ran the story.

Minutes later the phone rang again. This time it was the Duchess complaining that she had not seen me for a couple of months. A week or so later I found myself attending yet another meeting in the House of Lords and as arranged I met up with Margaret for dinner. Her maid answered the door and pointed me in the direction of the sherry decanter. Margaret called me into the study where she had just received a copy of her granddaughter's latest record. Lady Teresa Manners had joined a pop group. I wasn't overly impressed – it sounded like a load of monotone crashing noise to me and Margaret agreed.

We found a wonderful new restaurant where she lectured me. She said, "James, I want you to cut all this charity work and socialising down by half. It's not good to be seen at every social event in town." I accused her of sounding like my mother. She also said she didn't like the attitude of that fellow in my office (Barry Gray). "I don't like his tone of voice." I told her she wouldn't be speaking to him any more and explained the reason. She was furious and horrified. Margaret could swear like a trooper when she got mad.

Margaret was a remarkable woman and she had lived an astonishing life. Many years before when she was married to Sweeney, Cole Porter wrote the song "You're the Top" about her. Her divorce from the Duke caused the biggest scandal in modern British history at the time. It was the most expensive and public divorce ever known. The famous "headless man" photograph caused outrage and gave the Duke the ammunition he needed. What is not publicly known is that when the Duke married Margaret he had very little money. Inveraray Castle was in a severe state of disrepair and Margaret set about spending huge amounts of her own fortune on renovating the castle. She modernised the plumbing and had the place rewired. She restored the furnishings, paintings and the armour. She had decorated and interior designed the place in a way that only someone with her exquisite taste and eye for detail could do. All of that was forgotten when they banned her. The fact is that the Campbells did rather well out of their relationship with Margaret.

Upon my arrival home, Granada Television wanted to do a little film with me. I arrived at the location at 11a.m. and the crew turned up at 2p.m. That's showbiz !

Toward the end of April, I was staying with my dear friend, Gerald Rand, Lord of Lynford. Lynford Hall at Mundford in Norfolk is a magnificent house with over a hundred rooms, some of them bigger than most people's houses. It is in similar style to the Queen's house at Sandringham. Edward VII wanted to buy Lynford but was prevented by Parliament because it had a tiny Roman Catholic chapel within the grounds.

From the driveway you approach an open courtyard separated by the most enormous and very splendid cast-iron screen and gates. An avenue of massive Wellingtonias (California Redwood trees) stretch as far as the eye can see, punctuated half way down by a plinth with two bronze fighting bulls on the top.

The front elevation of the house overlooks immaculately kept Italian gardens which sweep down to a large man-made lake. The island in the lake is connected by a Japanese half round bridge and in the centre is an oriental tea house. Gerald and I have been known to take tea there on warm summer days. In the hall, Gerald has always reserved a suite for me and now Sebastian was given his own bedroom, complete with his own cot and toys. My suite consisted of the rooms Squire Osbaldeston had occupied in the nineteenth century, and more recently they were reserved for John F. Kennedy as a boy, when his father was the Ambassador to London.

In the evening Gerald and I drove to London to attend a reception in the Fusilier Army Headquarters in the Tower of London given by Willie (Viscount) Whitelaw, the Deputy Prime Minister. It was a lovely evening and a group of players performed for us in the Tower Yard while we all watched from the steps.

A few days later I was due to return to the opening of the Domesday Exhibition with the Lord Chancellor, Lord Hailsham, (Quintin Hogg), but for various reasons it was impossible for me to return so soon and I wasn't essential to the ceremony.

It was April 29th 1986. I had stayed at Robert's house in Kennington the previous night. We had arranged a private viewing of the Domesday Book at our exhibition in Chancery Lane, and some of the nation's Lord Lieutenants and High Sheriffs were there along with Members of Parliament. As Northern Chairman it was my duty to entertain Colonel John Timmins, High Sheriff of Greater Manchester and Mr. Dickson, High Sheriff of Lancashire. It was a thoroughly enjoyable evening, I plied them with Champagne and both agreed to attend my Charity Domesday Dinner in Manchester. The next day was to be one of the big days in the year's calendar.

Needless to say I didn't sleep well, I never do in that basement bedroom in Kennington. I arose early, made myself some tea and got into the bathroom before anyone else.

Robert, Nirj and myself posed on the steps for photographs in our top hats and tails and within minutes a beautiful Rolls-Royce glided to a halt in front of us. A liveried driver wearing gaiters opened the door and took us to Westminster Abbey. As we arrived at the main entrance, a policeman stepped forward and opened the car door for us. The last of the street barriers were being erected and already there were hundreds of tourists and onlookers jostling into their positions to get the best view. As we got out of the car people behind the barriers took photographs; God knows what they do with them.

Fleets of mayoral cars arrived in lines from all over the realm. Every Lord Lieutenant, High Sheriff, Lord Mayor and Mr. Mayor in the country had been invited to celebrate the founding of a unified nation and the forming of local government in England. Mayoral chains, swords, buckle shoes and tricorn hats; the stage was set, over two thousand of them. In the Abbey the State Trumpeters practised their fanfare, the orchestra tuned up and the Westminster choir hummed.

Only five of us were to be presented to Her Majesty the Queen Mother and we stood in a neat little line close to the door. Then panic set in! Sir Colin Cole, Garter King of Arms, had two of Her Majesty's Heralds at Windsor and they were unable to attend. He called Gerald and myself to one side. He appointed me as Portcullis Pursuivant and Gerald as Rouge Croix Pursuivant and we quickly went through the format of the ceremony; there was only minutes to go. Most of the two thousand were seated by this time. Everyone kept turning to see if the royal car had arrived. One or two sheriffs and mayors were seen scurrying down the aisle with ushers urging them to hurry up!

A great cheer was heard from outside. The Queen Mum was a tiny lady and I was slightly amused to notice that her stockings were all wrinkled around her ankles. She was dressed all in black that day because she was due to attend the funeral of her old enemy Mrs. Wallis Simpson, Duchess of Windsor. I was introduced to her. It is difficult not to bow from the waist down instead of the head only. Because she is so small you instinctively felt the urge to make a grander gesture. The protocol is that the top hat is held in the left hand along with the glove from the right hand, allowing your bare hand to meet hers in a handshake, always remembering not to squeeze the royal fingers too tightly or to shake the royal arm too vigorously! We engaged in the usual inane conversation and it ended with "Thank you Ma'am."

The service begins! A great trumpet fanfare bellows out and the Sergeant at Arms leads the way carrying the facsimile of the Domesday Book. The Queen Mother, Sir Colin, Gerald and myself walk slowly up the long aisle to the altar and take our places there. The orchestra plays and the choir sings. I kneel by the Queen Mum and glance back down this vast room. The congregation is a sea of black, scarlet and gold, which glints and flashes in stained-glass sunlight. The heads of every county, city and major town are there and I pause to think, "What the Hell am I doing here?"

The great book is placed on the altar and the first commemorative service for Domesday takes place exactly nine hundred years after the event. I take a microscopic place in England's history; I was Her Majesty's Herald for a day!

The service ended and a small handful of us retired to the Jerusalem Chamber in the Abbey to have drinks with the Queen Mum. We all chatted with her and she made it very obvious she was enjoying herself and the last place she wanted to be was at Mrs. Simpson's funeral. Her equerry continued to interrupt our conversation every few minutes by saying, "We are running late Ma'am", and she continued to ignore him. She then turned to Gerald and said, "I've got them all in a tizzy, I'm late you know, tee hee hee, they'll have to send a helicopter for me."

I have been with several members of the Royal Family over the years and I don't envy their job one bit. It has got to be one of the most tiresome jobs on earth, having to engage in inane conversation with armies of ghastly people and pretend that you are interested in them all individually. To have to do that every day of your life is a big price to pay for privilege.

After drinks, our chauffeured Rolls-Royce took us to Claridges where we had a magnificent luncheon. I drove back to Manchester still in my tails.

Meanwhile, Kelly had started a new job with Cal Air and was going to Gatwick for her training. I brought Sebastian along to say goodbye to his mummy and we all had luncheon at an Italian restaurant. His behaviour was terrible that day: he shouted, cried and threw his food everywhere. He was so disruptive that the waitress had to take him for a walk while we tried to finish our meal. We put it down to his teething but it was a landmark day for Sebastian; he got his first good smack from his mother and he jolly well deserved it. It never happened again!

In May, I received a call from John Richards enquiring as to whether I'd received my invitation to the Royal Windsor Horse Show as a special guest of Mr. Finn Casperson. Finn is an American billionaire who owns the Beneficial Corporation Banking Group. He was a man desperate to become part of the British upper echelons, and to the undoubted pleasure of Her Majesty, he offered to sponsor the Horse Show for the following five years. He wanted to meet all the toffs and the politicians. John asked if I would bring Margaret and if I could think of any politicians I thought Finn might be interested in meeting.

I phoned Winston Churchill MP, whom I knew well (he was MP for Urmston) and asked him what he could do to help. If Finn expanded his banking business to Britain it would mean jobs! Winston phoned me back a couple of days later to say he had arranged to meet Finn at the House of Commons, where he would take him to luncheon, give him a tour, and try to introduce him to Mrs. Thatcher.

Margaret Argyle was thrilled to come as my guest, and Finn had arranged to send a car to pick us up from her place on Park Lane. I arrived at Grosvenor House at 11a.m. The door was answered by her lady's maid who, although it was still morning, seemed bleary-eyed and somewhat drunk. She wobbled her way into the sitting room, pointed me in the direction of the salver of decanters and said, "Help ya bloody self," so I did!

Margaret ignored her and we left without acknowledging her at all. Parked outside was a black limousine as long as a row of houses, waiting to take us to Windsor Great Park. In the back of the car, Margaret and I laughed until we cried. She has a love-hate relationship with the maid who regularly tells Margaret to "fuck off". Margaret fires her, then reinstates her an hour or so later. She is often drunk and just before I arrived she had called Margaret "a miserable old bitch". The police escorted us and we were driven up to Finn Casperson's marquee. There we signed the Visitor's Book, a carnation was pinned to my lapel and we were handed a glass of Champagne each. John was competing that day and his wife, Helena, had gone to watch him.

I was told that the car and chauffeur were at my disposal all day. After pleasantries with other guests I asked Margaret if she would like to see John drive the horses through the water event which can be a dangerous part of the trials. Our driver obliged, and we started to drive through the crowds in the park. We came to a part where there was a long open avenue of parkland flanked by barriers on either side, behind which there were thousands of people. Ahead of us was a party of four people all alone, one of which was a small lady in a Burberry coat, headscarf and green wellies. As we pulled up alongside them, our driver jumped out and opened the door. Just then Margaret realised where we were. "Oh my God, James, it's the Queen, what the hell should we do now?" I said, "Brass it out, Margaret, we're not driving back past thousands of people with our tails between our legs, looking bloody stupid!"

The Queen was accompanied by Sir John Miller, the Crown Equerry, Prince Andrew and Sarah Ferguson, his new girlfriend. As I got out first, the Queen smiled and politely said, "Good afternoon," to which I replied, "Good afternoon, Ma'am." When she saw Margaret, never have I seen such an instant mood swing to absolute horror. Margaret had been a friend of the King, Edward VIII (the Queen's uncle) and Mrs. Simpson, and she had been part of their inner party set.

In addition to that, Margaret brought shame to the establishment with her dreadful and scandalous divorce from the Duke. The Queen could stand it no longer and ordered Sir John into the Land Rover; she drove. I would love to have been a fly on the wall of that Land Rover as the two of them drove off. We were left with Prince Andrew and Sarah who were very chatty and friendly and obviously oblivious to the incident. Our driver had long gone but as we all stood around chatting, a Range Rover arrived. The driver said, "Mr. Casperson thought you might care for some refreshment." He had sent a picnic basket with Champagne and some sandwiches for us. Now that is what I call looking after your guests!

John came through the water event but he was far too busy to notice the four of us.

This was one of the first days that Sarah was seen out with the Queen and so it indicated that a royal engagement would be announced soon. Sarah was a pleasant enough girl to talk to and Andrew seemed to be besotted. We were informed that the Queen really liked her. I thought at the time she had quite a manly gait. She didn't do much for me, a bit over-boisterous.

I spent the next few weeks in and out of radio stations and doing press interviews. One day I was on the Susie Mathis Show at 10a.m. and at 10.45a.m. I was opening the Manchester Schools' Domesday Exhibition at Castlefield. That was a wonderful day. I was met by the directors of the Manchester Education Authority and hundreds of children and their teachers. The Moss Side children had laid on their school Caribbean steel band to greet me. I was delighted that children from immigrant families were being taught about the foundation of our country, its history and its culture.

It is of paramount importance that people who settle here are made to feel that they belong, that they are British and proud to be so. A prime example is the Jewish community who came here in the late nineteenth and early twentieth centuries, many with nothing more than the clothes they stood up in. They prospered, and have contributed enormously to the nation. There are no people more loyal to our Queen or proud to be British than the Jewish community. I have always felt strongly conservative about these matters; all are welcome, but those who are not with us are against us. It is important to people that they retain their cultural identity while embracing the laws and traditions of their adopted country. We cannot escape the simple fact that humanity is a herding animal. My great hero Muhammad Ali made the point so poignantly when he said: "In the day, all the birds sing in the same tree, but when the evening comes, the Blackbirds go where the Blackbirds go and Sparrows go where the Sparrows go." If we are to be totally honest, the unequivocal fact is we can't help ourselves and no amount of crackpot political correctness or forced socialist ideology can change it.

Thursday, May 29th 1986. The Royal Courts of Justice. This was another major day in the Domesday celebration calendar. A huge amount of work and fine detail goes into the preparation of any royal event. This day was no exception and all credit to Robert Smith who had organised everything with split-second precision. We were all well primed as to our roles and the protocol of events. The usual fanfare of State Trumpeters announced the arrival of Her Majesty the Queen. Immediately Professor Geoffrey Martin, Keeper of the Public Records, lunged forward and started to introduce members of his staff, including typists and tea ladies. The entire thing went into chaos. The Queen lingered and chatted to all of us for quite some time. After a short ceremony only the committee were meant to go and have refreshments with Her Majesty in a side chamber. Geoffrey Martin bulldozed his staff into the chamber and Michael (the Earl of Onslow), the Earl of Cork, Viscount Masserine, the Laird of Teallach, Gerald and myself had the door closed in our faces. Robert Smith was furious that Geoffrey Martin had scuttled the entire proceedings and as Chairman instructed the whole committee to write a formal complaint to Robert Fellowes (the Queen's Private Secretary).

To my knowledge, Gerald and I were the only two dumbos who followed the instruction of our Chairman. In quick response I received a reply from the Queen's Private Secretary. I was informed that Her Majesty had read my letter personally and was upset to learn its content, as she had had such an enjoyable afternoon.

It is almost a prerequisite that a retiring Keeper of the Public Records receives a knighthood. Geoffrey Martin retired a month later but got a CBE. He was absolutely furious . . . we were all thrilled!

June 21st 1986. My Charity Domesday Dinner: Margaret phoned to say she would be arriving at Manchester Piccadilly Station at 2.45p.m. By 1.30p.m. I still didn't have a suitable car to pick her up in. My Land Rover, which was full of hay and horse shit, was hardly the carriage to collect a Duchess who was once engaged to His Highness Prince Aly Khan, the eldest son of the Aga Khan. She was later to refuse the hand and break the heart of the Earl of Warwick. It wouldn't have mattered really, Margaret was the least snobbish and most down-to-earth person you could meet.

I spent all the morning rushing round attending to detail for the night's dinner. Time was pressing when I suddenly had a brainwave; Arthur Gresty, Funeral Director! He had a huge black Silver Cloud Rolls-Royce. I raced to his office and told him of my dilemma. Thinking Margaret was royal he immediately agreed and arrived fifteen minutes later in full chauffeur's livery. I also had time to phone the Station Master at Piccadilly and inform him of our arrival.

The only profound thing my father ever said to me was, "Always remember, son, bullshit baffles brains." Much to my amusement, as I sat in the back of this funereal Rolls-Royce and arrived at Piccadilly, the Station Master had arranged for the Police to escort us up onto the platform of the station! It was hilarious. Crowds of commuters started to gather round. Margaret arrived with Cecile Robinson, who was a lady friend of Sir Colin and a member of the Royal Household. What was even more ridiculous was that as we arrived at the hotel, the manager and staff were all lined up in reception so that Margaret could be introduced to the whole lot of them! Perhaps I went a bit overboard on the bullshit. The manager showed Margaret to her suite and I had arranged press and radio interviews for her in order to keep her occupied while I attended to important things.

Sir Colin and Gerald arrived at 4.30p.m. followed shortly after by soldiers from the 5/8 Kings, Manchester Regiment, resplendent in their beautiful red tunics and spiked helmets. Behind the top table stood a row of heraldic shields and the hotel had arranged magnificent table displays. The guests all arrived, the order was black ties with decorations. Outside, soldiers opened car doors for people and inside they served everyone with a welcoming glass of sherry. Other soldiers stood on sentry duty on either side of each door. It was the grandest dinner Manchester had seen in a very long time and as good as anything you would see in the capital.

As the guests all gathered, the Toast Master announced the arrival of Margaret and myself. There were 400 guests and I had organised the entire thing alone, including selling all the tickets.

Over dinner Margaret became increasingly concerned over the wellbeing of the soldiers on sentry duty. The room was getting hot and she kept saying, "James, will you please dismiss those soldiers. Their uniforms and helmets are very heavy and I'm worried some of them will faint." I refused. She kept nagging me and in the end I called the sergeant over. He agreed to change the guard every ten minutes and Margaret was happy again. I was pleased with my speech but Sir Colin gave the most boring speech I can remember. TV funny man Stuart Hall did the charity auction; you can always rely on Stuart to liven things up a bit. Someone suggested that everyone should throw an extra ten pounds each into a pot. The soldiers went round collecting money in their helmets and by the time they had finished there was well over £4,000 in notes. I was astonished.

Because I was with the Duchess, Kelly had Lewis Collins as her escort. I had previously asked Christine, Johnny Briggs's wife, to come but she refused. Johnny was not thrilled at arriving alone and so we suggested he could come with Kelly's best friend, Hilary McMillan. Hilary was twenty-one and absolutely drop-dead gorgeous. Johnny couldn't believe his luck!

It was still in full swing at 2.30a.m. and by 3.30a.m. some of the former stodgy guests were dancing on top of the tables. By 5a.m. the hotel couldn't cope any more and they finally got to go home.

In the morning I had to get Margaret back to the station. Luck was with me and I managed to commandeer yet another Rolls-Royce and chauffeur from one of the guests who had stayed in the hotel overnight.

After getting Margaret safely on her way, Kelly, Sebastian and I had to race to Frodsham in Cheshire where I had to perform the opening of the Town Festival.

Later that day I got a call from Johnny. He had arranged to meet

Hilary for luncheon at Mere Golf Club; he was besotted. He described
the meeting. He got there early and was waiting for her in the Jaguar
he used in *Coronation Street*. The vision of Hilary cycling toward him
on a sit-up-and-beg bicycle, wearing a peasant girl dress with her long
hair flowing in the sunlight, was more than any red-blooded man
could resist. It was like watching a shampoo advert. From that minute
on Johnny, Hilary, Kelly and I would go out together two or three
nights a week. It all became too public and it was to end in tears.
Johnny tried to take Hilary secretly on a charity golfing week to
Barbados but the press were waiting for them when they got there.
Christine, Johnny's wife, always blamed me for it but I refused to
accept the blame. I'm not my brother's keeper, and if a fifty-one-year-
old man wants to fall in love with a twenty-one-year-old gorgeous girl,
what can I do about it?

Wednesday, July 23rd 1986. Prince Andrew married Sarah. I had
been asked by Susie Mathis if I would do the commentary on BBC
Radio for the Royal Wedding. I arrived at the BBC studio only to find
that I was sharing the show with Frank Foo Foo Lamar. Frank was a
very well-known Mancunian transvestite artiste, of the Danny La Rue
ilk. Frank's target audience was seventy-year-old blue-rinse ladies,
who gorged themselves on a banquet of sexual innuendo and smutty
jokes. In fairness to Frank, and whatever his motive, he did raise vast
amounts of money for every good cause in the city, and bless him for
that. The show ran smoothly enough, with me explaining about
things such as the tabard worn by the Garter King of Arms and him
saying he once had a frock like that. You get the picture! Last week I
was Her Majesty's Herald. This week I'm Foo Foo Lamar's straight-
man!

I felt the time had come for me to look for a suitable home for my
new little family. I had fallen in love with a beautiful house in
Nantwich, Cheshire, called Willaston Hall.

The Hall is a fine listed Queen Anne Manor House, built in 1713 by
the Bailey family. It has a splendid William Kent chimneypiece in the
sitting room with two ladies on either side depicting night and day
and in the centre is the head of Apollo. The sitting room and some of
the bedrooms still retain the original oak panelling, which, from the
1930s onward, had been painted. This was probably done because
over the years the coal fires would have blackened the oak and the
rooms would have been gloomily dark. The very large banqueting
room is south-facing with three floor-to-ceiling Georgian windows

making the whole room light and airy. The house was perfect. There was sufficient land to keep horses and sheep but not too much to require high maintenance.

To the rear of the building was a rubble-filled courtyard. The minute I saw it I knew exactly what I was going to do with it. A few years previously I had had luncheon with Roddy Llewellyn. Roddy had a long and much publicised affair with Princess Margaret. At the time that I met him, that was all over and we were joined by his new and very attractive fiancée. Roddy was a landscape gardener and designer and over luncheon he showed me a book of his townhouse garden designs. One of them stood out in my mind's eye and it would be perfect for this courtyard! Over luncheon Roddy told me that the one thing he really wanted was to have his own gardening show on television. It would be a dream which I would fulfil for him many years later. Also joining us at the luncheon was the swashbuckling Hollywood movie star, Stuart Granger. I found his company to be as dull as dishwater, as he talked incessantly about himself.

After much negotiation and with considerable financial assistance from my dear mother, I bought Willaston Hall.

Kelly, Sebastian and I moved in. We bought a Great Dane puppy and called him Lord Nelson because he had a patch on one eye. Albeit very briefly, it would be for the next couple of years the happiest time of my entire life.

It was in this year that I decided to found the Northern Child Care Trust in conjunction with the Domesday celebration. Johnny Briggs and I presented the Manchester Royal Infirmary with a respirator from the first of the proceeds.

In addition to that, at a charity dinner I was delighted to meet a wonderful lady from Salford called Kath Smith, who had recently set up the Royal Manchester Children's Hospital Research Equipment Fund, the aim of which was to raise the money to ensure that Manchester children's surgeons got the very latest theatre equipment.

I was deeply touched and honoured when Kath asked me if I would be their Patron, years later to be joined by Sir Ben Kingsley. Kath and I, along with a small band of truly remarkable and dedicated helpers, would work together for the next twenty-four years. During that time we raised over two million pounds for the hospital. Kath was awarded a BEM a few years before she died, but I was deeply disappointed. It was totally inappropriate for such selfless and dedicated service – she should have been made a dame!

One day I was standing at the urinal in the House of Lords gents, a place where many of the most famous toffs in the nation's history have also hung out.

There I got chatting to my chum Michael Farrow. Michael was an historian and an expert on feudal law. He informed me that he had checked manuscripts and discovered that one of my predecessors in title was granted a Royal Charter in 1254 by Henry III to hold a Saturday market within the Manor of Alderley, and extending to a 6.67 mile radius as the crow flies, and also to hold a three-day fair there at the feast of St. Lawrence. A Royal Charter overrides local council authority, providing things like planning, safety and the Road Traffic Act are complied with. Councils protect their market rights ferociously, and there was no reason why I shouldn't do the same.

Michael owned a company called Victoria Markets which resurrected dormant Royal Charter markets. The market at Alderley had eventually proven not to be financially viable in those early days in the thirteenth century. Historians believe it was most likely held in the fields adjacent to St. Mary's Church at Nether Alderley. As the local lord with a grant of "all ancient rights and privileges" I was the owner of that Royal Charter by right of title. Market rights are known as "franchises" but to give it its proper definition it is "a royal privilege or branch of the royal prerogative subsisting in the hands of a subject, by grant from the King". What fun it would be to reopen it after 700 years! I knew I would be putting my hand into a hornet's nest. The self-important councillors at Macclesfield, the local snobbery and the stuffy parish councillors at Alderley would go ballistic. I wasn't to be disappointed! I informed the local press of my intentions and my next move was to submit a questionnaire to all the shop owners in Alderley. To my surprise they were overwhelmingly in favour. The press started to do their own survey, which agreed with mine; war was declared. What was laughable was that the councillors were quoted as saying that a market would lower the tone of the village and bring undesirable people into Alderley Edge!

The market was opened in August 1987 with all the razzmatazz I could muster. We had fire-eaters, jugglers and jesters. The press and radio stations arrived en masse. In addition, I appointed an official Town Crier to Alderley in the form of Tom Clarkson who was also our local crier at Nantwich. Tom rang his bell and announced the official opening to all the townsfolk. Neil Hamilton, who was the MP for Tatton, was appointed my personal Ale Tester and his wife Christine

Chrissie, at the time we got engaged in Las Vegas.

Sue Hodgson, my new love, 1976.

The Powder House, Porthmadog, North Wales.

Thermovac Plastic Products Ltd – the factory in Trafford Park.

Adele, my secretary.

Kelly. I took this photo of her in a bar in Mexico.

Lewis Collins – the Godfather!

Rosamund de Tracy-Kelly's portrait of me before it became bronze.

Her Majesty Queen Elizabeth the Queen Mother. Sebastian accuses me of trying to head-butt the Queen Mum in this photo!

Kelly, Sebastian, Lord Nelson and me at our new home – Willaston Hall, Nantwich.

Margaret, Duchess of Argyle and myself at the Domesday Dinner.

Kelly and me at home on my birthday.

Looking for castles in Scotland.

Johnny and me at the time we got banned for arm-wrestling in the Film Exchange Club.

was sworn in as the official Hangman (the first Lady Hangman of England). To this day I address Neil as "Ale Tester" and he addresses me as "My Lord". I was having great fun, and the funniest thing of all was that predictably the council didn't see the funny side; the press were loving it. People came from as far away as Blackpool and Birmingham. The village was packed and parked cars lined the streets like tentacles stretching out in every direction.

I saw the market as a vehicle to help my many charities at that time, in particular the Royal Manchester Children's Hospital Research Equipment Fund, but several weeks later I felt I had to close it. The location at Queensgate was dangerous due to the fact that it was on a blind bend with no pavement, and someone could get seriously hurt or worse, but my point had been proved!

In my last interview with the local press, like Arnold Schwartzenegger, I told the Council, "I'll be back!"

Not long after this, my dear friend Ruth invited Kelly and me to attend a mid-day soireé at her cottage in Hale, near Altrincham. I was astonished to find my father and his wife, Ivy, there. I had no idea that Ruth even knew my father. As late evening approached and guests began to disperse, Ivy went upstairs to get the coats for my father and herself. She made the fatal mistake of putting her own coat on before descending the stairs. Her stiletto heel pierced the back of her full-length raincoat on the way down, and she was catapulted to the bottom of the staircase. Her head hit the wall with the full weight of her body behind it. At first she seemed dazed but was still quite lucid in her conversation with the paramedics, who were on the scene in minutes.

Ivy died within a couple of days. It was a dreadful shock to all concerned, not least Ruth, who was deeply distressed for quite some time afterwards and felt an element of responsibility by the mere fact that it had happened in her home. The one thing none of us can alter is our destiny; if Ivy had carried both coats, she might be here today. I had the unfortunate task of officially identifying the body at the morgue. Neither my father nor Ivy's two daughters, Yvonne and Avel, were in a fit state to perform such a task.

I knew my father wouldn't be alone for long and although by then he was in his late sixties, he got himself a thirty-year-old girlfriend. She had two young children, and the one thing my father was always extremely successful at was avoiding responsibility, so she didn't last!

In September, Sebastian and I drove to Lynford Hall in Norfolk. Kelly by this time had returned to her job flying short-haul. Gerald had invited our dear friend, Dr. Gordon Teall of Teallach as the principal guest to the annual meeting of the Norfolk Celtic Society. By 7.30p.m. the guests began to arrive. Gentlemen wore their kilts or black tie with tartan trews and I wore the kilt of my mother's ancestors, the McQuarries of Mull. Lynford is the perfect setting for such an occasion.

All the way down the magnificent avenue of Redwood trees could be heard the distant sound of the pipes. With all the guests assembled, Gerald made the announcement, "My Lords, Ladies and Gentlemen, will you please welcome the Laird of Teallach."

A single piper could be heard from the distant rooms upstairs, then he was joined by another, then another until the sound became almost deafening. It was the most splendid sight as Gordon descended the great staircase flanked by all his pipers. He wore full Highland dress and his tam-o'-shanter was adorned with three golden eagle feathers, signifying his rank as Clan Chief. Gordon gave a brief talk on the history of the tartan and his Pipe Major explained about the pipes. We all enjoyed a raucous evening of Highland dancing accompanied by an adequate sufficiency of malt whisky. Sebastian slept through the entire event!

By October I found myself heading back to Santa Barbara, California, to attend my sister's wedding. Kelly and I decided that Sebastian was just too young for me to take him on such a long journey. My sister was marrying a lovely chap called Josh Weisman and on the afternoon before the wedding the "Maitra Clan" were to meet the "Weisman Clan" at a rehearsal of the wedding. The groom's father was small, quietly spoken, down-trodden and gentle in manner. His mother was huge, loud, pushy and overbearing. At the risk of being extremely unkind, I can honestly say I'd never been in a room with so many incredibly ugly women before. In a strictly private moment of contemplation, I thought to myself, "If God had made these women as his 'chosen people', why on earth would he make them so ugly?" I was introduced to all the nieces and daughters by their respective parents as, "This is my little princess Miriam" etc. I'd never met so many princesses before.

After this, all the men headed into lower State Street where we were introduced by my brother Paul to the worst dead-beat Mexican Bar in town. Every Mexican bandit there seemed to know my brother. We rolled home at 5a.m.

On the morning of the wedding I felt remarkably well, all things considered. In America black tie and dinner jacket is the order of the day for weddings. Mother looked fabulous and I spent days before convincing her to wear a hat. "They don't wear hats at weddings in California," she said. I said, "It doesn't matter what they do, no self-respecting English lady would be seen without a hat." Mother complied and was bombarded with compliments by the Jewish ladies who felt they had breached protocol by not wearing one. I somehow feel that Mother has set a precedent in Santa Barbara for the mothers of all future "Princesses".

As is tradition in California, the service was conducted outside, amidst the lush tropical vegetation of the central courtyard of the Biltmore Hotel in Santa Barbara. The sun shone and the palm trees gently swayed as if in a ballet. This wedding was unusual in that it was conducted jointly by a Christian priest and a Jewish rabbi. This religious duo had only taken one joint service before, for the singer Sheena Easton and her Jewish husband. The family photo-session seemed to go on forever and my brother, who arrived late, was still drunk from the night before. Mother was furious with him.

My stepfather, although handicapped by his failed operation, was determined to fulfil his last duty as a father and give his daughter away. He linked her tightly and with great dignity he made it up to the beautiful canopy which was festooned with flowers. There wasn't a dry eye in the place, including my own, as everyone knew the tremendous effort it took for him to walk that short distance up the aisle. It was reminiscent of Earl Spencer and Princess Diana at her wedding. Andrea, my sister, looked stunning and Mother had spared no expense, as the bill for it all was down to her! It was a magnificent and most memorable day.

1987-88

From the Highlands to California • Letting go of the Powder House • Family break-up

We bid 1986 adieu! January and February show no mercy, the snow is a foot deep and Kelly and I wake each morning at the Hall with half an inch of ice on the windows; that's on the inside!

The heating doesn't work and the chimney in the sitting room smokes the house out. Our local chimney sweep is defeated by the chimneys at Willaston Hall. There is a parapet walkway all around the roof of the house and myself and a worker put ladders up from the parapet to the chimney pots. It is an additional 20ft up from the parapet to the top. Heating engineers had sealed them with concrete. He and I have to balance on the very top with a road drill to free it. Hey presto! The fire roars away.

1987 was a blissfully happy year and in September we all went to the Highland Games at Balmoral. Kelly and I were becoming terribly fond of Scotland and after staying at Gordon's estate near Pitlochry we started to tour the Highlands looking at castles for sale. We trudged round a great many bleak and miserable castles and although it seems a thoroughly romantic idea, the reality is something very different. Firstly, they are almost impossible to heat. Then, there is the additional fact that you have to endure four months of winter where there is very little daylight and in the summer there is very little night. The distance from civilisation and the fact that you would have to turn it into some sort of shooting or holiday destination in order to have some company made the romantic notion fade.

The memory of Thermovac Plastics, Gray and Sherrington had all but faded by this time, when out of the blue a letter arrived. It was from their solicitor saying that they were considering suing me for luring them into the original business. My solicitor wrote back saying their claim was nugatory, spurious and utterly ridiculous. There were no depths too low that Gray wouldn't stoop to. Sherrington would be just doing what he was told. I was mindful of the fact that with his minor shareholding, when the time was right, no doubt his execution would ensue. The problem with the judicial system is that the minute two solicitors write to each other, the wheels of litigation begin to grind. It is always in their interest to attempt to make a case, even if there really isn't one, as long as they are aware that you have the money to pay them. If you don't, and there is no chance of legal aid, they'll drop you like a stone.

Kelly, Sebastian and I went to California to spend some time with my mother. It was such a wonderful and happy time, showing Sebastian Disneyland, and we gave Mother time alone with him. She loved the idea of looking after him while I took Kelly to Las Vegas and then I hired a car and drove her to Mexico.

Upon our return I decided I would sell the Powder House. We had started to spend a great deal less time there and more time at the Hall. When we did go, much of the time was spent cleaning the place or fixing the roof, and the settees were being eaten by mice in our absence. It was sad to sell it but everything in life moves on. By October of 1988 I had a buyer for it but Kelly was insisting she needed another holiday. I pleaded with her to hang on until the sale of the Powder House was through and I promised her I would take her to India upon completion of the sale, but she was having none of it.

We spent an entire afternoon at a travel agents in Crewe and finally decided she and Sebastian could go to Barbados while I attended to business here.

Upon her return I was instinctively aware something was wrong. Her mood and whole demeanour were different. I had promised we would all go to Lynford for that weekend as it was Gerald's birthday but she refused and I took Sebastian. The day after I got back, she flew to New York. It was then that all hell let loose and people were crawling out of the woodwork to tell me she had met someone else in Barbados. I received calls from her sisters and Penny, my godchild, all telling me she had been flaunting him around while I was away. Even my own live-in house staff, Les and Tracy, told me they felt it was their duty to tell me that Kelly had allowed him to stay at the Hall in my absence.

I was totally devastated. When she returned from New York her suitcase was packed and standing by the door in the hall. We argued bitterly and in a fit of utter frustration, hurt and anger, for the first time in my life I slapped her across the face. It was the one and only time I had ever hit a woman.

The break-up of my family was the very last thing on earth I wanted and I spent many a tearful moment blaming myself. More than anything I didn't want the same thing to happen to Sebastian as had happened to me and now history was repeating itself.

The day that Kelly left me, taking Sebastian with her, our much-loved dog, Lord Nelson, ran down the driveway and was killed on the road.

It was a bad day. A very, very, very bad day.

I was about to embark upon a journey of constant and relentless litigation from Kelly, lasting twelve years. I was always to be the defendant and never the prosecution. Being a defendant is a debilitating, all-consuming experience. It drains you mentally, physically and financially. I was to be bombarded by an endless volley of accusation, distortion of the truth, public humiliation at a national level and financial demands. In addition to this I was also receiving regular letters from Gray and Sherrington's solicitors, who were continuing to build a case against me. A lesser man than me would have crumpled under the intense pressure of it all. I have to admit, I came very close. It was to be twelve years of living hell!

Through all this torment I still had all my charitable obligations to fulfil. I was founder of the Northern Child Care Trust and Secretary General of Happy Days, a new children's charity formed in Luton, Bedfordshire. In addition I was an active Patron of the Royal Manchester Children's Hospital Research Equipment Fund. I was Chairman of my local branch of the Conservative Association and Governor of the local village school. Trying to juggle all this and make a living for yourself was a heavy load indeed and nobody knew of the inner turmoil I was having to endure.

1989

Fighting for my title • Fighting for my son • Alice • Russian royalty

At the beginning of 1989 I received a deeply distressing notice that the validity of my title was in question. Robert Smith, who was unquestionably a leading expert in such matters, had been unaware of the chronology of succession. I believe he had written to Lord Stanley (now deceased) believing he was the rightful owner of the title. Robert failed to be aware of the Stanley–Richards–Hadfield-Hyde connection and believed at that time that the title had returned to the Crown via what used to be known as Law of Escheat. Because the Crown is the fountain of all noble titles, they return to it when there is no known owner. I then found myself involved in yet another legal battle, only this time it was with the Crown's Treasury Solicitor. In a local newspaper the Crown Solicitor, Malcolm Davis, who was the chap handling the matter, described it as "one of those unfortunate things". When asked whether the situation had resulted from a mix-up of the records, he replied, "Oh, something like that." The matter was resolved at cost. The result was that I am possibly one of the only men in modern English history to receive a Feudal Lordship from the Crown. John Richards, who is the most honourable and decent man I know, felt partly responsible for the mix-up, and contributed considerably to all my legal costs, and bless him for that. He was later to become the High Sheriff of Cheshire and to be awarded an OBE.

My previous inclusion in *Debrett's Distinguished People of Today* had suddenly become an exclusion from that year on!

In a desperate attempt to be loved, I went on a sexual crusade. Some of the happiest of married women came to my bed at the Hall, at the drop of a hat. It would be disgracefully ungallant of me to mention their names, but you know who you all are, don't you ladies!

Kelly had been gone for quite some time and I only had Les and Tracy to look after the house, the grounds, the livestock and myself. Understandably I was going through a period of considerable sleep disorder. Many a time I would rise at 3a.m., sit at the computer and continue with legal response to the constant demands of Kelly's lawyers.

A pattern began to develop. Les and Tracy lived in what has always been the servant's quarters in the Hall. During my nights of insomnia Tracy would appear in the kitchen to enquire if I required a cup of tea or whether I needed anything. The sight of my nineteen-year-old chambermaid at 3a.m. wearing nothing more than her dressing gown started to get the better of me. Then one day when she was doing her rounds of changing all the beds, without thinking about it or its possible consequences, I made my move. Her response was instant, passionate and with more than a sense of urgency and approval. After the event not a word was spoken and the two of us got up and went about our business: it was an animal moment; highly recommended! Historically it is almost a prerequisite that the squirearchy seduce their young housemaids and I can hear all the modernists and feminists screaming abuse at me as I write.

Another time was in the Banqueting Room. Our banquet table was about sixteen feet long, which as you can imagine, requires a considerable amount of polishing. Tracy was busy with that chore when I crept up behind her. I could see Les in the circular driveway in front of the Hall with his head under the bonnet of a 1965 classic Jaguar car I owned. While Les attended to the carburettors and big ends and the like, I was attending to a different type of big end in the banqueting room. I agree, it was a dastardly caddish thing to do, to seduce a man's woman while you watch him fix your car is awful, but the devil in me made it twice the fun. This book is about honesty and I'm not going to lie.

When Kelly and I were together it was a family tradition that each morning around 7a.m. Sebastian would come running down the corridor and jump into our bed for a huge family snuggle. Not wanting to be left out, Nelson would come bounding up the stairs the minute he heard the patter of Sebastian's feet. Nine stone in weight and over six feet tall when he stood up on his hind legs, Nelson was as big as a donkey. We would all hide under the sheets as the thunder of his arrival got closer, until his giant head and body would push and shove its way between us, frantically licking and kissing everybody. I had never experienced such overwhelming happiness before, or since.

Kelly moved into a flat in Altrincham with her new boyfriend, Ian. She had purchased an investment property in Crewe and was working on it with him while at that the same time Sebastian was attending a day nursery school nearby. One day when I was picking him up he told me that in the morning he had jumped into Mummy and Ian's bed for a big family snuggle, "just like we did Daddy!" The pain of that thought was unbearable; it did more than break my heart. I remember my mother once saying, "A bird may sing with a broken wing, but never with a broken heart," and I was certainly in no mood for singing that day. I drove straight to the house; I was going to beat the living daylights out of this man, even though it was no fault of his: it's a man to man thing! Kelly had described him as six feet four inches tall, extremely muscular and athletic. That meant nothing to me at that moment; I was still going to beat the crap out of him. When I got to the house and Kelly answered the door, she knew from my expression there was going to be trouble and I brushed her to one side. I found him up a ladder. He was so scared he started to whimper and beg for mercy as I pinned him up against the wall. Kelly was pleading for me not to hurt him but secretly I think she enjoyed the fact that men would fight over her. However, it wasn't her I was fighting for, he could have her, but not my son. Victory was stolen from me by his cowardice and I suddenly felt like a bully, rather than a man fighting for honour and his family. In his favour, many years later, Sebastian said Ian was always kind and caring toward him, but I still always refer to him as "the wimp".

Again I returned to California, only this time it was just Sebastian and me. One of the first ports of call was, naturally, Disneyland. As we entered the gates the first character we saw was Mickey Mouse. Sebastian ran as fast as he could toward him shouting as loud as he could, "Mickey, I'm back, I'm back!" as if he were a long-lost friend. Once again Mother wanted to have time with Sebastian and so I flew up to Toronto to visit family and some of my old haunts. Canada in February is not for me. Niagara Falls was frozen solid and I was more than pleased to return to the palms and beaches of Santa Barbara, but not before nearly being involved in a plane crash. I had missed my flight to Chicago and decided I would go to Dallas in Texas and try to get a connection to Los Angeles. The door seal blew just after takeoff and we had to make an emergency landing. It was a scary moment but I'm here to tell the tale, thank God.

Upon our return, along came Alice. I had invited a handful of friends to a barbecue in the courtyard at the back of the Hall. Among the guests were Ray Teret the disc jockey and a lady friend. I will never forget the second I saw Ray and Alice as they made their entrance through the courtyard gate. She was slender and immensely pretty with the most glorious smile I could ever remember. When she first spoke to me I couldn't help observe how wonderfully sensual her lips were. Throughout the entire conversation all I kept thinking about was how much I wanted to kiss them. The little man inside me kept saying, "For God's sake James, control yourself." She was delicate, feminine, highly intelligent and very much at ease with my company.

Before long I was a regular visitor to her house in Sale, but the fact of the matter was that it was too soon for me to start a new and serious relationship. I should have continued hopping in and out of bed with women with no strings attached, and the happily married ones were the best. Alice smoothed my furrowed brow, cared for me, caressed me and offered me her love. I on the other hand wallowed in a pool of self-pity and yearned for what was by then a lost and hopeless cause. Understandably this little bird flew away and I couldn't blame her for that.

Some time later, I was out for the evening at a wine bar in Hale with my chum, Colin Gurley. I was introduced to what appeared at first to be an agreeable fellow called Roy. He looked at me for several seconds and then said, "I know exactly who you are, you and I have something in common." What was that, I enquired. "We have both slept with my wife!" It was Alice's husband. The evening conversation was a little subdued after that.

If I was to learn any lesson in life from this, it is that you must let the past go and move on as quickly as possible. Pursue every dream and ambition you have, build and create as many wonderful memories as possible. Toward the end of your days, no matter how rich or poor you are, memories are all you'll have. They'll keep you going when you are old, so make them worth talking about.

About this time I received a letter from an acquaintance of mine by the name of Gregory Lauder-Frost, a nephew of Sir Harry Lauder, or so he told everyone. He was asking me if I wanted to come to a small private dinner party with His Imperial Highness the Grand Duke Vladimir of Russia and Her Highness the Duchess. The Grand Duke would be the present Tsar under different circumstances. I thought that sounded quite interesting. It would be intriguing to meet this man as at that time the Soviet Union was collapsing and in the throes of *perestroika* under Gorbachev. I asked Gregory if I could bring along John Richards, who had an interest in the Russian Royal Family because Helena, his wife, was closely related to them. He agreed.

Upon our arrival, John and I were greeted by Gregory and we were immediately introduced to a very tall, charismatic and charming man who referred to himself as Count Nikolai Tolstoy. After a short time of small-talk we were suddenly startled by the ear-piercing blast of a trumpet fanfare, announcing the arrival their Imperial Highnesses. It seemed somewhat over the top considering there were only a handful of guests for dinner. The room was classically elegant and the occasion was undoubtedly formal, but it certainly didn't warrant such audible overture, even for defunct heirs to a throne. I was immediately struck by the amazing similarity between the Grand Duke and Earl (Dickie) Mountbatten. As for the Grand Duchess, she reminded me of a Russian shot-putter. I had visions of her, after a few vodkas, challenging everyone to arm wrestling contests at the dinner table.

John and I were seated immediately in front of the Duke, and after an enjoyable meal and much polite conversation, the Duke said he would like to say a few words.

Sitting on the Duke's left was an enormous Russian man, completely bald and with no eyebrows, like Uncle Fester in the Adams Family. He started to make the most astonishing facial contortions and both John and I couldn't take our eyes off him.

I leaned over and whispered in John's ear, "I believe he is His Imperial Highness's Minister for Gurning." At that, the two of us got a fit of the giggles. In the meantime, His Imperial Highness produced his speech which looked like a copy of *War and Peace*. He placed it on the table, apologised for forgetting his spectacles, pressed his nose to the paper and started to read and descry every individual word. An hour later I had not heard a single word of it and the whole time the gurning continued. By this time John and I were crying and desperately trying to subdue our laughter. To make things worse and even more hilarious, as we looked around the room, all the guests including the Duchess were fast asleep! As the Duke raised his head, our rapturous applause ignited everyone from their slumber.

I had a pleasant chat with His Imperial Highness in which he politely corrected me over my pronunciation of his family name. It isn't pronounced "Roman-off", it is "Romarrn-off", so that put me in my place!

Gregory also tried to entice me into joining the Conservative Monday Club because of my very active support of the Conservative Party. In those days I was known as a "Tory Wet" and I felt that the Monday Club was just a little too close to the extreme right of a conservative ideology. Some time later I received a call from John telling me that there was an article in the national newspapers saying that Gregory Lauder-Frost had been prosecuted for fiddling Social Security benefits or some such thing; you've got to laugh.

1990

Fire! • Carriage driving • Loneliness and a difficult Christmas

In June of 1990, I received a deeply upsetting phone call from Mother in California. She was crying and utterly distraught. An arsonist had set fire to someone's home in the town and the flames got out of control causing a massive bush fire. It couldn't have been at a worse time of the year in that part of California, as it's when the hot easterly winds come from the desert. They are known as the Santa Anna winds, named after General Lopez de Santa Anna, the Mexican President in the 1820s.

The sparks leap from one hill to the next and in the arid climate ignite new fires as they spread. Our magnificent home on top of the hill was destroyed in minutes, leaving nothing but the stone chimney stacks standing. Mother, my stepfather, my brother, Penny Gibson my godchild and Mother's dog Bonnie, escaped in the car with nothing but their lives. Six hundred multi-million-dollar homes were destroyed that day in Santa Barbara. Mother said that to see queues of some of the richest people on earth at the Salvation Army being handed a meal and some clothes to wear was a remarkable sight indeed.

They had initially observed the fire on a distant hill and noticed it spreading toward them. My brother climbed onto our roof with the garden hose in order to try and dampen the house as much as possible in the vague hope of preventing the possibility of any rogue sparks landing. He was unaware that a fire had already started at the bottom of the hill behind the house. From the roof-top he could see our eighty-year-old neighbour, Mrs. Darling, trying to get her old classic Lincoln Continental out of the garage. She didn't realise that one side of her home was ablaze and the electric doors to the garage were jammed half open. In a desperate bid to save her life he raced to her and amid heavy protests threw her over his shoulder and ran. By the time they got to the end of her driveway her whole house was a raging inferno. Within minutes our house was the same. All those timber American ranch houses only take two to three minutes to be engulfed in flame, and flames climbing up the side of a tinderbox hill can reach four hundred feet high. The following day all traces of Mrs. Darling's Lincoln had disappeared; this massive car had melted in the intense heat.

The President declared a national emergency and sent in the National Guard.

Mother was asked to attend a meeting by a local politician of all these very rich refugees. There they were encouraged to all hold hands and have "group hugs". Mother stormed out saying she'd never seen such a bunch of pathetic soppy wimps in all her life. She had experienced the receiving end of Hitler's bombing! My mother was forged from the steel that had built our Empire and she wasn't into public displays of weakness!

Our neighbour Mrs. Darling was a cantankerous old bird who had outlived three millionaire husbands. Mr. Darling's family had arrived in the town nearly a hundred years ago, and had bought up great chunks of Santa Barbara before it became some of the most expensive real estate in America. She decided she was going to shed this mortal coil on her own terms, and so she told a select number of her friends to come round for drinks while she killed herself.

Needless to say she wisely refrained from inviting Mother, knowing full-well that she would have nothing to do with such an event.

Apparently she poured herself an extra large Scotch, took an overdose of pills and said goodbye to them as they all sat round having a jolly time. I believe her hairdresser had a lump of money left to her. Mother, who did more for her than anyone, got nothing.

After the departure of Alice I threw a late-in-the-year barbecue where a number of friends brought people I had previously not known. Remarkably enough I managed to bed three of the women who had attended! It didn't really make me any happier.

At that time I didn't know whether I wanted to go through all the emotional stress of another full-time relationship. My mental escape was carriage driving and I would drive out with my chum, Jean Lloyd. Jean was the finest judge of horse flesh in the county. Between us we had six driving ponies, two at the Hall and four in livery at Tatton Park. Several days a week I would come home from driving the horses and my elderly housekeeper, Mrs. Hilton, would bring my food to me in the banqueting room and return to the kitchen. I remember sitting and looking to the end of the table and beyond. The clatter of my knife and fork on the plate echoed around this enormous room. I must have looked a thoroughly miserable solitary soul, but you can be surrounded by people sometimes and still be lonely. The kitchen door would open little more than ajar; it was Mrs. Hilton. "Is everything alright, may I clear the table now, Sir?" "Yes, thank you Mrs. Hilton," and I would retire to the sitting room where she would have stacked the fire high with coal. My plight at that time reminded me of something my mother said just after my stepfather came out of hospital and life was pretty dreadful. She was sitting under the palm trees in the sunshine with a glass of wine in her hand when I phoned. I asked her how she was. Her reply was, "Oh, it's just another shit day in Paradise!"

Kelly had promised to spend a few days at Christmas with us, but when it came closer she had arranged to go to Thailand with the wimp. I had begged her not to go before Boxing Day for Sebastian's sake, but my plea fell on deaf ears. Christmas Eve was particularly upsetting. We had spent the day sorting the presents out and Sebastian was so excited that Father Christmas was coming that night. By 7p.m. she asked me to drive her to Crewe Railway Station. Sebastian was in my arms and as we got to the train she burst into tears saying how much she loved us. Before long, all of us were upset and she hugged and kissed us both. Sebastian was heartbroken and it took me another couple of hours to get him happy again and excited over Father Christmas's forthcoming visit down the banqueting room chimney. They were nothing more than tears of guilt on her behalf. After leaving Father Christmas his glass of sherry and some carrots for his reindeer we finally retired to bed. It was a wonderful Christmas in the end and we had dinner with my aunt Phil at White Hall where Sebastian was overindulged with presents and affection.

1990 closes its door and apart from emotional and financial blackmail, lawsuits flying in every direction, being dumped by Alice and the house burning down, it's been reasonably uneventful. My father has got married for the fourth time; he seems to have developed an irrepressible taste for wedding cake. His fourth wife, Alve, is almost a clone of his third wife, Ivy, and at the wedding the photographer they employed forgot to put film in his camera, and the only record of the day was from out-of-focus snaps taken by guests.

We have had various social events at the Hall which have been gentle respite from the doom and gloom of things. Last week we had a party in which a number of local friends and acquaintances came including Gerry Grosvenor, Duke of Westminster.

1991

Keeping Sebastian settled • Protestors • Media fame • Another roadtrip • Domestic quirks • Worm charming • A sad loss • A trip to St. Louis

On one of my trips to and from London on the train, I found myself sitting opposite a young mother and her eight-year-old son. He was a chatty little fellow and he told me his teacher had taught him a poem and would I like to hear it? He said he really liked poetry. I suggested to him that I would write a poem for him and he could help me. He could hand it in to his teacher when he got back. During our conversation I mentioned the word "bizarre" and he asked me what that word meant. I said, "Let's write a poem with the word bizarre in it." This is the result of our effort:

IT'S QUITE BIZARRE

Tiny ants n' ele-phants,
Don't shop at Marks, for underpants,
N' a big boiled sweet, is no treat,
For little birds that say tweet tweet,

An orangutan, n' a brown field mouse,
Never sang at the opera house,
N' a striped zeb-ra, won't drive a car,
I wonder why? It's quite bizarre!

For the strangest of reasons, and I'm not entirely sure as to the exact chronology of events, about this time Kelly moved into a ghastly terraced house in the Cromwell Road area of Salford. It was a seriously deprived area in those days and I was horrified when I became aware of the fact that my son should be living in such a place. A mutual business associate of ours referred to it as "Cockroach Hall". Thank goodness it was only a temporary stopover, and before long she acquired a very smart apartment in Bowdon in Altrincham where Sebastian started to attend the nursery school. Legal proceedings, in order to fight for custody of Sebastian, were put into motion at Trafford Magistrates' Court but my solicitor didn't hold out much hope of my success. In those days it was almost unheard of for custody to be given to a father even though I was in a position to offer him all the love and stability he required. You would have to prove the mother was either a prostitute or a drug addict and I could never accuse her of that. Apart from the fact that I adored him and wanted him always in my life, what concerned me was the idea of unsettling him. Kelly is by her nature a nomadic creature and I hated the idea that he might be shipped from pillar to post. The judgment was that she would have custody but I was granted equal parental rights. I was informed by my solicitor that I was the first father to fight such a battle under the recent new Children's Act.

Kelly was making plans to go and live in the South with the wimp and for several months I had the joy of having Sebastian all to myself at Willaston Hall. To prevent him having any further trauma I kept him at the Bowdon School, even though it meant me driving thirty-five miles each morning from Nantwich and picking him up at three in the afternoon. We made going to school fun. The first child to arrive at class in the morning had the privilege of changing the daily calendar, and even with a thirty-five-mile handicap, Sebastian made it every time. All too soon Kelly came to take him to her new place near Ascot. Over the next several years, and by the time he passed his entrance to Harrow, I counted twenty-six different addresses she had occupied with him. Every time he came to stay, I was careful to maintain his bedroom at the Hall exactly as he always left it, in order to give him the secure knowledge that Willaston was always his real home.

Then a new woman came into my life; she was 26 and I was 42. She was tall, beautiful, generously proportioned in all the right places and had an explosion of natural curly flaxen blonde hair. She had a country girl quality, Kim Basinger, *au natural*. In addition to all these physical attributes she was intelligent, witty and funny. She worked as programme secretary at Granada Television and her name was Vanessa Williams. Vanessa also had an evening job at a restaurant near her home in Knutsford and I was unaware that she had noticed me dining there. As a matter of fact I had been out on a few dinner dates with the actress Sally Whittaker who plays Sally Webster in *Coronation Street*, and on two occasions we dined in that restaurant. Continuing with the *Coronation Street* theme, my relationship with Vanessa started when I called at Granada TV to see two of my tenants, Charles Lawson (he played the part of Jim McDonald) and Phil Middlemiss (Des Barnes.) As I left the Old School which was Granada's Bar and Social Club, I noticed a group of girls standing outside. The beautiful one approached my car and tapped on the window. She said she had a bet with her friends that I was the Lord of Alderley. I confirmed, and not being the sort of chap who is backward at coming forward, I suggested it would be a wonderful idea if she came to dinner with me; she agreed!

Back home, and in my capacity as Branch Chairman of the Conservatives, we had invited The Rt. Hon. David Hunt, Secretary of State for Wales, to dinner. I happened to be driving to Manchester on that morning when I got a phone call from Alan Richardson OBE, a Cheshire County Councillor and Chairman of our local Conservative Patrons. He said, "James, are you aware that there is an article in today's papers saying that The Secretary of State is attending a private dinner party at Willaston Hall, where he will be met by angry Poll Tax protesters?" I went into panic mode and immediately phoned the Chief Constable, demanding that I have sufficient police protection to deal with the matter.

By the time I returned in the early evening the lynch mob were already gathering at the main gates to the Hall. The Poll Tax was a highly contentious piece of legislation, introduced by Mrs. Thatcher and bulldozed through both the Commons and Lords by getting all the Tory back-woods peers to come and vote in its favour. I had only just changed for dinner when I received a phone call from David saying he was lost somewhere near Stoke-on-Trent. I advised him that there were about a hundred protesters at my gates baying for his blood. The cavalry arrived in the form of half a dozen burly plod from Crewe who came straight to the Hall for a cup of tea.

I suggested that perhaps if I went out to talk to the protesters and recommend that they nominate four spokespersons to come and have a private chat with David, it might help defuse the situation. That was agreed and I duly marched down to the gates escorted by two policemen. At first the crowd were having none of it and just screamed abuse at me, but after employing all my diplomatic skills and giving them my word, they agreed to comply. I said I would give them time to select their representatives. Before long David's car appeared. As he tried to manoeuvre through the crowd they jeered and bashed his car with their placards. David went upstairs to get changed into his dinner jacket and I went back out to the crowd. This time I was escorted by four members of the strong arm of the law. A motley crew, including some woman who had appeared in a debating television show the week before with David, returned with us to the Hall. The police advised that we take them away from the banqueting room and our other guests, for fear of trouble and a bout of toff-bashing. David sat on the old four-poster bed in "Squire Bailey's Room" and gave them twenty minutes of his time. When dinner was over, late in the evening, the mob were still out there and David's car got another bashing on the way out.

The week before, I had received a call from a young female reporter called Linda Lamon, who worked for the *Manchester Evening News*. She asked me if she could do a story, "A day in the life of" about me. I agreed, and it was decided that I would spend the day teaching her how to drive a team of horses. She was thrilled, and arrived at the Hall with a photographer. Mrs. Hilton made luncheon for us and I phoned Sue, my groom, to harness the horses for me at Tatton. We had a thoroughly pleasant afternoon, Linda was a keen student and I enjoyed it as much as I think she did.

On the Saturday, the article appeared as a full page in their

"Lifestyle" section. It was so staggeringly flattering that my head wouldn't go through the doorway. It was full of comments like "now that he is no longer with Kelly, he must be one of the most eligible males in the country", and "he's a tall, dark and handsome million-aire". Although it massaged my vanity and inflated my ego to the stratosphere, the important bit about the horses totalled about three sentences. Someone sent the article to Kelly!

"Hell hath no fury as a woman scorned." Kelly phoned the *Evening News* and from that minute on, the sh-1-t hit the fan. The press hunted me, followed me and photographed me. There were articles in numerous national and local newspapers saying what a mean rotten bastard I was, and that I'd refused to pay Kelly an extra £5 per week for the maintenance of our son.

I received a call from Linda Lamon saying, "James, this is just the start of it. They are going to go for you in a big way and the tabloids are going to expand this story." I pleaded with her, "Why me? I'm not a movie star or a footballer. I just live a quiet little life in the country-side looking after my chickens, I'm not that interesting!"

She assured me that I lived a lifestyle a million miles removed from the daily lives of 90% of the population, and that made me perfect fodder for the tabloids. It contains money, sex, powerful and famous friends, grand houses and fast living. I thought the whole thing was bloody ridiculous. Although she was kind by warning me, I had no idea at that point just how intrusive it was about to be.

Les and Tracy had long since left my employ by this time and I didn't know that their relationship had ended. Afterwards, Les had gone to Ascot to work for Kelly and upon reading the article in the *Evening News* the two of them had obviously had a tete-à -tete. In the demise of their relationship, Tracy must have blurted out the facts of our little indiscretion on top of the banqueting table while he fixed my car.

I opened the front door to reporters from the *Sun* newspaper and Cavendish Press. The *Daily Mirror* and others were in my front field with telescopic lenses. The *Sun* informed me that Kelly was demanding £20,000 for her exclusive story, and that she was using her sister to do the negotiating, so she wouldn't look so bad. I've since learnt that one must never believe too much of what a reporter says, but who knows.

The headline in the *Sun* was "Bawd of the Manor, Lord Lust seduces young girls".

Even Adele was included in the sex romp stories. At 3a.m. I received a telephone call from her husband informing me that he had a gun and was on his way down to shoot me. I informed him that I had a cabinet full of guns and I would be waiting! The fact that my little liaison with Adele had happened years before he even met her seemed to be of little consequence to him, but I can understand the poor man's displeasure at reading all about it in the national newspapers.

Franklin, the *Sun*'s cartoonist, did a cartoon of me in bed with five maids and the butler on the phone saying, "Ring later. All the downstairs are upstairs at the moment!" The newspaper gave me the original copy of it as a present.

The *Sunday Mirror* paid Tracy for an exclusive story but she said such kind and truthful things about me, I really didn't mind and I know she needed the money. I found out years later that she was living in one of those hostels for single mothers.

Poor Vanessa didn't know what to make of it all – I'd only being going out with her for a month when all this happened. The first time I invited her to the Hall for luncheon, I took her out driving with the horses and I think she thought she'd met a poor man's Mr. Darcy, although all this publicity thing wasn't too removed from her previous boyfriend's lifestyle. He was Gareth Evans, manager of the pop group Stone Roses.

She was the centre of attention at Granada and at the butt-end of many a joke. Even the producers, directors and management started to address her in jest as "Lady V". The press just wouldn't leave me alone and I decided to make my escape to California until the dust settled and they would lose interest in me. It doesn't really work like that. I was to be referred to for ever more by the Press as "Lord Lust" and every word they ever write, whether it be fact or fiction is there in perpetuity, to be regurgitated at any time in the future. I was to be "Lust, for life".

I received a call from Lewis Collins saying he'd read it all and he suggested I come down and hide out at his place for a while. I told him my plan and he said he would take me to Heathrow. He was laughing about Franklin's cartoon and said he had two of them done about him. "James," he said, "when Franklin does cartoons about you, you know you've made it." I couldn't quite agree with him at that point in my life. He suggested we should form the Franklin Club where membership is exclusive to all the rogues Franklin has ever made fun of.

When I got down to Lew's house near Chalfont St. Peter there were two cars with pressmen waiting outside his gates. How they find out these things is a mystery to me. We laid low for a couple of days and then I got my plane to Los Angeles.

After a few days of retreat at my mother's in Santa Barbara I returned to Santa Monica and my sister's house. There I decided to do the most therapeutic thing I could think of, that is, riding a motorbike through the desert.

My brother-in-law, Josh, and I loaded the bikes onto the back of the truck and headed out over two hundred miles deep into the California desert. We eventually arrived at the most God-forsaken little settlement consisting of a few old aluminium caravans, the odd shack and a bar called "The Iron Door". In a couple more weeks the temperature would be over 45 degrees every day until October. At that time it was only 40 degrees. Upon our arrival we were met by Skip, a friend of Josh who knows this part of the desert well. Out here you wouldn't survive more than a couple of days at most. I was warmly greeted by the black wrinkled faces and toothless smiles of the locals and apart from a number of Navaho Indians they all seemed to be of English or Irish stock. I was introduced to "Beer Can Bob" who survived by collecting beer cans from the side of the roads and at places where people camp. Thirty empty cans would buy you a full one.

It's not much of a living.

Like the sea, the desert is so beautiful and yet so unforgiving. Although it was early morning, the temperature was already 30 degrees and you could feel that hot Santa Anna breeze hit your nostrils. We set off rough-country riding. The vastness of the place is awe-inspiring; it is only punctuated by the occasional cactus or joshua tree. As I rode up the dried river beds, created by thousands of years of desert flash floods, there erupted an explosion of magnificent butterflies; there must be several million of them, the like of which I have never seen before. It was remarkable.

I parked my bike on a high point next to a mud spring where boiling hot mud spits and gurgles its way up to meet the earth's surface. Josh and Skip had gone off and left me for a while and I was glad of a few solitary moments. In silence I stared out over the vastness of God's creation and felt an overwhelming sense of freedom. All too soon they were back and it was time to go screaming off deeper into the desert.

We had not travelled too far up over some dunes, when in the middle of nowhere, we looked down upon an array of mock wooden buildings with no backs or sides. There was plenty of activity going on and so at full throttle we went down to investigate. We certainly weren't made welcome. Warren Beatty was there, and they were making a film called *Bugsy* about the gangster Bugsy Siegel, who created Las Vegas. Our hostile reception culminated with the director referring to Josh, Skip and me as "three fucking stooges ruining the film!" A coffee break was called on set, to allow us to get far enough away for the sound of our motorbikes to be undetected by the sound man. We went back to the settlement and had a few beers in the Iron Door. We'd caused enough trouble for one day!

I returned to Santa Barbara and in the quiet of my mother's house, I had time to collect my thoughts and make a few decisions. In view of all of my scandalous publicity I felt that the honourable thing to do was to send letters of resignation to all the charities and honorary posts I held. My letter as Branch Chairman of the Conservative Association was first to go. You can't beat a good sex scandal to allow you to gracefully bow out from a number of things you no longer have the time nor inclination to be involved with. I have to admit, being a Governor of the local school was certainly one of them.

I received a total and categorical refusal to accept my resignation from each and every one of them! Damn! Oh well I suppose it shows, somebody loved me!

In the midst of writing my resignations I received a phone call from Chris Quinten in Los Angeles. "James, I've been reading all sorts of naughty things about you in the English papers!" he said. Chris had played in *Coronation Street* for years until they finally killed his part off in the show. At a celebrity charity telethon in New Zealand he met a beautiful American TV star called Leeza Gibbons and the two of them fell in lust and got married. I don't think at the time Chris realised just how powerful and important Leeza was in Hollywood. She did a coast-to-coast TV show called *Entertainment Tonight* and her critique on a new movie could have a serious effect on its success. Everyone who is anyone in Hollywood was friends with Leeza.

They invited me to their magnificent home in Los Angeles and Leeza said she would make dinner for me.

When I got there they had also invited some big movie director called John (can't remember his last name) to talk business with Chris. From childhood Chris had been a keen martial arts and gymnastics enthusiast, and he also had the sort of chiselled good looks which go down well in Hollywood. Over dinner John explained how he had an action movie script for Chuck Norris and he wanted to include Chris as Chuck Norris's partner in the movie. Leeza had arranged for Chris to attend the Drama School in Hollywood to improve his acting skills and to learn to "speak American". Through Leeza's influence Chris was on the threshold of major stardom but, as is his wont, he blew it!

Leeza and Chris had a baby by this time and they were in the process of selling their house and looking at buying an even more magnificent house in Bel Air, Hollywood. One evening Leeza came home to find Chris cavorting in their swimming pool with a load of naked girls. That was the end of that. Leeza was a girl from South Carolina and had had a very Christian upbringing; marriage was totally sacred. Chris lost custody of their little girl, Alexandra, and he returned to England. Years later he became a meet and greet doorman working for Peter Stringfellow at Stringfellow's Club in London.

Before returning to England, I lay alone on the beach in Santa Barbara, contemplating the cloudless sky, and gathering my thoughts. I wrote the following:

> No cumulus, nor cirrus cloud,
> Do flaw the blue ethereal shroud.
>
> As chicken on a roasting tin,
> I sizzle brown and sip pink gin.
>
> Centigrade begins to soar,
> I baste with oil, just once more.
>
> A fleeting thought occurs again,
> The gentle kiss of England's rain.
>
> Her emerald hills, her meadow smell,
> Should I return? should I hell!

When I got back to Willaston I found that my housekeeper, Mrs. Hilton, had abandoned me. The media attention had proved too much for her. Thank goodness my dear chum Jean Lloyd had come to the rescue and stayed at the Hall to look after things in my absence.

Mrs. Hilton was a strange woman, tall but slightly stooped, in her sixties, highly academic and well read, but not so much as a micro-dot of common sense. Like her predecessor Mrs. Dickinson, she was the most appalling cook.

I can give you an example of the sort of things I used to have to put up with.

I remember once coming down to the kitchen early in the morning. Mrs. Hilton had started cooking breakfast for two Australian guests and myself when I noticed the frying pan brimming over with sausages.

Me: Forgive me Mrs. Hilton, but just how many sausages are you cooking?

Mrs. H: 24 Sir!

Me: I'm quite sure our guests would be more than happy to receive two sausages each for breakfast, Mrs. H!

Mrs. H: Yes, but aren't you having any?

Me: I also would be quite content to receive two sausages Mrs. H! Why don't we remove some of them?

As I pricked a sausage to remove it, all 24 were still joined together!

Mrs. Dickinson, who was also a woman in her sixties, was a dab hand at opening tins of Fray Bentos pies. Cooking fresh vegetables and making decent wholesome food didn't come naturally to her. However, smoking, drinking my best vintage port and sleeping with young village boys did!

Mrs. Dickinson came to me via a Domestic Servants' Agency who had been known to supply staff to the Queen. She had previously worked for Gerry Grosvenor, Duke of Westminster, God knows in what capacity. If it were cooking, I'm amazed that Gerry looked so healthy! During the first week of her employment she told me I must call her Susan, as the Duke always called her Susan. I informed her that I wasn't the Duke and we would stick to Mrs. Dickinson.

A few days later, Sebastian and I arrived home after spending the afternoon driving our horses. The door was opened by a very drunk Mrs. Dickinson. Assuming she had spent the afternoon in the village pub, I chose to ignore it and not chastise her in front of Sebastian. Later that evening he became confused and enquired of me as to why Mrs. Dickinson was speaking in a very funny way, and why she left a trail of soup from the kitchen to the banqueting table, followed by a trail of gravy. Afterwards, while I bathed Sebastian and put him to bed, Mrs. Dickinson retired to her quarters.

It was then that I discovered an entire decanter of my vintage port had completely evaporated! I went up to her and laid the law down.

The next thing was to find her drunk and fast asleep in bed with a handsome 22-year-old boy from the village. Mrs. Dickinson was certainly no oil painting, and the thought of waking up with her makes me queasy as I write. When I removed him from the premises he said he'd had a few drinks and had offered to walk her home. I said he would need a lot more than a few, and recommended he visit the opticians! Fortunately she left soon after that.

My next encounter with domestic staff was Mr. and Mrs. Binfield, or Mr. and Mrs. B as they preferred to be addressed. As a matter of fact they even addressed each other in that way.

Mr. and Mrs. B were from the Derby area and had very strong Derby accents. Mr. B acted as my butler and Mrs. B was cook and house-keeper. The pair of them could have had doctorate degrees in malapropisms. It was just glorious to listen to their conversations. Many a time I would be in the banqueting room with floods of laughter tears streaming down my face, as I tuned into their kitchen chat.

Mrs. B: Mornin' Sir, we've ad abit o' rain last night, I'm glad to see that allergy 'as gone off the pond!

Me: Good morning Mrs. B, and how is Mr. B this morning?

Mrs. B: Not too good Sir, eez bin consummated all week!

Mr. and Mrs. B viewed the world from a totally different angle to the rest of us, and their understanding of things was both charming and very funny.

One day Mrs. B requested that Mr. B return to their home in Derby for a few days in order to do some jobs around their house. If it was all right could her sister come and help with the housework here at the Hall? I agreed and the sister duly arrived.

After a day or so I remarked to Mrs. B how shy and quiet her sister was.

Mrs. B: We don't like to talk about it Sir, only not long ago she lost err uzband!

Me: Oh that's sad, did he die suddenly?

Mrs. B: Yes, 'e 'ung himself in the kitchen!

Me: Oh that's dreadful Mrs. B, did he leave a note or give any reason for doing such a terrible thing?

Mrs. B: Not a word Sir! 43 years of marriage and not a goodbye. There was one thing though Sir, 'e left iz spectacles on a newspaper article that said "85% of people in Nottingham, 'ang themselves"!!

Vanessa, who had moved into the Hall with me by this time, hated the idea of having live-in domestic servants. She was not used to it, and found it intrusive into the privacy of our lives. Some time later when Mr. B started to find climbing the stairs more difficult they graciously retired and returned to their home in Derby.

Vanessa became a wonderful stepmother to Sebastian, insisting that photographs of Kelly, Sebastian and me remained in place for at least another year, in order not to cause Sebastian any additional upset. I was deeply touched by her thoughtfulness. She was young enough to have fun with him and sometimes I would come home to find the pair of them dancing around the room with pop music blaring full blast. She also insisted that we all sat at the banquet table for dinner as a family, when Sebastian was with us. She didn't believe in eating on your knee while gawping at the TV in the sitting room. Dining together was "quality time" as our American cousins would say.

Kelly, on the other hand, continued to bombard me with litigation and emotional blackmail. I find it difficult to resurrect the details here on paper, the thoughts of it are so painful to me. Looking through all my files and court papers brings it all back, and I don't want to bore the reader with my tales of woe, or dig myself into a depression.

It was at this time that they started filming *Robin Hood* at Tatton Park and they needed about half a dozen men to be noblemen and to ride horses in the stag hunt scene of the film. I was asked to be in it. The film starred Patrick Bergin as Robin Hood, Uma Thurman as Maid Marian and Edward Fox as Prince John. Most of the film was done at Peckforton Castle near Chester but Tatton was perfect for the hunt scene. I was sitting in the chair next to Patrick Bergin in makeup and I attempted to engage him in conversation but got monosyllabic answers. He was far too grand to talk to a lowly Extra such as myself. Uma Thurman was adorable and very friendly. I took Sebastian along one day and she offered to look after him for me. She made him sandwiches and drinks and the two of them went off together. Whenever we see Uma in films, Sebastian reminds me of the fact that he has kissed Uma Thurman and I haven't!

Patrick Bergin was a "luvvie". The weather was bitter and damp and at one point they had to send for a Range Rover to take him to the other side of the park to his caravan so he could have a cup of tea and a warm. The rest of us had to stand around in the freezing cold for an hour, waiting for him, and the horses got more and more restless. In the scene we had to do several cavalry charges across the open land and then there were lots of shots riding down through streams and woodlands. It was great fun but we were in the saddle all day. I enjoyed it though.

This version of Robin Hood unfortunately came out around the same time Kevin Costner did *Robin Hood, Prince of Thieves.* That one proved to be a smash hit, aided by its opening theme tune, which was in the charts for months. I thought some of the things in Costner's version were utterly ridiculous. In one scene he is crossing the English Channel under the White Cliffs of Dover and he declares, "This night I shall be in my father's house!" Nottingham? He would have needed a bloody Ferrari to get there! The next minute he's standing on Hadrian's Wall! Only the Americans could come up with such nonsense.

By the beginning of October 1991 and since returning from my voluntary exile in California, there have been a series of dinners, balls, presentations and all things charitable. In the summer I have to fulfil my annual local duty as Squire of the village, presenting the gold and silver prizes at the Willaston International Worm Charming Championships. Willaston claims to be the founder of Worm Charming worldwide, and it attracts potty people from the four corners of the globe. The format is as follows: the school football pitch is marked out into squares. Each group of charmers buys a square and in thirty minutes one has to charm as many worms to the surface as possible without removing the turf. There are very strict rules, as laid down by Mike Forster (our village policeman) and Gordon Farr (Headmaster of Willaston School and Master of the Worm!). The pitch is guarded throughout the night before, to ensure no tampering or foul play, e.g. heavily watering your square!

We've had Worm Charming tap dancers and even a Worm Charming horse who banged the turf with his hoof. Local farmer Tom Shufflebotham held the World Record for years, charming 511 worms in the thirty minutes.

It's late October and I find myself back in California, only this time it's for a very different reason. John Richards and myself are to be guests of the Claytonshire Coaching Club in St. Louis, Missouri, of which we are honorary members. I had no idea how prestigious the Coaching Club was at that time. Some high-flying Americans have waited as long as twenty years to be accepted as members, but we were what was called the English Branch.

November 1st 1991. Oh such grief, such heartfelt sadness. Little did I know that, as I wrote my diary in the early hours of the morning, in the very next bedroom my stepfather's life had slipped away. As the Bible says, it came as a thief in the night.

It was about 7a.m. and I put my head around my mother's door. She was up but whispered, thinking my stepfather was still asleep. The room was in semi-darkness and it was difficult to see. Mother and I went into the kitchen to make tea and have our morning chat and after an hour I suggested we check to see if he was all right. He had grown considerably weaker since I had last seen him in April. Mother was concerned not to wake him at this hour for fear he may have had a restless night. In the recent years, and because of his illness, he had to have a special bed, separate from Mother. It was only when she gently touched his forehead that the sad reality dawned. I shouted Paul, my brother, and we all wept bitterly. My sister was called. It would take her a couple of hours to drive up from Los Angeles.

We made phone calls to all concerned and before long the doctor arrived. Mutually, we decided to leave his body in bed and asked the Funeral Director not to come until after dark at 6p.m. The day was spent in and out of the bedroom and close friends came to pay their respects. All too soon at 5p.m. Mother, Andrea, Paul, Josh and myself went in to sit with Dad for our last hour together. It was so desperately sad, and yet even in that final hour we could find fond memories and amusing anecdotes to tell.

He looked as if he were peacefully asleep. Many may think it morbid to leave the corpse in bed throughout the whole day, but somehow it made the goodbye that much easier. It gave us all time to come to terms with the transition from life to death.

His memorial service was held in the magnificent Temple above Montecito, Santa Barbara, where his nephew, Amit, gave the most moving eulogy to his uncle. Months later, my mother, Andrea and Paul flew to India, his birthplace, to sprinkle his ashes in the River Ganges, as is Hindu tradition. The men sprinkle the ashes and the women scatter the river with rose petals, sometimes from boats or from the end of a purpose-built jetty.

The following week I drove down to Los Angeles in order to get my plane to St. Louis. After the warmth of California I had not thought about the fact that St. Louis would be in the midst of winter snows, and the plane landed in a blizzard. I was totally inappropriately dressed. I was met by a delightful rotund southern gentleman called

Michael, who informed me he was my full-time chauffeur for the next few days. Helena, John's wife, arrived minutes later and I know she was relieved to see my welcoming face. John had flown there from Texas in his friend Stewart's private jet and was already at the Missouri Athletic Club awaiting our arrival.

The following morning Michael arrived promptly and was instructed to show us the sights of St. Louis including the famous 630-foot high Gateway Arch. The city has a wealth of magnificent old-money mansions still in the hands of the cotton- and slave- trading families, and Confederate flags fly everywhere. In the evening the three of us attended dinner at the University Club where John gave a most enlightening talk to the Missouri carriage-driving fraternity.

I can't remember a time when I ate so much food. After an enormous breakfast we were then taken to the Noonday Luncheon Club, but the most bizarre event of our trip was about to happen. We had been invited over to the family home of the Busch family. They are undoubtedly among the richest people on earth and their wealth started when they arrived in St. Louis as poor immigrants. They founded and own the Budweiser Beer empire along with God knows what else.

We drove into their estate of open countryside and rolling hills. The sun shone with not a cloud in the sky and the trees were still heavily laden with snow. It was the sort of day Christmas cards are made of. The Busch mansion was not overbearingly large, more of a substantial French chateau in style. As we drove into the courtyard we were immediately greeted by Trudy Busch, the matriarch of the family, and her son Andy. A great line of house staff stood to attention in the snow. What was utterly remarkable was that two enormous Indian elephants flanked the staff on each end. These creatures proceeded to greet the three of us by kneeling, shaking our hands with their trunks and rolling over in the snow! It was the kind of welcome usually reserved for the Queen of England or the President of the United States! We were naturally amazed by it all. Andy invited us to view the "Trophy Room", an endless corridor of cabinets filled with polo trophies, cups, shields and gifts from kings and presidents the world over. As we returned to the courtyard the grooms had harnessed a carriage and four to take us on a drive around the estate; Andy drove. We were about to board when we were met by the late arrival of some more of the family, Billy Busch and his very pregnant wife, Christie. Our first stop was a modest log cabin, home of the great Civil War General and 18th President of the United States, Ulysses S. Grant. As a matter of fact the Busch family estate is known as Grant's Farm. As we clip-clopped through the snow, wrapped in blankets and chatting together, I admit to momentarily forgetting the grief my mother was enduring at home in Santa Barbara.

Andy stopped the carriage and in total silence we admired the amazing beauty which surrounded us. The solemnity of the moment was broken: Andy began to shout, as if in some Tarzan movie! The earth began to shake and a rumbling thunder began to stir. From over the hills came a herd of American bison, zebras, wild Grand Canyon horses, Scottish deer and a host of other exotic animals. They pushed and shoved against the carriage – it was amazing. Andy fed the beasts from the back of the vehicle and we then made a leisurely return to the chateau. When we got back, the servants had prepared yet another meal for us in the family "Animal Trophy Room". This magnificent room was home to the stuffed heads of every animal you could raise a gun to. The walk-in fireplace, which was the size of the sitting room of an English terraced house, was ablaze with tree-trunk logs.

The following day we went on what the American carriage driving enthusiasts call a "Tool". This is a gathering of horse-drawn vehicles. There were around ten horses and carriages involved in this Tool, and we drove in convoy through the streets of St. Louis wearing our top hats, much to the delight of the local populace.

In the evening the Busch family had arranged a farewell dinner-dance in our honour.

For once, I had the appropriate attire. Aware of the fact that at some time I would be attending a black-tie dinner, I brought my kilt and full Highland dress. My strategy in doing so was purely to pander to the Americans. John, who is not quite as extrovert as myself, stuck to tradition and Helena looked stunning as always.

Fully togged up and kitted out, our car pulled up at the venue. To my utter amazement, standing in line at the main door were four buglers, dressed as Palace Guards in bearskins, who bugled the announcement of our arrival. In the foyer we were greeted by Trudy and some of the dignitaries. The doors to the main dining area were opened and accompanied by two Scots Highland pipers, we were piped through the room and up to the top table, to a standing applause.

There were 400 of the richest and most powerful people in the mid-western states of America there, and I can truthfully say I have shaken the hand of each and every one of them and been photographed with most!

The whole experience was surreal, thoroughly enjoyable and totally memorable. When it was all over, John and Helena flew to New Hampshire and I returned to California.

A week later I was back in England.

1992

A room with a view • *That* dress! • Ostriches • Reggie Kray

I had been neglecting Vanessa, and within weeks of my return we decided to have a weekend in Rome. I know the city reasonably well, and as Vanessa had not been there before it was a joy to show her around. Apart from nearly losing my passport, wallet and money to a bunch of tourist-mugging street urchins, it was a wonderful weekend.

Unsuspecting tourists suddenly find themselves surrounded by these little devils who pull at your clothes asking for money. There are so many of them that they distract you from all sides. I felt my wallet go from my inside jacket pocket and immediately grabbed the nearest little soul by the throat. I wasn't going to let him go. In the end they became afraid of me and my belongings were duly returned. The one who steals it passes it straight away to another and then another and they all take off before you realise what's happened. They live in the caves and ancient Roman ruins and survive on their wits only. I gave them some money when they returned everything. Some people just have a lousy start to life; you couldn't help feeling sorry for these kids!

We also went to Florence and, unbeknown to me, Vanessa had arranged for us to stay in the little Pensioni by the Ponte Vecchio, where they filmed *Room with a View*. We stayed in the actual room! Very romantic.

A quick visit to the Leaning Tower of Pisa, which was closed because it had started to lean just that bit too far for everyone's liking! Then home.

Life wasn't all "Beer 'n' Skittles". I was still enduring a constant bombardment of litigation. I received a call from my lawyer, Nick Johnson, who informed me that Kelly had been helping Barry Gray with his case against me. I spoke to her sister who said that she would never go to the trouble of helping Gray unless there was something in it for her. What on earth had I done to make these people so vindictive? I could only conclude that the motivation was nothing more than envy and greed. They had set the date for the case, May 13th – my birthday!

As I arrived at Leeds High Court, the national press were waiting for me. Sherrington, as I predicted, had also received his execution from the company and was standing as a witness for me. Adele came, and to my pleasant surprise, so did her husband. I was most appreciative of their support. My barrister insisted that my mother fly over, also to stand as witness. This was in order to show that we had ample funds and that money could not be the motive for me to deceptively lure Gray into the business. That was actually to turn the case against me, along with my recent publicity. I knew that the judge looked upon Gray as a hard-working industrialist who offered employment to the people of Leeds. I was a worthless, rich, no-good, womanising playboy. I lost the case and was ordered to pay all costs plus £54,000. My barrister assured me I would have up to twelve months to pay, but within three days I received notice from the bailiffs informing me they were coming to clear Willaston Hall of its contents. I paid within seven days thanks to the help of my dear mother. On the way to court a black cat ran out across our path and everyone including my solicitor said, "That's good luck, it's a good omen." Bollocks! I'll never trust another black cat!

Kelly had put Sebastian into Stubbington School in Sunninghill. It was a wonderful school and boasted several Victoria Crosses among its former pupils. Its most famous pupil was Captain Scott of the Antarctic. Kelly then insisted Sebastian become a boarder, despite the fact that the school was only 200 yards from her home. I informed Mr. Learoyd, the headmaster that I would pay half the fees directly to him. I am well quoted in the press as saying "I have no intention of sending any money to her and help fund her Joan Collins lifestyle."

On the subject of finance, I had sacked my long-time accountant, the Rt. Hon. Lord Barnett and replaced him with Eddie Nugent, a local accountant based in Eccles, Manchester. I invited Eddie and his wife, Rose to dinner at the Hall, along with Lewis Collins. Lew was paying vast amounts of money to his accountants in London and I thought Eddie might be able to help him also. Eddie and Rose were quiet, shy and a little reserved, as you would expect anyone in the accountancy business to be. As we were about to sit down to dinner the phone rang. It was none other than Chris Quinten with his new girlfriend. "I'm on the M6 near Nantwich, any chance of a cup of tea and a bed for the night?" he asked. I told him he was in luck, dinner was just about to be served on the table. When giving dinner parties it is always the concern of the host as to whether the guests are going to gel, and I had my misgivings on this night. Lew and Chris were two of the wildest men on, and off, television. By 2a.m. Lewis Collins, Chris Quinten and Rose were running around my woodlands shooting and playing Cowboys and Indians! It's amazing what alcohol can do and it ended up a thoroughly enjoyable and successful night. Eddie became Lew's accountant and all worked out well.

Months later, Lew decided to pop the question to his long-standing girlfriend, Michelle. They already had a little boy together, Oliver. I suggested to him that he should get *Hello* magazine to fund the wedding in exchange for exclusive rights to the story and photographs. It just happened that the week before, Vanessa had filled out a competition form in *Hello* and had won a wonderful prize. It was an outfit designed by Bellville Sassoon for Princess Diana. An appointment was arranged and she and I went to London to meet the fashion designer for her fitting. It was perfect timing, just in time for Lew's wedding. I told her not to mention to *Hello* whose wedding she was going to, just while Lew was in the throes of negotiating with the magazine, but Lew phoned to say the deal was off. *Hello* had only agreed to pay money to a charity of his choosing and so naturally Lew was annoyed and disappointed.

The night before the wedding Vanessa and I went down to Alford in Surrey to meet Lew and join him for dinner. In the morning, I picked him up in the car to take him to the church of St. Nicholas for the service. Michelle was adamant, she didn't want a showbiz wedding and was not keen on the idea of it turning into a media circus. The fact was, it was already the talk of the village and the local press were already on to the story. In order to prevent a local reporter making a killing, in the car on the way to church, Lew phoned the nationals. Within minutes the press were swarming. They arrived on motorbikes en masse.

It was a tremendous wedding and it was there that we became

friends with Mike and Rowena McCartney and a great mountain of a man called Big John Newton.

Several days later Vanessa received a call from *Hello* to see how she had enjoyed her outfit. Now that the wedding was all done and dusted, Vanessa felt she could mention the wedding she had attended. The following week *Hello* magazine did their wedding feature, with the main picture being Lew, Vanessa and me. The story attached was more about Vanessa's dress than Lew's wedding and naturally Lew was hopping mad.

We had a major fallout over that!

At Christmas I still continued to treat around two hundred handicapped children to the pantomime. I felt I just couldn't let them down, having done it for so many years, but I was becoming seriously concerned over my finances. For years, I was constantly having to fork out money to a hungry bunch of parasitic barristers and solicitors. It was bleeding me dry. The property market had all but collapsed and the bank interest rates were stratospheric. This was not a time to be property rich and cash poor. In addition I had lost touch with Sebastian. Kelly had removed him from Stubbington, owing them thousands of pounds in fees. She had left the address she was at and I was unable to find out where she had gone. I was in a panic and spent weeks phoning every school and authority to see if she had registered him in any school. Mr. Learoyd phoned me to tell his sorry tale and suggested I contact Social Services Educational Welfare, which I did. Eventually, I got a little note from Sebastian saying "Daddy, I'm at Sunningdale school." I phoned the headmaster, Mr. Dawson, and immediately drove down from Cheshire to the school. Sebastian couldn't have been in a better place. It was the most wonderful homely little boarding school, where the masters even bring their dogs into the class. He was safe and happy, he loved it and that's all I was bothered about. He entered the school with two other boys, Hanbury-Tennyson, son of the famous explorer and His Serene Highness Prince V. Mahidol, grandson to the King of Thailand, who has remained one of his closest friends to this day.

After all the trauma of recent events, Vanessa and I decided we needed a break, and escaped to the south of France to stay in a lovely old house in the village of St. Cesere, owned by a television presenter friend, called Shelley Rohde. Shelley only rented the house to friends she could trust and as we moved in, the writer Alan Bennett moved out. It was just what the doctor ordered. We drove the length and breadth of the Cote d'Azur and Monaco, drank wine and made love. The day we returned, Mike McCartney and Rowena invited us to their house for the first time for dinner: Scouse 'n' Red Cabbage with as much red wine as you can drink! Scouse, as everyone knows, is similar to Irish stew. However, it is only Scouse when it has meat in it. When it doesn't, it's called Blind Scouse!

On the theme of food, at about this time I was seriously thinking about going into the ostrich business. This was almost unheard of in Britain but was beginning to take off in America. South Africa had had ostrich farms from before the turn of the twentieth century, but that was to cater to the feather market. As you can imagine they did a boom trade during the roaring twenties and the time of the Charleston, when everyone wanted ostrich feathers, but their high value goes back much further than that. Knights throughout medieval Europe adorned their helmets with ostrich feathers as part of their crest, the Prince of Wales for example. The feather is quite unique in that the plume is perfectly equal on both sides and just as we use a set of scales as our symbol of justice, the early Egyptians used the ostrich feather.

More recently, meat is the marketable product along with the skins, as used in designer luggage. Fully grown, standing at nine feet tall and weighing three hundred pounds with a brain the size of a chicken's, an ostrich can be a formidable and dangerous creature. Their intellectual limits extend to eating, sleeping, defecating and procreating.

I purchased my first birds, imported from Zimbabwe. This caused great hilarity and the press had a field-day with me, although I couldn't see what all the fuss was about. I ended up going on endless TV shows including bringing them on the *Richard and Judy Morning Show*, where I got Richard and Judy to attempt to taste the difference between pork, beef and ostrich. I studied the subject, went and visited ostrich farms in California and went on a crash course in Belgium. While in Brussels, on the last night of the course, we were treated to a dinner at the Palace Hotel. Naturally, the set meal of the night was ostrich steak, and this was served with a tarragon sauce. Most people who have never eaten ostrich before can't believe it is not fillet of beef. One would normally expect a tarragon sauce to accompany a chicken dish, but the reason was simple. When the hotel chef was informed he was cooking ostrich, he assumed the meat would be white, like chicken or turkey. It still worked perfectly and was a wonderful and enjoyable meal.

I supplied our local fish and chip shop, the Willaston Fish Bar, with ostrich meat, thus declaring that it was the first chip shop in the world to serve ostrich, chips and peas (gravy optional). People who enjoy eating ostrich meat are known as "Struthophogists" (I just thought you would be impressed with that little bit of trivia). My own academic achievements are almost nil, while most of my friends have the walls of their homes emblazoned with framed certificates declaring their Bachelors, Masters and Doctorates. The one thing none of them have is a Diploma in Ostrich Management!

In addition to this, I had a couple of horses in livery at the Hall and one of the owners was a horsey girl called Gina. She and I decided to get our heads together and start doing private riding lessons for adults. She owned a wonderful docile sixteen-hand chestnut gelding, which would be perfect for the job. When you are advanced in years and you want to learn to ride, there is nothing more embarrassing than going to your local riding school and having the humiliating experience of having to trot round with a load of ten-year-olds, who look as if they were born in the saddle. Our secluded one-to-one tuition was the answer. All was going swimmingly and we were building a regular client-base until one of Gina's old enemies decided to report her to the council.

One day, before leaving, Gina came to me and informed me that one of the male ostriches in the other field was looking decidedly peaky. The problem with birds is that they require stones in their intake of food to assist with their digestion. With the absence of teeth, they build stones in the gut to help grind the food. Nobody seems to know the reason, but sometimes they overfill the gut, it prevents digestion completely and they die very quickly.

It couldn't have happened at a worse time. Within the hour, I was due to interview some prospective tenants for a flat we rented out, in the rear wing of the Hall. The ostrich paddock was close by and I didn't think it would bode well for them to find an ostrich with its legs in the air outside their door. A three hundred pound dead ostrich takes quite a bit of manoeuvring, and I called on Vanessa to assist with its rapid removal. With much pushing and shoving and the long neck flopping all over the place, the dead carcass was going nowhere. Vanessa did a lot of crying and I did a lot of shouting and swearing. I then came up with Plan B. The day before, I'd bought a new washing machine and still had the large cardboard box it came in. By putting the open box on its side we could get the bird in it and this made it easier to slide the box over the wet grass. Just when we thought we'd successfully got it to the steps of the kitchen, the box fell apart, and to make things worse, rigor mortis had set in, with the legs in the ten to two position. This caused a real problem, as the outstretched legs were wider than the kitchen door! Mustering all of my strength and with one leg in my shoulder and both my arms forcing the other closed, I managed to get the corpse into the kitchen. The doorbell went as the carcass tumbled down the cellar steps and into the wine cellar. Mr. and Mrs. Bigelow were greeted warmly as if nothing was untoward!

Ostriches are incredibly stupid and even when you are bringing their food into the field, a large male sometimes considers you to be a threat. They fight in a similar way to a kangaroo but their four-inch claws on the end of each foot can be lethal weapons. They invariably give you warning when they are about to attack by puffing up their feathers to make themselves look even larger, and doing a little on-the-spot dancing. I've always adhered to the fact that attack is the best form of defence, and the second they'd start the dancing bit, I'd lunge at them with an uppercut and a right hook. If that didn't work I'd hit them with the bucket. That usually flustered them, they'd take off in the opposite direction and the fight was over. I've never lost a fight with an ostrich so far, but I might meet my match one day.

As with most large or predatory animals, the worst tactic you could employ is to take flight. You either play dead, or attack whilst making as much noise as possible, as it confuses them. Predators are usually cowards and that can apply to humans. If you take flight, an ostrich can run at a top speed of 55 miles an hour, so you're not going to get very far.

The ostrich-farming business in Britain was in danger of being a non-starter, as long as the birds were classified as "exotic wild animals" instead of "farm game". This meant that the birds, the meat and the eggs were subject to VAT.

I made an appointment with the Minister for Agriculture, John Gummer, at his office at Whitehall. The place had all the trappings of a once-great Empire and I received a friendly welcome from the minister and his staff. I felt I was attending an interview for a job, as I was quizzed by his army of "Sir Humphries". It was just like the TV show, *Yes, Minister*. After a lengthy chat, he came round to my way of thinking and assured me that VAT would be removed immediately and the birds would be re-categorised. He also told me that his department was at my disposal and whatever he could do to get the industry going would receive his backing to the fullest extent. By this time I was on my fourth cup of tea and I suggested that, as this was still a "fledgling" industry, he could start by giving some government grants. "Ah!" he said. "In this office we are jolly good at giving cups of tea but grants we struggle with." I returned home feeling I had achieved my goal as VAT had been the main stumbling block.

From the late 1980s I had been receiving regular written correspondence from the infamous gangster, Reginald Kray. I first made his acquaintance through a book I was researching and from then on we became pen-pals. For many years, and almost to the point of his death, he never failed to phone me at Christmas time and for my birthday.

The first conversation I had with him was early one morning. Sebastian was at home when the phone went and he ran to answer it. At that time I assumed it was my mother, phoning from California, as nobody else would be calling us at 7a.m. Sebastian was a very chatty little boy and throughout their half-hour conversation, in passing, I kept hearing snippets of their chat. At one point I heard Sebastian say, "Do you think you could draw me a picture of an ostrich?" to which I believe Reggie said, "Sebastian, I don't think I can remember what an ostrich looks like!" He then replied, "All right then, I'll draw a picture of an ostrich for you and I'll get Daddy to send it to you," which he did. Reggie agreed that in exchange, he would draw Sebastian a picture of a cowboy and a sailor, which duly arrived in the post three days later, signed and addressed to Sebastian. I admit to being a little surprised when Sebastian shouted to me to say it was a friend of mine called Reggie on the phone, and not Grandma. He and I chatted at length. At that time I had been unaware that he could phone out from prison. He told me that there was a big queue behind him waiting to use the phone. Let's face it, who's going to tell Reggie Kray to get a move on!

Weeks before, I had sent Reggie a cheque for £100 for a young boy called Paul Stapleton. Paul was suffering from Ducheens Disease, which is the worst form of muscular dystrophy, and Reggie was raising money to send him and his family on holiday to Disney World. Later that day, I received a call from a lady called Mrs. King. She was organising the Stapletons' holiday and she phoned to thank me for my kindness. She told me she had spoken to Mr. Kray earlier in the afternoon and he was very upset. As a matter of fact, she said, he wept on the phone. I was astonished and enquired why. She said he couldn't stop thinking about his long chat with Sebastian – he hadn't spoken to a little boy like him in over twenty years!

Some time later he sent me a copy of a book of poems he had written. His poetry told of a strong man in sadness, regret and melancholy. In it he wrote, "To James, God Bless friend, Reg Kray."

Mrs. King called again to give me an update on the Stapletons' holiday and said Mr. Kray was thrilled with the drawing of the ostrich, sent to him by Sebastian, and he had it up on his cell wall! I believe the next contact I had was when he called to tell me he had been moved from Blundeston Prison in Suffolk to Maidstone.

I was also really pleased for him when he told me he had met a lovely girl called Roberta. He was to marry her in prison, and she was to be with him in his final moments of life. I spoke to her on a number of occasions, and when Jack Straw MP finally released him, to die in hospital in Norfolk, I left messages on Roberta's telephone to see if I could visit him. She failed to return my calls and I suppose I can understand why. She would have been bombarded with people pestering her at that time.

Reggie once told me that sometimes he would receive as many as fifty letters in a day, many from young offenders and inmates from around the world. He would write back to all of them, telling them not to be stupid and waste their lives.

There are many who will disagree with me, but there was a very decent and good side to Reggie Kray, and over many years of conversations with him, I can truthfully say I have witnessed it first hand. Reggie did further drawings for me, in order to help me with my charities, but the press wouldn't be interested in that. *Julius Caesar*, Act 3, Scene 2: "The evil that men do lives after them; the good is oft interred with their bones."

When Sebastian was later at Harrow, his Master gave the class an essay to write about a famous person they knew. Bear in mind that most of the boys in his class were the sons of famous people. Sebastian wrote "The day I made Reggie Kray cry!" His Master was so utterly astonished that Sebastian knew Reggie Kray personally that he got an A+ for that one!

1993

A giant Christmas pud • From MPs to MBEs • *Chaplin*
• Bob the pot-bellied pig

Iwas asked, along with the Liverpool Labour MP Jane Kennedy, to go
to the theme park Camelot, near Preston. Jane and I were to be
witness to, and verify, a European record balloon launch for the
Guinness Book of Records. I can't remember just how many balloons,
but it was thousands. There I bumped into Big John Newton whom I
had previously met at Lewis Collins's wedding. Big John was
something to do with the management of some of the gladiators,
from a muscle-bound competition show on TV, very popular at the
time. He introduced me to a number of them, including Mike
O'Hearne, alias Warrior. Big John said that if ever I needed some of
the gladiators to attend any of my charity functions, all I had to do was
call him. From then on, Mike and Big John became regular visitors to
the Hall. In addition to that, they introduced me to some people who
ran an organisation called the Children's Support Foundation Ltd.,
who asked for my help with fund-raising ideas.

As Christmas was approaching in a few months I said, "Why don't
we make the Biggest Christmas Pudding in the World?" The wheels
were put in motion and at that time the world's largest pudding stood
at a mere three and a half tons. "If we are going to do this then let's
do a proper job and blow the existing record out of the water," I said.
"Let's make a ten-ton pudding!"

We gave the task of writing the recipe and calculating the ingredients to the TV chef Keith Floyd. He came up with the following;

    20,000 eggs
    2,500lbs of flour
    1,875lbs of brown sugar
    2,500lbs of candied peel
    5,000lbs of currants and sultanas
    2,500lbs of bread crumbs
    2,500lbs of suet
    288 large bottles of Guinness
    30 large bottles of brandy
    134 litres of cider

We got an engineering company in Birmingham to build a large steel globe, after the size and volume required was calculated. At first we were offered a ship's boiler to cook it in but the hygiene people weren't too happy about that. It's amazing how whenever you come up with an utterly potty idea, suddenly everyone wants to get involved!

On November 12th 1993 the mixing of the pudding began at a location in Birmingham, and school children helped us break the eggs, all twenty thousand of them. A motorway cement mixer mixed the ingredients and JCB lent us a new digger to load it. Midlands TV came to film us and the pudding was cooked for ten days and cooled for a further ten. The idea was that, when cooked, it would tour the country, and be broken up into thousands of tiny puddings which people could buy as part of the Biggest Christmas Pudding in the World. The proceeds would go to the Children's Support Foundation, along with two of the charities dearest to my heart, Happy Days and the Royal Manchester Children's Hospital Research Equipment Fund, and also a Liverpool-based children's charity called MAP.

The TV presenter, Anneka Rice, kindly lent us her huge lorry from her show, *Challenge Anneka*, along with Paul her driver, to take the pudding on tour. The first stop was "The Rover's Return" on the set of *Coronation Street*. There I had arranged for a party to be held for some of the children who would benefit from the proceeds. As the pudding arrived at the studio, Granada TV featured it on their evening news show.

The following morning I had arranged to take the pudding on Richard and Judy's *This Morning* Show in Liverpool, to allow the two of them to be the very first people to sample the Biggest Christmas Pudding in the World! The thing was, at that point nobody had actually tasted this pudding. It was purely fortuitous that I thought I'd better check that it was edible before Richard got a taste of it. If it wasn't up to scratch, he would blurt out on screen that it was bloody awful and the whole charity event could collapse!

We had to chisel our way through the first six-inch layer of charcoal and it seemed to be a total disaster! By the time we managed to dig our way past that, it did start to taste quite delicious, but we daren't take any chances. As the steel frame of the pudding resembled an "Atlasphere" from the TV show *Gladiators*, I phoned Mike (Warrior) and told him of my dilemma. I asked him if he wanted to come on the show with me, but not before going to Marks and Spencer to buy half a dozen Christmas puddings to stuff in the top of ours.

On the show, Mike climbed up on top of the pudding while I chatted to Richard and Judy. He handed down three bowls of it for us to sample. "Goodness me, this is absolutely delicious!" said Richard, and Judy enthusiastically agreed. A sigh of relief on our part. Our pudding went on to raise about £60,000 for the children. Sometimes, an economy of truth is shamefully necessary!

At home all things were as well as could be expected, and my relationship with Vanessa was in full bloom. Sebastian had become a little TV personality, thanks to our friend Russell T. Davies. Russell was producing a children's programme called *Children's Ward*. He got Sebastian to appear in the opening credits, and so he was on the TV every week for the following three years.

I continued holding events every few weeks at the Hall, in support of the Conservative Party, inviting members of Mrs. Thatcher's Cabinet and the like. We invited Peter Brook MP for breakfast one morning. Peter had previously been the Secretary of State for Northern Ireland, but at this time he was the Heritage Minister. The week before he was due to arrive, I got a visit from Special Branch who went through the house and grounds like a dose of salts. I was given special instructions, and informed that they would return on the morning of his arrival. Peter was due at 10a.m. At 5a.m. the Special Branch arrived in force and started to almost take the house to pieces, yet again. Everything was searched, there wasn't a drawer, cupboard or floorboard they didn't look into, twice. When Peter finally arrived, I had eight armed men in the house, one on the roof parapet and one pretending to walk his dog in the field. As we sat down for breakfast there were more men toting guns in the room than there were guests! I vowed I wouldn't invite any more Northern Ireland Secretaries of State again; it was a bloody nightmare.

A couple of weeks later, we had Jeremy Handley MP who was the Armed Forces Minister, but thank goodness we didn't have a repeat of that lot.

There followed a procession of Tory high-flyers to the Hall, including Neil Hamilton MP. Neil and Christine Hamilton were great fun, and they were to become among my closest of friends, as time went on.

Another great devotee of the Tory Party was Bill Roache MBE, the longest performing actor to appear in *Coronation Street*. Bill came to numerous events at the Hall and could always be relied on whenever we needed a star to appear.

I seem to recall that in the earlier part of 1993 the film *Chaplin* was released. Although it was completed in 1992 it didn't have its Manchester premiere until the following year. It starred Robert Downey Junior as Charlie, and it was directed and produced by Lord (Dickie) Attenborough; I was invited. After the show, I happened to be having a drink with "darling little Dickie", as one does! I mentioned to him that my grandfather and Charlie were great friends when they were boys, and when they were in the little touring dance group "Eight Lancashire Lads". To my absolute astonishment he said, "I've got a photograph of your grandfather and Charlie, I'll send it to you. You must give me your address!" A cigarette packet was ripped in half (in those days you could smoke at liberty), and he pushed it into his handkerchief pocket. I thought to myself, "That jacket will go to the cleaners and that will be the end of that!" However, to my most pleasant surprise, about a month later, the photograph arrived along with a most charming letter. Recently I have been frantically looking for it to include in this book and no doubt I'll find it after the damned thing has been published.

I'd had several appearances on *This Morning* with Richard and Judy and one day I received a call from the producer, saying that Judy wanted me to bring my ostriches on again. I flatly refused, it was far too much trouble trying to catch the bloody things and load them into a lorry, then drive them to Liverpool. In addition to that, they easily become stressed, and you might open the lorry door to find a load of dead ostriches. The only safe way to transport them was to load them the night before and let them sleep in the lorry. You could then transport them, still in the dark and they'd be fine. She insisted that Judy really wanted me to come on the show again, so I said, "I'll bring a pig instead." I got a call back saying, Judy says, "What the hell are we going to do with a pig?" I said, "We can give it away on the show, because I'm fed up to the back teeth with him, he's a Vietnamese pot-bellied pig called Bob!" "OK, great!" said the producer. It was December 1993.

How I came to own Bob: I had a visit from a fellow who worked for me on occasion, and he told me his sorry tale. The landlord of his local pub in Nantwich had a collection of rare ducks, and also a pig. The pig broke in and killed all his ducks, and so he decided he was going to shoot him. His execution by firing squad was due the following day. My workman pleaded for a stay of execution and loaded the pig into the boot of his car, to take him home. Upon arrival, his wife threatened him with divorce. The obvious place for him was James, at Willaston Hall!

My workman's name was Bob, and so we named the pig after him.

It just so happened that the week before, a fox had broken into our hen house and slaughtered all our chickens, so that could be Bob's new home, until we could think of something else. Bob was an ungrateful swine and every few days he would break out and take off into Nantwich. Our local police got to know Bob well and I was forever getting calls from them saying, "James, Bob's been spotted at such and such a place, chasing cattle." He was a nightmare to catch, because he could run like the wind.

I phoned Richard and Judy and asked them to get their carpenter to build a pigpen in the studio. Bob arrived on the back seat of my car, but during the whole journey he kept insisting on climbing over and getting in the front seat with me. You couldn't help but like him though, because he had such an intelligent and interesting little personality.

In the first five minutes we received over 50 calls from people wanting Bob, and toward the end of the show, Judy and I decided we would give him to a special needs school in Blackpool. It was a wonderful school, where they had a little farm attached and the children had responsibility to care for the animals.

A week later we did an outside broadcast for the show. Bob was leaving his home at Willaston Hall and arriving at his new home at the seaside! Sebastian had to come with me and had to fight with Bob to keep him in the back seat.

On the day, the weather was like a hurricane, with a ferocious wind and the sea crashing in. I was filmed on the beach with Blackpool Tower in the background, carrying Bob, who weighed a ton, and was squealing his head off. I was wearing Wellingtons and had a knotted handkerchief on my head. I can honestly say, I was greatly relieved to hand him over to the excited children.

1994

Times are hard • Depression sets in • Down, but not out
• The passing of a friend • Tom McNally and the
Atlantic record • Plas Teg

In January 1994, it was Mike McCartney's 50th birthday, and Vanessa and I were invited to the party. The theme to it was simply black and white. Mike and Ro had arranged for a magnificent marquee to be erected in the grounds of their house on the Wirral. I seem to remember the entire interior was black, with the ceiling draped in star-studded curtaining. Mike's brother Paul and his wife Linda came. The McCartneys are a very large and close-knit Liverpool family, and Vanessa and I were very touched by the fact that we were included in their inner circle of friends, and always made to feel part of the family. Scousers are without doubt the funniest people in the land. I know of no other city where all the people, from the Lord Mayor to the road sweeper, have a sharper, more razor-like wit, and everyone has a joke to tell. It's impossible to leave Liverpool without someone making you laugh before you go. I have a great affection for the city, the splendid architecture, the magnificent harbour front, and its deeply loyal and passionate people. It must be the Irish in them.

The music was provided by a band of boyhood friends of Mike and Paul, who called themselves The Chip Shop Boys. They only get together as a band for friends or charity events nowadays. In daily life, they are solicitors or accountants or some such thing, with bald heads and beer bellies. They were great fun, as you can imagine, and the highlight was when Mike and Paul got up on stage with them, and opened up with "Blue Suede Shoes". The whole place erupted. Paul told me later that it was the first time he and Mike had sung together on a stage since their mother entered them in a singing competition when they were little boys. Paul then sang some of his Beatles and Wings songs and then he got us to sing with him; it was amazing. What is so lovely, as an outsider looking in, is the way the family seem so dismissive of the fact that their close relative is one of the richest and most famous people on earth. To them he's just "arr kid, Paul".

The food was a carnivore's delight, an amazing display of every kind of meat and savoury you can imagine. Paul made no comment, merely raised an eyebrow, but Linda said it was a vegetarian's worst nightmare.

The only slight downside to the evening was that Lewis Collins and his wife, Michelle, turned their backs on Vanessa and refused to acknowledge her, although they did talk to me. They still haven't forgiven us for our appearance in *Hello* magazine to this day!

At home, our new tenants, Mr. and Mrs. Bigelow, or Big-earlobes as we'd taken to calling them, were settled in nicely. Mr. Big-earlobe was a small stick-like creature with a balding head, and what appeared to be a nailbrush placed above his lip. He was in his late thirties and laughed raucously at every single word I ever uttered. If I said, "Good morning Mr. Bigelow," he would split his sides. Mrs. Big-earlobe was to be congratulated for her resounding victory over anorexia, and it would be true to say that you could fit two Mr. Big-earlobes down each leg of her astonishingly tight Lycra trousers. She stood head and shoulders above him, and although I may seem a trifle unkind in my description, they were delightful and charming people, albeit comical to look at.

To the outside world, my life seemed to be one of privileged fun and frolics, but beneath the calm surface waters, it was desperately dark and filled with predators. The endless bombardment of mindless, unnecessary litigation from Kelly, and the vastness of my overheads and responsibilities, began to wear me down. I managed to sell ten houses I owned in the centre of Manchester, at a time when the market was at its least buoyant, and made little or no profit. I'd sold the small factory I'd owned up in Oldham and also some houses in Crewe. I even put Willaston Hall up for sale, but the market was so depressed that I only had one interested party. He was a tall, charismatic man named Jeremy Sale. At that time, he also wasn't in a position to buy, until he offloaded a magnificent chateau he owned in France. Our meeting was the beginning of a great friendship between us, and some weeks later, he introduced us to his petite and very attractive wife, Lynda.

My beloved driving ponies, gigs and carriages also had to go and I will always cherish those memories of Sebastian when he was no more than six years old. He would hang onto the back of the carriage shouting, "Gallop them, Daddy, gallop them!" whenever we came to the mud-filled road through the woods at Tatton. The pair of us would return home caked in mud from head to toe. They were wonderful days. An additional fact was that the Tatton Estate had new management. A case of lots more chiefs and less Indians. They decided that I no longer had the freedom to drive the horses wherever I pleased in the park, and restricted me to only driving along the woodland pathway. My driving partner, Jean, and I were given keys for several gates along the route. Constantly having to stop and unlock and lock gates took the joy out of it all. They didn't seem to realise that we were a free tourist attraction for them. We would often give people free rides just for the fun of it, and people used to love seeing us. We were forever posing for photographs while trotting through the park and we didn't mind at all; it was all part of it.

In March of 1994, I received a call from Big John Newton. He said he wanted to introduce me to a remarkable man called Tom McNally. "You and Tom will get on like a house on fire. He's right up your street, you're both completely nuts and he needs some help."

The previous year, Tom had successfully crossed the Atlantic Ocean in a boat measuring five feet, four and a half inches (1.64m), thus breaking the world record for the smallest boat to cross an ocean. He had constructed it partly from an oak wardrobe he found on a skip in Liverpool. The masts were three scaffolding poles, and the batten-down hatch porthole was the window of a washing machine.

His journey basically followed the Columbus route, from Portugal to Madeira and on to Puerto Rico and then Florida.

Tom did indeed sound like my sort of chap.

At this time, I was beginning to show the classic symptoms of depression and nervous breakdown. I was comfort eating and drinking excessively. I was piling weight on which made everything worse, and I had less energy to cope. I had begun to feel that I was a complete failure in every aspect of my life. I'd failed to go to university, I'd failed in my relationships with so many women, I'd failed in my business. Depression creates a chain reaction and your self-esteem hits rock bottom. I saw a picture of myself in the *Manchester Evening News*; my face looked like a football. Sometimes when I was alone, and I would be doing some totally mundane task, for no reason whatsoever I would burst into tears. For the life of me I couldn't understand what I was crying about. I remember thinking, "The one thing I must never fail at is to be a good father." The thought that my son might grow up to think his father was one of life's losers was the very thing that kick-started me into action. My cousin Jim had studied hypnosis and I am forever in his debt. He hypnotised me, and gave me a hypnotic tape recording he had made, which I played each night. After three weeks, I was a new man. He restored my self-esteem, and although the problems hadn't gone away, I was able to cope with each as it came along.

I went to Dr. Shapiro, a dietician in Bowdon, Altrincham, and he put me on a strict diet. I was answerable to him every Thursday. By August I'd lost two and a half stone: I was back in the ring – down, but not out.

I continued through it all with my squirearchal duties as normal. In April Warrington Council asked if I would open the Business Connections 94 Exhibition. Around four hundred companies were exhibiting there on the sight of the old American Airbase at Burtonwood. The day after that, I was cutting the ribbon at the opening of a hairdressing salon in Altrincham, and on the Sunday I was presenting the cup and medals to all the players of our local football team.

Sebastian and I finally managed to get up in a hot air balloon. We had tried before, but inclement weather always got in the way. Vanessa, Sebastian and I were dining together one evening when we noticed men inflating a balloon in the front field to the Hall. "If you hurry up and eat your dinner, we'll walk over and watch them take off," I said. The field was full of onlookers by the time we got there and as we approached, the owner ran over to me and said, "Is this your little boy? If you hurry, I've got room for two more." We ran as fast as we could to tell Vanessa where we were going, and get warm coats. Within minutes we were two thousand feet above Nantwich and heading toward Market Drayton. I had to hold Sebastian by the seat of his pants, as he fearlessly hung over the edge of the basket, pointing at the tiny sheep and cattle below. We soft landed in a farmer's field in Shropshire and then we all helped fold the balloon and load it into a Land Rover. I think it was about eleven at night by the time we got back to the Hall. The end of a lovely, unexpected evening. On a previous similar occasion, I had taken Sebastian up in a glider, flying over the Pennine Hills, with him sitting on my knee. He was then only about four years old.

Sebastian spent almost the whole summer holiday of 1994 with me at Willaston. We religiously did our homework, and I was very pleased with his progress. Although he was troubled with dyslexia, he has a very sharp inquisitive mind and a high IQ. But, like myself, I believe him to be more artistic than academic. During that summer, Mother flew over from California. The day after she arrived, I dropped her and Sebastian off at Chelford Cattle Market, to buy some laying hens. At the auction Sebastian was bidding for the biggest and most evil-looking, yellow-legged cockerel, who had spurs four inches long. You could only use him as a fighting cock (if it was legal). Sebastian bid to £4 for him, when the hammer went down, but he didn't want it at that price, and the auctioneer let him off.

Mother bought him a tent, which was erected in our paddock by the woods. He and his cousin, Paul, camped out in it on the first night, and the following day, Mother, Vanessa and I were invited to a luncheon of campfire-cooked sausages. You could have them very well done, burnt, very burnt or charcoal burnt, dependent on your preference.

About this time, my dear friend, Peter Platts-Judd, had been admitted to the Royal Devonshire Hospital in Buxton and I made regular visits to him there. He was 68 and he was to spend a total of twelve months in hospital. At one point the surgeon told him he might have to have his leg removed from the knee down. Peter insisted that if that happened, he wanted the leg to be packed in ice and sent to a taxidermist to be stuffed: it was his leg, and he could do what he wanted with it. As I mentioned before, Peter used to be one of Her Majesty's jewellers at Garrards in London. Being a master jewellery craftsman, he was going to make a beautiful silver top for it, and have the leg standing next to his favourite armchair, as his ashtray. He said to me that, in the shooting season he would put a tartan sock and a brown brogue shoe on it. Then, if they invited people round for dinner, he would change it to a black sock and a patent leather evening shoe! Peter died peacefully with his long-suffering wife, Patricia, and his closest friends by his side. What moved me greatly was that the three nurses who had cared for him over that year, stood by his bedside and all wept bitterly. Peter was buried in Ireland, the land he adopted and loved. Farewell old friend.

In November of 1994, Vanessa and I attended Bonfire Night at Hulgrave Hall, near Tarporley, which is the home of my old chum, Keith Hopwood, from the pop group Herman's Hermits. Keith and his wife Marie always put on a fabulous show. It was a night with lots of mulled wine, laughter, meeting old friends and fireworks.

Much of my time was now being spent assisting Tom McNally with his plan to bring the Atlantic world record back to Britain after an American, Hugo Vilhen, had beaten his previous record. I had started to try and interest large corporate sponsors in the project, but it was an uphill battle. Tom had blotted his copy book with some of them before, because he proved to be too much of a loose cannon. They couldn't control him, and in retrospect I don't know why I thought I could. I set up a company for Tom, called Atlantic Challenge Limited. Through Big John Newton, I was asked to have luncheon with Hugo de Ferranti, at Portals Golf Club near Tarporley, to discuss Tom. I'd never met Hugo before, although I had met his father, Sebastian de Ferranti many times. Sebastian and his family lived in the magnificent house they built near Macclesfield, Henbury Hall. Hugo and I decided to meet again in London where I would introduce him to Tom. The night before we were due to drive down, Tom stayed with us at Willaston. Hugo phoned to say he was going to try and bring a prince along to the meeting. The prince in question was Prince Rupert Ludwig Ferdinand zu Loewenstein-Werthein-Freudenberg, from the Bavarian Royal Family. To cut a long story short, he didn't come, but his daughter, Dora, or to give her full title . . . Princess Maria Theodora Marjorie Loewenstein-Werthein-Freudenberg, did!

Prince Rupert was a financial wizard and controlled all the finances of the Rolling Stones. When he met them in 1968, despite being second in line to the British pop throne, next to The Beatles, they were absolutely Rolling Stoney broke. He took complete control and built them into the giant pop corporation they are today.

We had arranged to meet Hugo and Princess Dora at the Groucho Club on Dean Street. As we arrived at reception, Sir Clement Freud was just leaving. "Hello Mr. Freud, remember me? Tom from Liverpool!" shouts Tom. Sir Clement politely acknowledged that he did indeed remember Tom from Liverpool, he had bought one of Tom's paintings. Among other things, Tom was an exceptional artist.

I was delighted to see Hugo seated alone, as Tom and I were fifteen minutes late. Dora then rushed in, apologising, the traffic was dreadful. Over luncheon, Tom was on form with his many tales of adventure and I knew that Hugo and Dora had taken to him.

As early evening approached, I decided that it might just be possible to drive at full speed to Sunningdale, in time for Sebastian's school Christmas Carol Service. It would be a nice surprise, as I had previously told him it was not going to be possible for me to come. As we drove into the driveway, in the dark, cold, wet weather, Sebastian was standing outside the school alone, waiting for his mother. Thank goodness I made it, because she didn't turn up. I could have wept at the sight of him standing there and he was so excited to see me. All the boys were thrilled to meet Tom, and Mr. Dawson, the headmaster, asked Tom if he would come again and talk to the boys about how he broke the Atlantic world record. It ended up as a lovely evening for all concerned.

It was two in the morning by the time we got back to the Hall and at 9a.m. I had a newspaper reporter coming to interview me about a recipe book I had started to write – *50 Ways to Cook an Ostrich*.

1994 was reaching its end and on December 10th Vanessa and I we were invited to another couple of friends of mine, for an early Christmas soireé at their home, Wenlock Abbey, in Shropshire. Gabrielle Drake is a very beautiful, successful and classically trained actress. Her brother was Nick Drake, the folk and pop singer who sadly died long before his time. Gabrielle's husband, Louis de Wet (pronounced Vet) is a slightly strange man. He's Noel Cowardesque, a very talented artist and an academic. He speaks with a South African accent and uses floral and Byronic English, always using ten scholarly words, when a couple of simple ones would do. His dinner conversation will suddenly drift into French for a while and then wander into German. This allows his guests to be amused and in awe of his linguistic muscle flexing. It reminds me of those little men who take up weightlifting and insist on wearing only a tee shirt in the dead of winter.

Being a simple soul myself, I find the constant bombardment of academic subjects from opera, to the sex life of the African dung beetle, while having to mentally translate half of it back into English, exhausting. I don't dislike Louis in any way, I'm rather fond of him. The abbey, where they live, is fascinating. It is reputed to be the finest preserved medieval Abbey in Europe, and I believe it. Louis lives there in Baronial splendour, with his wife and a live-in lady helper. The evening was splendid as always, with locally killed pheasant being the main course. Gabrielle is a wonderful cook and a most charming hostess. Dinner was served in the very grand Great Hall, which has remained unchanged since the thirteenth century. We were invited back for New Year's Eve.

I first met Gabrielle and Louis at a party in the home of another friend of mine, Cornelia Bayley. Cornelia lives at "Plas Teg" in Pontlyddyn near Mold in North Wales. The house is a large grey stone mansion, reputed to be the most haunted house in Wales. Plas Teg was believed to be beyond repair when Cornelia first bought it. As a matter of fact, I looked at it myself, but found the whole prospect of aiding its recovery too daunting. As you approach the front door, leading directly into the Great Hall, it is easy to allow your imagination to run wild. Ghostly figures appear at windows and with a second glance, they are gone. The previous residents had, over the years, retreated to living in one room, as the ceilings fell in, one after another. Wales owes Cornelia a great debt of gratitude for restoring one of their finest Elizabethan houses. Along the way they put stumbling block after stumbling block in her way, in order to prevent it happening, but Cornelia is made of sterner stuff. I know that in my years of being a landowner in Wales, I never found "A Welcome in the Hillside", from the "Men of Harlech".

Cornelia needed financial help, and I suggested she cash in on its haunted notoriety and open up to the public. For many years, she had lived with Chris Thompson, heir to the Thompson publishing empire. I think I recall that they bought Plas Teg together, but Chris then found a new, younger, American girlfriend. Cornelia was left alone in the haunted house, to fend for herself. She and Chris had amassed quite a collection of French Empire furnishings and artifacts, including some splendid Napoleonic baths, beds and bronzes. Poor Cornelia didn't have much idea, and at first, she allowed the public to wander round at will. They proceeded to steal everything which wasn't too big, too heavy or screwed down. She couldn't believe people would be dishonest!

Christmas had come and gone, and I'm delighted to say Sebastian spent nearly all of it with me. A few days later, Kelly phoned to say she was not sending Sebastian back to Sunningdale, as she hadn't paid her contribution toward the school fees. I immediately spoke to Mr. Dawson who said he would speak to her directly. He phoned me minutes later, saying, "Kelly says I'm not to worry about the fees because your mother will pay the shortfall!" I told her, in no uncertain terms, that the only way my mother would contribute more than she already had in the past, was if I had complete custody of Sebastian. To my astonishment, she said she was already considering it. Needless to say, it didn't happen.

1995

Indian adventures • Vanessa turns 30 and Sebastian goes to Thailand • The Atlantic challenge begins to sink

By New Year, Vanessa and I were suffering from party fatigue. The thought of facing another vol-au-vent or chicken leg was more than we could cope with.

Weeks later, in the January of 1995, we took off for India, stopping in Bahrain along the way. We arrived at Goa at a tiny military airfield. At that time, the country was still unspoilt, but I could see that in ten years or so, it would end up being a major package tour destination and its primitive charm would be destroyed. The endless miles of white palm-lined beaches, punctuated only by the occasional old wooden fishing boat, was exactly what we needed. The fishermen and their families live in mud huts under the coconut palms, just yards away from the sea. Small pigs and chickens run free. These people live a shared communal existence, and at that time were still not contaminated by money, greed or Western values.

A day or so later we arranged for a driver to take us inland into the country and deep into the jungle. We arrived at a small village which caused a great stir with the locals. Our driver said that they had only seen four white people before. An old lady told our Indian driver that she was very upset with him. Had they known we were coming, they would have made presents for us and all the people`in the village would have put their best clothes on. Vanessa was a particular curiosity to them. Standing at five feet ten inches tall, with her great explosion of golden hair, made her very special. These people are tiny: even the tallest man was only about five feet four inches tall.

We sat on the floor of a mud hut and they gave us rice cake and treacle, served on banana leaves. Vanessa was really not keen, but I discretely informed her that diplomacy demanded that she look as if she was enjoying it. I asked for seconds, which pleased them no end. They offered us hospitality and friendship and wanted nothing in return. These delightful people showed us the very best qualities of humanity.

Days later we flew up to Bombay by Moduluft Airways (I'd never heard of them either!). We didn't bother reserving a hotel in an enormous city like Bombay – surely we wouldn't have a problem finding accommodation? We had previously been told to stay at the YMCA. It was spotlessly clean and very cheap. After we had arrived at the airport seeking advice, we were told that the YMCA was in a remote part of town, and the desk clerk's brother owned a lovely hotel right by the Gateway to India Arch. The famous Taj Mahal Hotel, which is directly opposite the Gateway Arch, was fully booked. We arrived by taxi. The degree of poverty on such a massive scale is the first thing that shocks most Westerners. There is an endless sea of sprawling shanty towns. People in their tens of thousands live in the gutters and open sewers. For every person, there must be a hundred rats. The first thing we saw as we entered the city was an ox and cart with a crudely painted sign in English saying, "WE COLLECT DEAD BODY, ANY PLACE, ANY TIME". As we milled our way through the crowds, the next thing to make our acquaintance was a half-naked man, escorting two enormous brown bears, tethered by chains. He beat their feet with a stick to make them dance. This kind of entertainment has not been seen in England since the middle ages.

The desk clerk's brother's hotel was indeed close to the Gateway Arch. My chickens live in more luxurious accommodation. The building was decaying in every sense of the word. As we walked into reception, it was so dark I honestly couldn't see the man standing behind the counter. The entire ramshackle place was painted, floor to ceiling, in dark brown. A single 40-watt bulb hung above his head and even that had dead flies stuck to it. We wandered from hotel to hotel: they were either full or worse and the night was drawing in. Much of the time we were having to step over bodies, never knowing whether they were dead or asleep, and not bothering to find out. You quickly become immune to the plight of the individual. We eventually met a young boy who said he knew of somewhere to stay: I'll never forget it. He led us to the Sea Lord Hotel, on Arthur Bunder Road.

The hotel shared its main entrance with the Charcoal Merchant's shop, and you had to climb past sacks of charcoal before going up the stairs to the third floor, which was the hotel. As we ascended the stairs there was a body lying full length on every second or third stair. The place was white sanatorium tiles throughout. There was the most nauseating strong smell of disinfectant. As we walked down the corridor I glanced into a room, only to see a man pouring a bucket of it around the floor, while cockroaches the size of a baby tortoise tried to climb the walls. I distracted Vanessa from seeing it and we were led to our cell. It was either this, or sleeping on the streets with the corpses. It was a bare room with an iron bed frame and something that resembled a prison mattress. When I enquired if it were possible to have some bed linen, I was asked, "What do you want that for? It's hot here!" I insisted. I was given two neatly folded bed sheets and when we opened them they were full of holes as big as your fist. Vanessa and I lay awake the entire night, fully clothed, while I kept one eye on the cockroaches. Although totally unconvinced, I tried to make light of it and assure Vanessa that one day she would laugh about this night. The stench and the heat were unbearable, and it was unwise to open the window as there was an outbreak of malaria.

Every minute we waited for the dawn. As the city awoke, we decided it was better to walk the streets of the slums rather than be in this place. The toilet was a hole in the floor in a stinking tiled room, and a tap washed the excrement away. In addition, after stepping over more bodies sleeping in the corridor outside our cell, we found that the metal concertina door was locked. If there was ever a fire, this place was a fire trap. Eventually we got free. Vanessa just couldn't stand it any more and the possibility of spending the day looking for a respectable place to stay just wasn't going to happen. People everywhere cooked food for sale on the street in the dirt. Men and women urinated and defecated wherever they stood in the streets; I saw dozens of them. The canals, probably built by the British, were filled dry with garbage and people. Once magnificent classical Romanesque buildings were in tatters, a neglected legacy from their Imperial rulers. Vanessa demanded we go back to the airport later that day and fly back to Goa – she just couldn't take it any longer.

We returned to coconut groves, rice paddy fields and travelling into rural India.

We visited rubber plantations and cashew nut producers, and went out with the fishermen in their boats. Most of all, we successfully avoided malaria.

Upon our return Hugo de Ferranti and Princess Dora got the train up from London to have luncheon at the Hall with me, to discuss Tom's progress. I'd been busy writing Tom's biography, making endless tape recordings, which all had to be trimmed and edited, then written in long hand. With the invaluable help of Vanessa, who re-typed the entire thing four times, it was a major task. Coupled with that, Tom's concentration span was limited; he got bored quickly. When it was completed, Dora advised that I send it to her cousin, Sarah Lutyens, a publishing agent.

Tom's record-breaking boat, *VeraHugh, Pride of Merseyside* sat outside the Hall and we received a visit from Mr. Mathew Tanner from the Liverpool Maritime Museum, with a view to buying it. It was to remain at Willaston for a further two years. Atlantic Challenge consumed much of my daily diary of events.

In May 1995, Reggie Kray phoned me as usual, to wish me Happy Birthday. He said that he had been told that he wouldn't be released before the end of his thirty-year term. I did write a letter on his behalf to the Home Secretary, but got the same conclusive response. Reggie suggested that when he got released, he and I should go into the property business together ... an interesting proposal. At least we wouldn't have the problem of tenants defaulting on payment of rents! I suppose not everyone gets asked to go into business by Britain's equivalent of Al Capone. Reggie said he instinctively knew I'm an honest and honourable man.

In June I received a letter from Her Serene Highness, Princess Sujarinee Mahidol Na Ayudhya, saying that the Thai Royal Family would like to invite Sebastian out to Thailand during the summer holidays, and would I give them permission. They would fly him out on August 19th and return him on August 30th. Prince Vatchrawee was Sebastian's best friend at school. The Princess continued in her letter, "I shall, of course, have the pleasure of defraying all expenses in this connection." I wrote immediately, thanking her for the Royal Family's kindness. Later, she telephoned me to say that she had prepared a wonderful itinerary for his visit and that the night before he returned, he would attend the fifteenth birthday of her eldest son, Prince Juthavachara, the future Crown Prince, in the Nonthaburi Royal Palace. Her Ambassador in London would liaise with me to confirm the details. In speaking to the Ambassador, I asked him if it would be an impertinence to ask if Sebastian could have a photograph taken with the Royal Family, while staying with them. He assured me that during his entire stay, the royal photographer would be following him constantly.

July 10th was Vanessa's 30th birthday. We had a party to beat all parties, and in the planning, Vanessa's meticulous eye for detail paid off. The mode of attire was past, present and future and as most of the guests, apart from family, were her work colleagues from Granada Television, there was no shortage of extravagant and bizarre ensembles. We had a West Indian steel band which filled the far end of the banqueting room and the sounds of the Caribbean could be heard as far as the town. Sebastian was dressed as a Beefeater and ceremoniously brought out her cake. They were still dancing on the lawns at six in the morning. It was the most wonderful and memorable night and the birthday party she had always dreamed of. At that time I felt so lucky to be loved by such a wonderful girl, and in return I loved her deeply.

Vanessa and I went to Cornwall for a week, and in August Sebastian returned from his trip to Thailand. The Royal Family flew him around the country in royal jets, he did everything and went everywhere. He was allowed to join them on a trip down the river in the Golden Royal Barge, he walked on red carpets and inspected ranks of royal soldiers. He returned with gifts and three enormous photograph albums of his every move. The Royal Family sent gifts to me, in the form of shirts, ties and large boxes of exotic fruits. Before leaving, Sebastian asked me what I wanted him to bring back as a present. I said, "You could bring me a coolie hat." While there, he told the Princess of my request. It was hilarious to see the photographs of the Royal Family, along with boatloads of generals and high-ranking military personnel, all in punts on the Bangkok River Market looking to buy a coolie hat for me. I was flattered that they should take the time out from running the country!

At home, it took Sebastian a week to get used to the idea that every policeman and soldier didn't salute him, and everybody else didn't bow or prostrate themselves in his presence.

September 1995. I had been working tirelessly on Tom McNally's Atlantic Challenge. The new boat was nearing completion, and although we managed to get the equipment and materials sponsored, finding the bulk of the money was a real struggle. Even though I had pecuniary shortcomings myself, mainly because I was funding the British judiciary, I still managed to pump a running tap of money into Tom's challenge. I really wanted him to bring the world record back to Britain. He had little or no appreciation of the massive amount of effort I was putting into it.

I am very fond of Tom but there is another side to him I find not so pleasant. I was forever doing interviews and making speeches, likening him to many of our other great heroes such as Scott, Shackleton, Lawrence etc., and there is an element of truth in all that. Tom is a remarkable man and you cannot remove his great achievements. Although I portrayed him as a deeply caring man, in reality he was nothing of the sort. There was an element of self-obsession with

Tom. His mother was the only person he was bothered about and she was elderly, frail and had cancer. I was very fond of his mum; like Tom, she was a real character.

I had arranged a deal with Granada Television to make a documentary about him. They were more interested in doing it their way, to include both of us. They liked the slant that I lived in a stately home with a butler, and Tom lived in a council flat in the toughest part of Liverpool, both men working together in different ways to bring the World Record back to Britain.

All was agreed and they employed a TV production company in Birkenhead to make the film. Atlantic Challenge Ltd was getting £4000 up front money, a substantial payment on completion, and 20% of the world rights.

Filming began, when Tom suddenly decided that he wanted the £4000 to be paid to him in cash. I was horrified – he just couldn't comprehend that everything had to be above board and go through Atlantic Challenge Ltd. He didn't understand that it all had to be part of a corporate structure. He told me the camera crew could "fuck off" and they weren't allowed to carry on filming unless they gave him the money. Dave Clapham, the producer, was in a total panic. He was contracted to Granada TV; if he didn't come up with the goods it was likely that Granada would never employ his company again. I said to Dave, "If you give Tom that money, he'll be drunk for months." He did, and he was!

At that stage I realised there was no further point in continuing to throw time and money at this project. I should have listened to Ian Wallace, his previous benefactor, who like me, abandoned him for the same reason. Tom is indeed a loose cannon.

I only wish him well, "Good Luck" to him.

About this time I was deeply saddened to watch the evening news and hear of the disappearance of Peter Bird. Peter was a similar seafaring adventurer. He had made several attempts at rowing across the Pacific, alone. I first met him when Tom and I were being filmed at the Earl's Court Boat Show for the documentary. Peter became my spy-in-the-camp at Sector Watches and had helped me with negotiations in order to secure the best sponsorship deal for Tom. He had confidentially told me all the tactics he was able to employ with Derek Salter, Sector's Managing Director. Many a time Peter would just phone me to chat about nothing. This trip, he was determined to succeed, and he phoned to say he had got the money out of Sector and it was all systems go! His last call to me was to say that he was leaving in the morning and stopping off in Canada to visit relatives before going on to Russia to prepare for the trip. I wished him "God Bless and Bon Voyage!" I shed tears as it was announced on *News at Ten* that he had sent a "Mayday" north of Japan. When a rescue crew were sent to him they only found his up-turned boat. They never found his body. He was an interesting, charming, articulate and heroic man. I'm honoured to say I knew him.

1996

The circus comes to town • A lie-down protest • Vanessa's career progresses

In February 1996 I received a call from John Richards. John and I seem to stumble from helping one good cause to another. It invariably costs us an absolute fortune in money, time and effort, and with all the best and most noble intentions, we often end up with the egg on our faces. John's latest good deed, among many, was to be roped into the Manchester Olympic Appeal.

At his home in Cheshire he put on a luncheon for a selection of high-flying Manchester businessmen. His Royal Highness Prince Michael came, not in a royal capacity, but as an old friend. John most generously flew him up in a private jet. Helena, John's wife, had arranged the luncheon and it was splendid. You would expect nothing less.

Being the sort of chap who enjoys his food, I shall give you the menu ... Baked cheese soufflés, followed by fillet of beef with Madeira sauce, roast potatoes, carrot and celeriac puree, broccoli florets and almonds. Treacle tart with crème Anglais. Cheeseboard, coffee, mints, and a selection of wines fit for a prince. Rolls-Royce at Crewe brought along their magnificent Silver Ghost, the most valuable car in the world at that time. I chatted at length with Prince Michael, mostly about his recent visit to Santa Barbara and our mutual interest in carriage driving. My only sadness was that he didn't bring Princess Michael along as I've never met her.

March was the beginning of Sebastian's school Easter holidays and

I arranged for him to fly up from London. The circus was coming to town, and it was to be built in the front field to the Hall. I asked the circus owner if it would be possible for Sebastian to help the men with the events and he said "most definitely". How many little boys get the opportunity to work in a circus for a week? King's Circus was one of the last proper circuses to have a full selection of performing animals, before the animal rights brigade and general spoil-sports/do-gooders got their way. Even the council were trying their best to prevent it happening. As a counter-attack, I got the owner to agree to give a free performance for all the handicapped schools in the area. That was then a big feature in the local press, and the magistrate who was due sign the council's summons wisely said he was unable sign until Monday, which was when the circus was due to leave! Victory for common sense and a jolly good time for all!

I managed to get it on the front pages of all the papers in Cheshire and it resulted in a complete sell-out at every performance. They photographed me riding elephants outside the Hall. Chico dressed me up as a clown with full make-up. The only slightly tricky bit was when one newspaper asked if I would be photographed in the cage with the lions. I obliged. Paul, the lion tamer, instructed me on how to get to know the lions for an hour or so before we chanced that picture. I'm here to tell the tale with all legs and arms intact. You must never give the adrenaline of fear to any animal, especially a lion. Sebastian was almost not so lucky. They had built a makeshift portable cage with very wide open bars. Paul, Sebastian and I were standing next to it chatting. From out of the corner of my eye I saw a lion leap toward us and in split-second reaction I grabbed Sebastian and threw him to one side. The lion was frantically clawing with his front legs outside the bars trying to get at him. Paul said he attacked because Sebastian was small and looked like easy prey.

It was all great fun and Sebastian became one of the crew, feeding and riding elephants and looking after the bears, tigers and lions – even the one that tried to eat him! On the Sunday, he helped them take down the Big Top and load the chairs into the lorries. That night as I got him ready for bed, we watched them leave the field from an upstairs bedroom window. We made new friends that week: Chico the clown, Paul the lion tamer and his wife Jackie, Polo the tightrope walker, Simon the ringmaster and Geoff and his wife who owned the circus. As they were leaving, Geoff's wife knocked on the door of the Hall with a bottle of brandy for me and a huge bouquet of roses for

Vanessa. It was kind and thoughtful of them. The driver of the last lorry closed the gate to the field and then they were gone! All was quiet again. We couldn't help feeling very sad. "Ah well, maybe next year!"

In April we had a new Conservative prospective parliamentary candidate, Michael Loveridge. I had been asked if I would hold a "Cottage Meeting" at the Hall in order for the Tory devotees and myself to get to know him. There was never more than a couple of weeks that went by when I wasn't having some event for the Conservatives. I had not been on the Selection Committee this time prior to the election and I was interested to see who they had approved. As far as I was concerned he was a charming fellow but as a Londoner and very rich old Etonian, I could see that Michael would go down with railway workers in Crewe like a lead balloon; they'd hate him. The evening was organised by Brian Sylvester, former leader of Crewe Council, and some sixty people were invited. Four turned up. Poor Brian hopped from foot to foot and there were many embarrassing silences. As council elections were also looming, I took the opportunity to ask Brian what exactly was he going to do about my "Sleeping Policemen". Since the building of the Nantwich Bypass our little country lane had become a shortcut for big lorries and it had become a serious danger to the village. Like all politicians he said, "I'll look into it."

I said, "Just to make sure you do. On Tuesday morning I will lie down in the middle of the road in protest and block all the morning traffic until I get a positive assurance from the council that something will be done." Brian, grasping at the perfect photo opportunity for his election campaign, said he would come and support me. The press are far too clever to fall for that one, and my protest was the main feature of all three local newspapers but they managed to exclude Brian from each picture. Frustrated morning commuters were furiously honking their horns. One lorry driver was shouting, "Run the bastard over." Every so often the council need to be shaken up a bit; they get bored otherwise.

In a melancholic moment when I was suffering from one of my occasional Churchillian "Black Dog" days, I was reflecting on my life of failure and lack of achievement. Because many of the things I did attracted much publicity, I have been the subject of envy, sycophantic admiration, jealousy and sometimes almost hatred, but I felt I'd never actually achieved anything of any true worth. I'm very aware that those of us who stick our heads above the parapet get shot at, but sometimes I felt that my life was rather like being on one of those pedal-boats at the seaside. You know, the ones which have two paddle wheels and look like a one-man Mississippi Steamboat. You can pedal like crazy, creating a great froth and foam which attracts the glances of the nearby swimmers and beached sunbathers, but you don't actually get anywhere! Vanessa's diagnosis was that I was suffering from the male menopause.

In July 1996, Vanessa, Sebastian and I flew to visit Mother in California where we were given a whirlwind tour of the state, mainly for Vanessa's sake as she had never been before. She was deeply concerned at the prospect of her new responsibilities when she returned to Blighty. She had been promoted to a producer of the newly formed Granada Sky TV. Vanessa had two shows to find presenters for; an antiques show and a gardening one. I said, "Fear not, I know two who would fit the bill." Roddy Llewellyn would be perfect for the gardening show! I also reminded myself that I'd once had dinner at Royal Windsor with a highly amusing chap called Tim Wonnacott. He is very televisual and looks like Terry Thomas. On top of that he was a director of Sotheby's in Chester, perfect for the antiques show. I suggested she give him a call and see if he wanted to go on television. To this day Tim is unaware that I am responsible for launching him into television stardom.

Upon our return I received a notice of investigation by the much-dreaded Child Support Agency. I was to endure twelve months of Gestapo interrogation into every facet of my life. At the end of it, in conversation with one of the female investigating agents, she concluded that I was one of the most loving and responsible fathers she had dealt with. She said it was apparent that I was the victim of a very vindictive woman indeed. I said, "That is the greatest understatement of all time." I was one of the soft targets which made up the Child Support Agency report figures. The real scoundrels, generally fathers of no fixed abode, or the like, continued to be able to shirk their responsibility. To date, six very decent soft-target fathers had committed suicide as a result of heavy-handed investigations by this agency. It was an abomination.

Heading toward Christmas I was busy arranging for my two hundred children to go to the pantomime and all the other things relating to the festive season.

1997

"Sticky Fingers" • A Tunisian break • Family reunion in the
Emerald Isle • Lord Lust's lovelies
• The parting of the ways

1997 began with Reggie Kray phoning me to wish me a very Happy
New Year. You feel awkward saying it back to someone who is to
spend at least thirty of them in the clink!

In March of 1997, Bill Wyman of the Rolling Stones was opening a
new restaurant in Manchester called "Sticky Fingers" and Vanessa and
I were invited.

We managed to wangle two extra invites, and I suggested we bring
Mike and Ro McCartney. It was a thoroughly enjoyable evening. Every
famous face you could think of was there. Boy George was acting as DJ
for the night and in a later conversation with Bill, he told me he had
paid Boy George £4000 for the night and he was not happy. I wouldn't
have paid him in tap washers for what he did. Dave Dee was Master of
Ceremonies and a comedian was employed to entertain us. His first
joke was about John Lennon being shot. Bearing in mind that Mike
McCartney and several other people there had known John Lennon
well, you can imagine how that went down. By his third tasteless joke
the crowd were booing him off the stage. Thank goodness for Steve
Coogan. Steve jumped up, took over and saved the night. He was
absolutely hilarious. Vanessa and Ro spotted Sacha Distel standing at
the bar and the pair of them started behaving like two lovesick
teenagers. After about ten minutes of listening to them drooling over
him, I made my excuse to go to the loo. I sneaked over and had a little
chat with Sacha and invited him to join us at our table. The look on
their faces when they saw Sacha and me walking toward them chatting
together was priceless. He sat between the girls with his arms around
them both and got them to sing "Raindrops keep falling on my head"
with him. It was a great night out.

In the same month I was in need of a new car, and so I got the train
to London and called to see Sebastian. Kelly was with her latest man,
Martin Gibbins, living in a lovely house at Berkley Square. Sebastian
was off school, and he and I walked to have luncheon at Planet
Hollywood. I told him we were getting another car but kept him

Vanessa — my flaxen-haired "Lady V".

Leeza Gibbons and Chris Quinten at their home in Hollywood.

Lewis and Michelle with little Oliver, the day they tied the knot.

Paul and me at Mike McCartney's 50th birthday celebration.

Tom McNally in his record-breaking boat.

John Richards, His Royal Highness Prince Michael, me (grinning like a Cheshire cat) and the High Sheriff of Cheshire.

"Lord Lust" and some of his "lovelies".

Mother and I discuss our safe return through Newry with troops.

The burnt-out carpet lorry the morning after.

Sebastian rolls on the ground in agony (left). Prince Harry runs off after head-butting him in the testicles.

I wore Sir George's armour; Vicky wore her sneakers!

guessing as to what sort. When we walked down the little mews to Wykehams, he was thrilled to see that it was a Morgan. It was British Racing Green with a brown leather strap over the bonnet, brown leather seats and a wooden steering wheel. There was a small enamel union flag on the bodywork. It was traditional British motoring in the truest sense. The day was glorious and sunny, and Sebastian and I drove all around central London with the hood down, showing off!

The following month, Vanessa and I took a break and flew to Tunisia. We did all the tourist things, riding camels with the tribesmen, visiting the Troglodytes and travelling the length and breadth of the country. It was a wonderful, romantic, and much-needed break. We arrived back just in time to vote in the General Election, not that it would have made a blind bit of difference. The Conservatives suffered a crushing defeat, far worse than we ever dreamed possible. Tony Blair was the new man in No.10 with his New Labour Party! Oh, woe unto the nation.

It was an odd sort of month. I received a call from a friend asking if I had seen the news. My chum, Colin Gurley had been arrested on suspicion of flying in drugs from abroad in his plane. It appeared on national television. I couldn't believe for a second that Colin would be involved in that sort of business. He kept his aircraft at Barton Airport near Manchester and I have thoroughly enjoyed flying in it with him. His incarceration at Strangeways Prison during the trial took almost a year. At the end of it he was acquitted and totally exonerated of any wrongdoing, but understandably the whole ghastly affair had a devastating affect on his life. You can be guilty merely by association, until proven innocent.

On a similar subject, about twelve months previous to this, Big John Newton brought along a couple of his friends from Liverpool to the Hall. The one who was obviously the boss was a very pleasant stocky chap, with the physique of a power lifter. He was most amiable, highly intelligent and obviously self-educated. He appeared to be well-read and had an extensive knowledge of art. He had the inevitable Scouse humour and razor wit and I found him to be extremely good company. His name was Curtis Warren. His friend was a much taller man with an interest in horses, and on one visit they called to discuss buying one of my carriages. The last time Curtis visited us at the Hall, he and Sebastian spent much of the afternoon lying on the floor of the banqueting room playing with Sebastian's train set. Unbeknown to me he slipped Sebastian a little gift of ten pounds before leaving. A week or so later I turned on *News at Ten* to see a mug-shot of Curtis. He had been arrested in Europe as the head of one of the largest drug empires in the world, worth hundreds of millions of pounds. The authorities were so in fear of him, they held the trial at a secret location. It said he was the most dangerous and wanted criminal in Europe. I found him to be most courteous and charming; I take people as I find them.

My cousin, Brian Leigh Jnr, got married to Sarah in July of 1997. As a consequence almost the entire clan flew in from all corners of the world. In the week that followed it was decided that some of them wanted to spend a few days in Ireland, visiting family-owned farms and long-lost relatives. I had no intention of joining them as it was Vanessa's birthday on July 10th, but Vanessa insisted that I must go. "It isn't one of my landmark birthdays and you rarely see your mother," she said.

It was decided we'd go to Dublin and hire a minibus there. As most of the group on this trip were North Americans, I was nominated as bus driver, being the only one who doesn't mind driving on the wrong side of the road. The group consisted of Mother, her sisters Betty and Andolores, her brother John and his French Canadian wife Michelline, my sister Andrea, and me.

We were oblivious of the fact that in Northern Ireland it was Orangeman's Week. From Dublin, we headed north toward Dundalk and along the way we telephoned a distant cousin in order to get instructions. In a panic-stricken voice, we were told we were mad to come anywhere near the place. All hell had been let loose and we were to go nowhere near the town of Newry. A relative would meet us at the "Checkpoint Charlie" at Dundalk and lead us via country lanes to Warrenpoint. Needless to say there were two Checkpoint Charlies at the border between North and South and we were at the wrong one. After much deliberation and waiting for an hour and a half, as bus driver and official tourist guide, I decided we had no choice but to take our chances through Newry; all agreed.

Upon entering the town we wondered what all the fuss was about. Children were playing in the streets, women were pushing prams, delivery men were going about their business. All was quiet and perfectly normal ... until I turned the corner. A huge armoured military lorry shot out from an alleyway, blocking my retreat exit. In front of us, a lorry carrying carpets was ablaze. Several cars and a shop were all on fire. Soldiers were running everywhere, crouching in doorways and behind walls, their machine guns pointing at every-thing and anything that moved. We were in the middle of a full- blown war zone. Bricks and debris lay everywhere. So intense was the heat from the burning vehicles that the tar on the road had melted. I could feel it and hear it sticking to the tyres of my bus as I gingerly drove through the chaos and carnage. It was terrifying, I felt I was the only duck in the pond at a duck-hunter's convention. I genuinely expected us to get shot at. My over-loquacious passengers were noticeably silent, save for one whispered comment from the back: "Oh my God, we're all going to die!"

We made it out of the war zone and into utter tranquillity, only three miles away. Warrenpoint hadn't changed; it was thirty years since I had last set foot in the place.

It is one of the most beautiful and picturesque parts of the British Isles, where as the song says, "The Mountains of Mourne sweep down to the sea". It was hard to realise that there was such turmoil and destruction only a stone's throw away from it. A party was held in a local hotel on the seafront where there were around a hundred people all claiming to be related to us. All the local newspapers covered the story.

Our first stop was Mayobridge, Auchnagon, where my grandfather had owned his two farms and my mother and some of her sisters were born. We visited cemeteries, schools and old haunts and ended up at a pub called Gorman's Bar. There the walls were covered with early pictures of locals, and numerous fascinating items of the area's social history. A sepia portrait of my grandfather and grandmother taken on their honeymoon in 1919 was included. Also there was the poster of the auction in 1937 when my grandfather leased out his farms and sold the last remaining livestock. It included a plough horse and mare (good workers) and a Morris motor car PMO (in prime motoring order!).

We drove to Belleeks village, which is not to be confused with the place of pottery fame. This place was serious bandit country. Telegraph poles were painted green, white and gold and cut-out letters, I R A, were nailed to trees and farm gates. Fortunately we were driving a vehicle with Southern Irish plates and they were less likely to take pot shots at us. We also had the advantage of lots of American accents emanating from our vehicle. They loved Yanks; I kept my mouth shut.

A cottage built by my great-grandfather and occupied by my great-aunt May until she died, now lay derelict. The farmhouse I used to stay in as a boy was also almost roofless and abandoned; it was a sad sight. My boyhood memories flooded back to me – farming life was so simple in those days. At the beginning of the twentieth century my great-grandfather had installed a generator powered by wind, but when I was a boy in the 1950s the idea seemed to have been abandoned and they reverted to lighting the house by Tilley lamps or candles. Although the house had a modern bathroom on the ground floor all the bedrooms were supplied with chamber pots. One minor irritation was to have to use the pot in the middle of the night. If you forgot to put it well beneath the bed you invariably put your foot in it when you got up in the morning. Another thing I remember vividly was climbing the dark stairs at night with your candle in its chamber-stick in one hand, and a brown stoneware hot water bottle in the other. The beds always felt cold and slightly damp and the stoneware bottle was too hot to put your feet on. You would periodically wake in the night having stubbed your toe on the damned thing.

The evenings were spent sitting round the fire telling stories, and sometimes men would come from neighbouring farms or the village to play the fiddle and sing songs with us. In the summer we would harvest the corn, wheat, barley, oats, flax and hay. I remember much of it was cut by hand, and we would gather it by the armful, using a few strands to tie the neck of the sheaves. These would be stacked in tricorns, and at the end of the day the field would appear to have the linear precision of a military graveyard.

In the middle of the day the womenfolk would come down to the fields with luncheon. I will always remember the wonderful Irish soda bread, hot out of the baking oven with lashings of homemade butter. I can taste it and smell it as I write. Things had been done like that for a thousand years or more. We did have a big old tractor with metal wheels, I think it was called a Fordson, but our neighbours, the Bennetts, who lived at the bottom of our lane, still ploughed with heavy horses. I watched Mr. Bennett with great admiration as he commanded his Clydesdales. You'd never find the slightest wiggle in Mr. Bennett's ploughed field. They were wonderful days!

Another job I used to assist with was killing the pigs. This was long before all the silly red tape, Euro-rules and health and safely nonsense. Farmers would kill their own animals as needed. Pigs were ringed and a single pig was led into the courtyard by the nose. Before it knew what was happening it was hit on the head between the eyes with a lump hammer. While unconscious, its throat was slit and the pig died instantly without pain or knowledge.

My job was to run in and out of the farmhouse with kettles of boiling water to shave the carcass. We used a man's cut-throat razor, as pig hair is like wire, and the animal had to be completely clean to satisfy the butcher. Hooks were put into each back leg Achilles and the pig was strung up in the barn, gutted and cleaned. By mid afternoon the butcher would come from Newry, the carcass was weighed, and the cash was paid!

When I was ten years old I was taught how to kill a chicken by wringing its neck, and I have wrung many a one since. My grandmother taught me how to pluck and gut them and get them ready for the oven. It was all simple and uncomplicated.

The next farm to Hughes's Farm was owned by James O'Hare. I remember being intrigued by him as a boy; he was a very interesting old chap. I believe he was somehow related to us but I couldn't tell you how. James had gone to America in the 1880s and made his fortune and returned to Ireland. He brought a Wells Fargo stage coach back with him and used it as his mode of transport. He would harness it up and drive his wife into the village to buy his chewing tobacco and provisions. When I knew them, I believe neither James nor his wife had ever bathed or had a wash in over forty years. James always wore a wide-brimmed cowboy hat, and both it and his clothes were so dirty they looked as if they were made of leather. As a child, I was always afraid of his wife. She wore full-length black clothes and a huge floppy black hat and I was convinced she was a witch. She never spoke to me, she just stared at me, which I found very unnerving. They both lived well into their nineties having never had a day's illness in their lives. On this trip, I wandered over the fields to visit James's house, only to find it also was derelict. The remains of burnt peat still lay in the grate from his last fire all those years ago. I said a little goodbye prayer to James before I left.

Upon our return, the clan all went back to their respective homes. *Cheshire Life* came to do a feature story about the Hall and me, and so did *Country Homes and Interiors* magazine. The press continued to hound me, but no matter what they wrote, there was always a sting in the tail in their articles. Vanessa advised me to do something to turn the whole thing into a joke. The "Lord Lust" label which they had attached to me was forever being brought up, but often in a nasty way. If I was to be Lord Lust then why not make it funny? She said,

"Self-deprecation and making fun of yourself is an endearing quality, and it will help change your public image for the better." I heeded her advice and had a meeting with Eamonn O'Neil at Granada Sky TV. Eamonn agreed that we should do a TV series called *Lord Lust's Lovelies Show* involving pretty semi-naked glamour models. It would be an updated version of Benny Hill. It hit much of the national press and within weeks it became the top-rated show on Granada Sky for the next year and a half. In addition to that I was invited on several chat shows, and even featured on the religious programme called *Heart of the Matter* with Joan Bakewell. Graham Norton did a programme about myself and Alexander, the Marquis of Bath, called *Royalty Unzipped*. The whole thing was gloriously tacky and great fun. It was a welcome respite from my personal problems and the constant bombardment of litigation from Kelly.

The saddest thing of all was that, since our return from California together, cracks were beginning to appear in my relationship with Vanessa. Not, I might add, on my part. I loved and adored her. As a producer, Vanessa was in a position to help me to procure more television work as a presenter, but she refused to do so on the grounds of nepotism. I felt that the instant success of the Lord Lust show didn't bode well with her. Although I don't want to sound too gleeful of the fact, nonetheless, I couldn't help inwardly feeling a degree of gratification.

In August of 1997, I was burdened by an overwhelming sadness. My darling Vanessa moved out of the Hall. She had bought a little house for herself on George Street in Knutsford. When I met her she was a slightly shy and under-confident girl; now she was a well-paid, very confident, and highly successful television producer woman. Over the years, she had to endure the constant intrusion of Kelly and the potty excentricities of myself. When she left I wrote the following to her ...

> The hours of which, forever gone,
> That precious dreams restore,
> Of flaxen hair in moonlight shone,
> Thy sweet soft lips, no more.
>
> N'er again shall we wake entwined,
> To hear that woodland dove.
> N'er again must my thoughts inclined,
> To yearning for thy love.

In the months that followed we continued to yoyo in and out of our relationship. Sometimes I would stay in Knutsford and sometimes she would return to the Hall.

The denouement was when she went to Cornwall with her mother and sister, Emma.

Again, I wrote a silly poem for her; I often wrote silly poems…

> A horse can't neigh, when his mare's away,
> A slug can't wink, with his antennae.
>
> A chair's no good, if it's got no seat,
> A bed can't run, though it's got four feet.
>
> A clock can't chime, if it's got no bell,
> A duck can't quack, if it's not very well.
>
> Cyclops dreams of having a pair,
> And I dream of you, when you're not there.

When I wrote it, I was unaware that in Cornwall she was in the arms of another.

What was to follow was another one of my sexual crusades, but in my heart I was to inwardly pine for Vanessa for years to come.

During filming at the Hall, I was to make the acquaintance of the husband of one of the girls being filmed by Granada TV. Jim was an interesting sort of chap. He had been university educated, after which he had joined the Parachute Regiment. His military career was short lived, and for some time he found himself at a crossroads as to what to do next. I'm unsure how he became a professional male stripper, but that's what he did. Sue, his stunningly pretty wife, was also in the same profession.

When Jim and Sue parted company, Jim was devastated, and so I employed him as my chauffeur and chum. Jim played the part brilliantly, and I would turn up at official functions with him in full livery, complete with chauffeur's hat. It was all a bit of fun really, we were just having a lark. He had a superb intelligent wit and humour, which I thoroughly enjoyed. He once described our mutual dangerous but insatiable attraction for beautiful young women as, "the pointy carrot of Damocles".

Both Sue and Vanessa had gone and Jim and I were, very briefly, in a state of romantic dormancy. We were buying groceries in the supermarket in Nantwich one day, when it struck us both that the public might perceive us to be two old queens, Dorothy and Doreen Dormant!

I penned the following to Dorothy and Doreen:

> Battenburg, each day at noon,
> A gingham dress well worn,
> Her red beret, a para's platoon,
> Far from that sergeant's scorn.
>
> Doreen condones her facial hair,
> Dorothy, to disagree,
> A flick of the head, a pugnacious stare,
> Doreen to mince and flee.
>
> The shopping cart, with buckled wheel,
> Doreen is wont to choose,
> Shrill the curse, blaspheme the squeal,
> Damn those stiletto shoes.
>
> For Dorothy, warm milk and one pink fancy,
> Slumber beckons her Doreen,
> Some may mock and call them nancy,
> Tedium plagues a sad old queen.

Before the summer holiday was over I took advantage of a few days alone with Sebastian. He had been studying the Roman occupation of Britain at school, and so he and I drove to Hadrian's Wall. There, we stayed at a little bed and breakfast in the village of Gilsland. Although the weather was predictably dreadful, we walked the Wall and visited the Roman museums in order for him to learn as much as possible. I must admit I learnt quite a lot myself. As he grows up we are becoming the best of pals, as well as father and son. I love him more than my limited vocabulary can express into words, and I'm always so proud of him.

August 1997 brought the saddest news of all. Princess Diana was killed in Paris. Never in the history of the world had so many tears been shed for one individual. I always thought it would be impossible for such a deep and heartfelt display of international mourning ever to surpass that for President John F. Kennedy, but this day it did. Even soldiers and policemen were seen to weep.

Back at the Hall, the usual calendar of events continued. Sir George Young came to dinner and as our suit of armour, which stood by the window in the banqueting room, was always called George, we decided to mark the occasion by knighting it.

We began to film the second series of the *Lord Lust's Lovelies Show* and life was returning to being fun, which is how I like it. I started to go out with Carole Davies, an old acquaintance. Carole was a stunning beauty and I had known her since she was fifteen, but it was not to get much past the first post. She was still seeing her sometime ex-boyfriend, Philip Jay. For a while she was enjoying the favours of both of us. Much as I was keen to get the relationship on a firm footing, I felt it was rather like trying to light a camp fire in a damp woodland. I wrote the following to her . . .

> Amidst the moist and leafy glade,
> Kindling strives to torch its fire,
> As love that isn't heaven made,
> A wretched fool can but desire.
>
> And e're so often a tiny flame,
> Will burst with joyous breath,
> But dew and lichen will to blame,
> In causing of its death.
>
> The sweet and burning fragrant air,
> Through wooded regions go,
> It tells that love must not despair,
> But will embrace that fire's glow.

Well it didn't, and I kicked the idea into touch.

That summer, Sebastian's school friend, the Hon. William Frankland, along with his mother and father (Lord and Lady Zouche) called to see us, to look at an eighteenth-century portrait we have hanging in the Hall. It is of one of Jimmy Zouche's ancestors, John Frankland. Jimmy said it was sold from his old family estate in 1920 and it was one of the items he had been trying to track down. I said his search was over and it was his for £2,500. He said he would go away and think about it. I got the impression that John Frankland would be staying with us for quite some time to come!

As Sebastian was about to return to school, Kelly and Martin insisted on taking him to Hong Kong. He had his Common Entrance Exam coming soon and I wasn't happy!

1998

Royal rugby • Mother's 70th birthday • The television cameras
roll again • The sting! • Another wedding • Harrow

In February 1998 I received a very excited phone call from Sebastian,
"Daddy, I've been made captain of the school second rugby team!
Do you think you could come on Wednesday and watch me play?" I
wouldn't have missed it for the world. I asked Mr. Dawson, the headmaster, if it were possible for me to come, and he said he would be
delighted to see me. When I arrived, I met Sebastian's Science Master
and Rugby Coach, who informed me that there was a change of plan.
He said that Sebastian was an exceptionally fine rugby player and he
had promoted him to the first team to play Ludgrove.

Prince Harry led the Ludgrove team onto the pitch. I was the only
spectator there, save for a very bouncy and vivacious girl who came
and joined me. She was chatty, very friendly, and introduced herself as
Tiggy Legge-Bourke. She was royal nanny to the two boys. Sebastian
played a terrific game. Ludgrove had some fine players, including
Harry, but I couldn't help feeling deeply saddened that his mother
was no longer there to support him. Princess Diana always came to
the school matches. She would have been just as proud of her son's
performance that day, as I was of mine. It would have been nice if the
Prince of Wales had come, but Tiggy was more than enthusiastic in
her support for Ludgrove, screaming and shouting whenever Harry
got the ball. In the last few minutes of the game, Sebastian was
injured, but he behaved like a real trooper. He received a very painful
head-butt in the testicles by none other than Prince Harry. When the
game was over, Harry ran up to Tiggy and flung his arms around her
neck, hugging and kissing her, and it was obvious to see that he was
greatly loved. At the end of the game there was much confusion as to
the final score but it didn't really matter. After drinks in the headmaster's sitting room with Tiggy and Mr. Dawson, and dinner at Chicitos
with Sebastian, I drove back to Cheshire, a very proud dad indeed!

March 11th 1998 was Mother's 70th birthday and my Aunt Phil and
I decided to fly to California and surprise her. It was the most dreadful
flight and we got the worst seats on the plane, right in the centre at
the back where we couldn't see the film. The staff were ghastly and

thoroughly unhelpful. The misery of the flight was soon forgotten and Phil and I made our way to Santa Barbara and checked into a hotel down by the beach. Mother's house is directly in front of the old Santa Barbara Mission. My mother's sister, Andolores and her husband, Brian and daughter Margaret were already there at the house, on holiday. We decided to give Mother a double surprise and Phil walked in alone. Brian, who was sunning himself, ignored her, thinking she was a friend of Mother's. Out of context, at first he didn't recognise his own sister-in-law! From down the road I heard the shrieks and yelps of excitement and laughter. Ten minutes later I made my entrance to a similar reception. Mother couldn't have been more thrilled. We had her party at the Biltmore in Santa Barbara, during which my brother, Paul, also made a surprise entrance. It was a wonderful couple of weeks.

I returned to England to a heavy series of filming engagements and in addition to *Lord Lust* I continued to be invited onto other TV programmes. In April we began filming four shows of an antiques programme called *Collectors Lot* for Channel 4, at the Hall. Sue Cook was the presenter and it was a four-day shoot. I was very handsomely paid. In casual conversation with a scouser, who was the film crew chef, he told me tales of when he was at sea. To my absolute astonishment he said he was once nearly shipwrecked mid-Atlantic on a ship called *The Empress of England*. He couldn't believe it when I said I was also on board. He explained that in the great swell all the below-deck crew cabins at the bow of the ship were completely filled with water.

This made the front end extra heavy and dangerously low in the water. He said that they were told under no circumstances were they allowed to give panic to the passengers, but another hour of swell would have sunk us. As all the doors were lashed, all souls on board would have been lost. We are both here to tell the tale!

During filming *Lord Lust* outside in the grounds of the Hall, I wore Sir George's suit of armour. In full armour, I rode my sit-up-and-beg 1910 bicycle in hot pursuit of glamour model, Vicky, who was wearing nothing more than her white sneakers! Villagers complained of my disgraceful behaviour to the police, but no police arrived.

I was later told by Paul, our local bobby, that all six of our policemen assigned to Nantwich station were hiding behind the wall of our ha-ha. Paul admitted that he climbed a tree to get a better view. Further complaints by the townsfolk were received, only to be told that the police were taking it very seriously indeed, and were dealing with the matter!

Roger Cook used to do a TV show called *The Cook Report*, an under-cover programme investigating criminals from around the world. One day I received a call from Philip Braund, the producer. He asked if he could have a meeting with me about the possibility of doing a "sting" at the Hall. A Derby-based solicitor called Paul Bowler had allegedly built an army of criminal chums through his work as a solicitor.

Roger had been tracking Bowler for over a year, and the yarn spun to Bowler by Roger Cook's researcher, Andy, who posed as an Eastender and small time crook, was thus . . .

Andy had, over a long time, won the confidence of Bowler and said that his sister worked for a country squire who lived in a stately home in Cheshire. There, a valuable painting had been removed from the wall for repairs. It had been sitting in the kitchen for weeks and his Lordship probably wouldn't notice it was missing for some time. Andy told Bowler that he had a buyer for the painting in Amsterdam, but his problem was finding someone reliable to break in and steal it. Bowler fell for the story hook, line and sinker, and he assured Andy that he had just the right men for the job. All of Andy's conversations were recorded on film via a mini camera in his shirt button.

Roger and the team discussed with me the best way of allowing them to break in. We decided that entry through the coal hatch and into the wine cellar was the easiest. Andy had several meetings with Bowler, and made it clear that all the paintings still on the walls were alarmed and linked to the police in Nantwich. Under no circumstances were they to open the cellar door more than eighteen inches as it would trigger a beam alarm in the corridor. Bowler assured Andy that his men were highly professional.

The following Saturday the Cook team returned to lay the trap. They placed a micro-camera in a box of teabags with a false bottom, and plenty of teabags on the top, in the event the thieves might be cocky enough to make themselves a cup of tea!

They brought a breadbin, loaded with a camera, from their props department at Carlton Television which gave a full scan of the kitchen. They also placed a further two cameras outside. One was in the courtyard and one in the wheelie-bin next to the coal hatch. They also delivered the valuable painting. The trap was set!

On the morning of the sting, the team arrived to check that all cameras were working properly and Andy had arranged to meet Bowler's men at the truck driver's "Butty Bar" just off Exit 16 on the M6. There they received their instructions and a detailed map. They followed Andy to the roundabout at the bottom of the lane to the Hall. Philip suggested that he and I should go to the Peacock Inn for a drink while the robbery was taking place, but I refused. I had no intention of leaving my house while it was being robbed, and decided to hide in the Squire's Room at the top of the first floor stairs. Philip agreed to hide with me.

Before settling down I loaded my 12-bore shotgun and Sebastian's 410, which I duly handed to Philip. He went into a total panic. "Christ almighty, you're not going to start shooting people," he said. I explained to him that if these chaps were as professional as Bowler said, then there was always the possibility they might be armed. The criminal mind doesn't stick to rules like the rest of us. If they were armed, and they broke the rules and came upstairs, I was not going to be caught sitting there like a tin duck at a fairground. Should they decide to risk coming up the stairs, by the time they reached the mezzanine, I would have a protected line of fire and they would have nowhere to go! They would have broken the rules, and would be fair game as far as I was concerned.

The Hall has a deathly silence during the day and Philip and I sat on the bedroom floor, guns at the ready. Thirty minutes seemed an eternity, then we heard the tyres of a car slowly coming along the crunchy driveway. Slowly, slowly, it turned around the circle in front of the Hall and then retreated. "They've gone! They smell a rat," said Philip. Just then, he went to look out of the window. I shouted at him, "Keep down, they'll be surveying the place, they'll be back!" Philip is a city boy, and he had much to learn about the patience of being a hunter. The Hall returned to silence, save for the pounding of our hearts and the chattering of Philip's teeth.

Then it came ... Thump, thump, thump, they were smashing the coal hatch door. I could hear them shuffling in the cellar. Every few minutes Philip would whisper, "Where are they now?" The door leading to the wine cellar had a distinctive creak to it, similar to one you would hear in a horror film. They were in the kitchen and we could hear them talking directly below us. I had to admit a rush of adrenaline at that moment, and my finger moved onto the trigger. Then silence returned. Fifteen minutes went by and then both of us nearly leapt out of our skin when Philip's mobile phone rang out! It was his team, saying they had spotted the thieves' car speeding down the Nantwich Bypass heading toward the motorway. Andy had arranged to do the exchange in the car park at Derby Football Club. What turned out to be the icing on the cake was that Bowler turned up to be in on the exchange. It was all caught on camera and a great success. It turned out to be one of their highest-rated shows, and at the time Roger was thrilled. So was I, I was a few thousand pounds richer from that little adventure!

A week or so after it was televised, I got a visit from our local Chief Constable, informing me that Roger Cook, Philip and myself could be charged with Entrapment. This was for creating a crime which would not have happened had we not created it. He said he wouldn't charge me, but he was working with Derby Police and they might insist on it. I wasn't bothered, it was all just a lark to me.

Some time later I got a distressed call from Roger. One of his camera team had been offered a considerable amount of money by the *News of The World* to do an exposé on the programme. He'd taken the money, and made out that much of the show was a set-up. Understandably, Roger was deeply hurt and upset by those spurious allegations. He had risked his life for years, exposing some of the most dangerous criminals in the world. At one point he had as many as six contracts on his life by international gangsters. I felt deeply sorry for Roger. I opened the *News of The World* to see a bloody great picture of Roger and me, along with the shotgun story!

His long-standing and high-value show was dropped not long after that. We rarely saw Roger on TV again, but he and I kept in touch.

A week or so later I was on the train to London to appear on a TV discussion show with John Singleton. They paid my hotel bill and a fee, as I was due on the show the following morning. When I got back to the studio at Granada I was told that the whole of Granada Sky staff had stopped work to watch me. Everyone was glued to the TV monitors except Vanessa, who continued working on her computer and refused to look up. Why?

Meanwhile, Sebastian had completed his Common Entrance Exam and had been staying at the Hall with me for the mid-term break. It was an anxious return journey. All the boys' exam results were posted on the school notice board. To his overwhelming relief it read ... SEBASTIAN HADFIELD-HYDE – PASS for HARROW. I was thrilled!

His years at Sunningdale had been exceptionally happy ones, and I am eternally grateful to Mr. Dawson, his brother, and their staff for all that they did for Sebastian. There were numerous fond and amusing memories.

One springs to mind. A couple of years earlier I had been acquainted with a wheeler-dealer friend of mine, who informed me he was in possession of four tons of dynamite, and could I find a buyer? It was totally inert, and only used for training NATO troops on how to handle explosives. It came in military boxes and each stick was marked "DYNAMITE!" but in small print it read INERT. Basically it was just normal plasticine. With the help of Vanessa's father, who was a brilliant salesman, we managed to sell a ton of it to Saddam Hussein! At that time he was still in favour with the Western world and it would be of no military value anyway.

We had several boxes of it in our wine cellar, and one day when Sebastian was returning to school, he asked if he could take a few sticks to give to his friend, Guinness (of the Guinness Brewery family) who collected military memorabilia.

At the end of the school term, I received a frantic panic-stricken telephone call from Mr. Dawson, saying that the Guinness family were returning to their home in Ireland when they were stopped and interrogated by security. Part of Heathrow Airport had been put on bomb alert! All ended well, but I don't think I was too popular with the Guinness family after that.

In July I found myself back in London, I had been invited to be a presenter on the *Collector's Lot* antiques programme for Channel 4. My job was to do an outside broadcast in St. John's Wood about a fellow who had a wonderful spoof stately home in a terraced house there. He was a remarkable eccentric and it was a joy to interview him.

By August, Sebastian and I were back in California. This time it was to attend my sister's second wedding. Sadly, things hadn't worked out for her and Josh. There are some people you instantly like, and Andrea's new man, David, is one of those. Not many of my mother's family came, as most of them were only in California in March.

My sister and her new husband are both Los Angeles stockbrokers, and apart from David's family many of the guests were their stockbroker work colleagues. In all innocence Sebastian made the most glorious politically incorrect faux pas. Charming as always, he approached the guests and introduced himself in that Prince Charles/Hugh Grant sort of way. One of Andrea's closest friends was a charming man of African American origins. Sebastian shook his hand

and said, "And what part of Africa do you come from?" There was a two-second delay of silence before the whole place erupted into laughter. The man took it in great humour and said, "Well Sebastian, I'm actually from Los Angeles, but you have given me an interesting project of finding out exactly where in Africa my ancestors did come from!" Later, I explained to him that Sebastian had only ever known a few black people at his school, and they were all the sons of African Kings or Prime Ministers. Andrea's friend was a lovely and charming man.

The heat was unbearable that day. The wedding was held on the terrace of the magnificent hotel on the hill above Mother's house and the old Mission. Sadly, my brother Paul and myself jointly gave Andrea away in the absence of their late father.

The evening before the wedding, my sister Andrea asked me if I would say a few words on the day. I quickly wrote the bones of my speech and in considerable haste, I wrote the following little poem for them.

> What sweet language do these lovers share?
> The smiles, the sighs, the pensive stare,
> For mortals struck by Cupid's dart,
> No torrent flood nor fire can part.
>
> But when e'er conflicting passions urge,
> And a moment's thoughtless anger surge,
> As pampas grass in storm or breeze,
> Must bend and yield with gracious ease.
>
> Blessed are those who tread this road,
> By loyal and steadfast vows have showed,
> Love's dancing flame shall live in thee,
> Til both of you shall cease to be.

Sebastian and I returned, and Saturday, September 5th 1998 was his first day at Harrow. He looked terribly grand in his tailcoat and straw boater. The black tie worn by the boys at Harrow is in mourning for the death of Queen Victoria. At that time, as a mark of respect, the school decreed a hundred years of mourning. I was deeply saddened to leave him at the steps of Bradby's, which was his House, but I was comforted by the fact that many of his chums from Sunningdale were there with him.

Back at the Hall, I opened the door one day to be handed a High Court Summons by a bailiff who had driven all the way from the capital to have the pleasure of presenting it to me. It's content was the size and thickness of the London telephone directory. This latest piece of crackpot litigation was an application for a High Court Order preventing me from ever mentioning our son's name on any television programme, on the radio, or in any newspaper or magazine. After much negotiation with Kelly's lawyers, I was assured by them that the matter would be dropped and I would hear nothing further. Completely without my knowledge, the Order was granted. It was only when dealing with another matter that my dear friend and barrister, Neil Hamilton MP, brought it to my notice. Having been tricked by Kelly's lawyers, I became acutely aware that at any time a story could be leaked to the press, and I could be blamed. I lived in perpetual fear of arrest and imprisonment for breach of a High Court Order.

1999

Jeremy defies the odds • Adventures in Kenya • Neil and Christine • The pink dame • The High Court for Neil – and for me

In February of 1999 I was to receive a heartbreaking call from Lynda Sale. Jeremy, her husband and my friend, had suffered a severe accident in an underground car park in London. He had fallen and split his head and was undergoing brain surgery. I was deeply upset for both of them. I telephoned Vanessa as they were our mutual friends, and she suggested I should come over to her that night, rather than be in the Hall alone. It would be the last night that she and I would ever sleep together.

I left for London the following day in order to offer whatever support I could. Over the next few weeks Jeremy endured a total of three brain operations and I went to see him on several occasions. The situation got to that dreadful point of finality. Jeremy's doctors suggested that family and friends be called to say their goodbyes, and he received the last rites. I arrived the following morning for what I believed to be the last time. As I walked the length of the ward, I could see him sitting up in bed. A big smile appeared on his face as I approached. Lynda ran up to me. "James," she shouted, "he has just opened his eyes and said to me, 'You didn't send me a Valentine card!'" As we approached his bed she said, "Jeremy, you can talk, you can talk!" To which he replied, "White man's magic!" I'm delighted to say he went on to make a rapid and complete recovery.

In March I decided that Sebastian and I needed some real adventure time together and I booked a trip to Kenya. The last thing I wanted was to go on a group tourist package, I wanted it to be special, just the two of us. Through a specialist tour operator I managed to arrange for us to have our own driver, who would take us around much of the country. We arrived in Mombasa and were met by our man, Osmund, who drove us to a camp in the Taita Hills on the banks of the Bura river. As we lay in our tent under mosquito nets, we got our first experience of the smells and the night-time sounds of the African bush.

We were awakened at 6a.m. in order to get an early start and after a few miles we came across our first encounter with a family of lions, blocking our path. We made a respectable retreat and found another route. Lions rise early, and catch their prey while they are still sleepy. After a hearty breakfast, they then sleep it off during the heat of the day. By luncheon we were heading for Ziwani on the border of Tanzania, and upon our arrival at a thatched camp we found that we were the only guests. By nightfall Osmund returned to take us on a night trip because our truck was equipped with search lights; it was fascinating. I didn't sleep too well as our lakeside tent was surrounded by baboons who break in and steal everything and you need eyes in the back of your head for those devils. Even with a stick to beat them off, they are not easily deterred. They just glare at you in a sinister way and await their opportunity. Our tent was pitched only a few yards from the crocodile-infested water's edge, and in the morning Sebastian left a message in a visitor's book for German tourists: "Wonderful location, a relaxing swim in the lake is highly recommended!"

The following day we met up with a young African botany student who took us on a long walk through the bush. I admit to being somewhat concerned that all we had for protection was a stick. After walking for about a mile we came across the remains of a hippopotamus. Our young friend told us that he had known that it had been attacked by three lions a few days before. Its long tusk-like teeth had already been removed by local bushmen as nothing is wasted in this part of the world. Our botanist friend was highly knowledgeable, and we learnt much about the local plants and medicines from him. We crawled through the undergrowth where we silently approached a watering hole full of hippos. We were only a few feet from these magnificent creatures. Hippos don't take kindly to uninvited guests and the minute they realise you are there, it's time to go. On our walk back to the camp we were suddenly startled by an enormous crocodile which ran across our path and slid into the water. Fortunately, crocodiles feel vulnerable on land where they are less likely to enjoy confrontation. Upon our return to the tent, outside it was the headless body of a baboon who had stooped to take a drink from the lake, but no sign of any Germans!!

Before long we were heading for Kilaguni in the centre of the Tsavo West National Park. Throughout our whole trip, there were several points where we had to pick up an armed guard who rode with us. This was not to protect the two of us from lions, but from armed militia and the possible prospect of kidnap. The roads were treacherous, as it was at the latter end of the monsoon, and on more than one occasion we had to ask for the assistance of local boys or tribesmen to help Sebastian and I push our vehicle out of the mud.

At one point, in the middle of nowhere, we came across a lorry stuck waist deep. An excited population of about thirty men were jumping up and down, shouting and waving their arms in the air. The confused driver continued to twist his wheel, digging himself in deeper. They had been attempting this manoeuvre for hours. Upon our arrival, Sebastian and I took control. I ordered the driver to keep his wheels perfectly straight and put his vehicle in second gear. Sebastian ordered all the men to the rear of the truck. Within a minute it was free and on dry land. Charming though these people were, the men all had the bodies of prize fighters but their brains were those of hyperactive children.

As for the Maasai, he is a different kettle of fish altogether, a proud warrior. He is known as "the noble savage" and takes pride in the fact. I told Osmund that under no circumstances was he to drive us to some Maasai village frequented by tourists, where they meet the buses and do their jumping dance in exchange for money. I only wanted to meet people who were unfamiliar with white people. I wanted to learn of their true culture and traditions. Osmund knew of one such tribe about half a day's drive away.

We approached the village and parked some distance from it on a hill. Osmund left Sebastian and me in the truck while he went to tell the chief that a very important white man Me-zay (meaning chief or elder) and his son were coming to visit them.

Within minutes we were greeted by the chief and his warriors, resplendent in their bright red clothing which is wrapped around their waist and thrown over one shoulder. They carried spears and at their necks was an array of beautifully coloured beads. Their hair was dyed with a red ochre. Some of them had their earlobes pierced and stretched and the removal of their bottom two front teeth added to their warrior status. We were warmly greeted and taken to the chief's house. The women are responsible for the building of the houses which are made from wattle and cow dung. Their duties include caring for the family and fetching the water. Men hunt and tend to the cattle, but mostly they sit around philosophising. The chief told me that they had only just finished a seven-year war with a neighbouring tribe, during which many of his young warriors were speared to death. Heaven forbid the day they get hold of Kalaschnikov rifles. The Kenyan authorities don't involve themselves with the conflicts between the Maasai. The chief remains the absolute administrator of law. For example, a person found guilty of murder will be hacked to death with a machete and the remains of his body will be unceremoniously thrown into the thorn bushes for the animals to eat.

I asked the chief what punishment he would inflict upon me if I was found sleeping with his wife. He looked at me for a minute and said, "You would have to pay me two cows!" The Maasai have never found a good reason to invent the wheel. Their nomadic existence follows a strict cycle of grazing from season to season, and they abandon their villages only to return the next year. Their tribal territories are clearly marked by tradition, going back thousands of years. When a neighbour's cattle is found grazing within their traditional grazing pathway, retaliatory action is swift and brutal. Cattle is currency, and a man's standing in the community is determined by the size of his herd.

The Maasai rarely become sick and they have little use for vegetables, grain or fruit. Their diet consists of mostly meat, blood, milk and water. They regularly bleed the cows for sustenance. This involves restraining the animal while a spear carefully severs a vein in the neck and each warrior takes his fill from the spouting blood. Before the cow becomes too weak, the wound is sealed with mud and the cow returns to the herd.

Herbal plants are gathered from the foothills of Kilimanjaro and made into a soup which they claimed cured everything but it tasted like mud water to me.

I attempted to teach them a slightly more sophisticated method of lighting a fire, rather than each warrior taking it in turn to spin a piece of hardwood into softwood with his hands. By making a simple bow for the hardwood stick, it would be more effective and less work. They nodded appreciatively and returned to the method of their ancestors.

I also explained the advantage of making a chimney in their houses, which would clear the smoke and create a draught for greater heat for their cooking. That also fell on deaf ears. I realised that my intervention would be a disruptive step toward destroying their ancient culture. We Anglo-Saxons have an insatiable appetite to control everything within our world. These people live in perfect harmony with theirs, just as God made them.

As I sat with the chief and the elders of the tribe, discussing our mutual problems, Sebastian went off to teach the young warriors how to play Harrow Football.

As we were seated, we were approached by a tiny child, no more than four years old. He had tied two long pieces of string to the back legs of a giant black beetle, which must have been the size of a large hen's egg. As the beetle took flight he was able to guide it by pulling on either string as a western child would fly a kite. It was hilarious to see and the chief and elders enjoyed the fact that I found it so funny.

As darkness approached I realised that poor Osmund had spent the entire day cooking himself in the truck. He assured us that the Maasai had given him something to eat and he had spent much of his time asleep under an Acacia tree.

Before leaving, I gave some of the women English coins to make jewellery with and we were given beaded bracelets in exchange. The chief was anxious for us to stay and live with them. He said he would teach us both to approach and kill a lion with a spear and Sebastian would go through the initiation ceremony of becoming a warrior. For Sebastian to have his earlobes stretched and beaded plates inserted, plus having his front teeth knocked out, probably wouldn't have been too well received by his House Master. But the offer was sincere and greatly appreciated.

We continued to travel extensively throughout the country, visiting the Shatani lava flow, Kilimanjaro, Emali, Voi and numerous other places. Everywhere we stopped we would distribute pencils to the children. Finally we returned to Mombasa and the comfort of the Silver Star Beach Hotel, where we were given the best rooms in the house. From then on we just relaxed and called to see local places of interest. One interesting one was the famous Mombasa crocodile Farm, home to over ten thousand crocodiles. There we dined on enormous Crocodile burgers. I can honestly say that crocodile meat was the best hamburger I have ever tasted, and Sebastian agreed. California bison burgers come a close second.

On the flight home, I wrote the following ...

> Oh noble savage, with whetted blade,
> Tribal scars, that ebony face,
> Remorseless pride in foes he slayed,
> Lion fears his stealthy pace.
>
> Cloaked in red, lean as willow,
> Rainbow beads and ochred hair,
> Wood and cowskin be his pillow,
> Dung and wattle is his lair.
>
> Goats and cattle to sustain him,
> Nomadic search for pastures new,
> No walls nor tolls, to retain him,
> Oh would that I could be as you.

While in Mombasa I met a charming old black man in his eighties; he was a cloakroom attendant. He told me that he had spent much of his life under British rule. "When the British came here, they built roads, they built schools, they built hospitals, they built railways, they cultivated the land, and they ruled us with intelligence," he said. "Now they are gone, we have reverted back to tribal hatred, chaos and corruption." He said that the British had given his country independence far too soon, and that they had left some of their African colonies before creating an educated civil service. He said he feared for the Africa his great-grandchildren are just beginning to grow up in. He was a devout Christian, and he was afraid of the rise of Islam and Islamic fundamentalism more than anything. He said he was only glad he wouldn't be here to see it happen. I was amazed at his knowledgeable understanding of the facts. I was always of the belief that they all hated and resented their Imperial masters, but I was wrong.

May 1999 saw my 50th birthday. I had no appetite to celebrate; as a matter of fact I was quite depressed at the prospect. On my fortieth, I had thrown a huge party at the Hall which was a joyous and magnificent occasion. Ten years later, I flew to the Isle of Man to join Gerald and his wife Clarrie. It was the dullest and most uneventful day in my living memory.

In June, Sebastian and I called to see Neil and Christine at their home in Alderley, Cheshire. I had an idea to produce a television programme for them called *Posh Nosh with the Hamiltons*. They thought it sounded fun, and I said I would go away and work out a format and synopsis. My idea was to turn them into "Fanny and Johnny Cradock". I felt there was a niche in television to resurrect the 1960s cookery duo, and Neil and Christine were perfect. In real life, Christine is a culinary whizz and Neil's knowledge of fine wines is unsurpassable. The format would be based on the Batman and Robin formula. The Bat-phone would ring, or in this case, the Food-phone, and the Hamiltons would race to the rescue and cook a banquet for someone. The idea was to find the oddest of people to cook for, e.g. the Pearly King, Queen and family, a party for transvestites, etc. I introduced them to my chum and working partner, Greame Oxby, an experienced TV director and producer, and it was all systems go. Our pilot show featured the Marshall family from Derby, a gloriously bizarre family of humorous misfits. It was hilariously funny and Graeme and I had huge fun editing it. Our major dilemma was deciding exactly what should end up on the editing room floor. The show received rave reviews from the *Daily Mail* and slivers of it appeared on shows like Louis Theroux and Anthony H. Wilson's programme called *Content*. Climbing the ramparts of the television world as outsiders is a formidable task. The corporate climbers within don't take kindly to good ideas from without, and we struggled to get it commissioned by the networks. It wasn't too costly to produce and we all had a jolly time in the making of it.

Neil and Christine Hamilton had become amongst my closest chums, although there was a price to pay. I had always been a highly active Tory supporter. I had assisted at every election campaign since Tony Barber at Altrincham in 1970, with my time, effort and considerable amounts of my money. After the massive Tory sleaze episode and Neil losing his seat at Tatton to Martin Bell, not forgetting the famous

1997 Battle of Knutsford Common, I was to receive numerous warnings to disassociate myself from the Hamiltons. Over the years I had almost become part of their family, and I was privy to the trauma and distress they all had to endure. They had become the most reviled couple in the country. So determined was Neil to prove his innocence and restore his integrity that he was prepared to lay everything they possessed on the line to that endeavour. I was to be among only a handful of people who were not prepared to kick them when they were down.

In August 1999 I received a telephone command from Christine. "James, luncheon at twelve, Barbara is coming, don't be late!" Dame Barbara Cartland was the Barbara referred to. "I am placing you at the table seated next to Barbara because I know she will be charmed by you," said Christine. The pink dame adored the company of men and hated the company of women. The former step-grandmother to the late Princess Diana, and one of the most successful authors in the world, arrived predictably looking like a pink blancmange. One of the richest women in Britain pulled up to the front door in a ghastly clapped-out thirty-year-old Mercedes, painted white, with a ridiculous turquoise blue stripe running along the side. I had last seen such garishness in Las Vegas. She was driven by her eldest son and her second son arrived in an equally old Ford, loaded with luggage. The car door opened, and first to appear was what can only be described as a white mop-head. Dame Barbara instructed it to do "wee-wees". Neil and Christine had placed a red carpet from the doorway into the driveway. The only other guest to receive such treatment was Mrs. Thatcher, when she popped in for luncheon at the height of her premiership.

The other guests to attend that day's little soireé were their dear friends Razzi, Bertie and Derek. Derek is a brilliant horseman, and the first black man ever to become Master of his County Hunt. He has the aristocratic tones and the demeanour of a duke, but he is very much a likeable queen. Neil and Christine are terribly fond of him, and refer to him as "Golly", which he quite enjoys. He often makes jokes about how some of his ancestors have eaten some of ours. Upon entering the house, mistaking Derek for a man-servant, the pink dame ordered him to escort her to the nearest lavatory.

I got on well with the near one-hundred-year-old dame. We chatted about all things pertinent to her. I asked the inevitable question, "Why pink?"

She told me she had been close friends with Lord Caernarvon and "darling little Howard", as she referred to him (Howard Carter) in the 1920s. She was amongst the first people to enter Tutankhamen's tomb. As she had reached nearly a hundred years of age, it rather knocks the "curse of Tutankhamen" theory into touch. She said she was so inspired by the pink walls and hieroglyphics that she decided she wanted to surround herself with pink from that moment on! We talked incessantly about her books and in one sweeping statement she said, "James, I have dedicated my entire life to love!"

She explained that the worst people at buying her books were the English. They only wanted crude sex and violence. "My books are about romance, bravery and honour," she said. Apparently the French love her books, but her favourite customers are the Chinese, who buy them in their millions. Dame Barbara said to me that she hated Tony Blair, and blamed him entirely for the new low-life culture in Britain. "Gone are the days when an English gentleman could travel the world and be treated with such great respect. Now all we are known for is loutish behaviour," she said.

Throughout the luncheon, her two Churchillian-looking sons endured a constant barrage of orders and instructions from the pink matriarch. By late afternoon, the Cartlands departed and continued their journey to their northern estate. It marked the end of an amusing and thoroughly enjoyable afternoon.

In November it was Christine's birthday. Neil, Christine and myself are all baby-boomers, born in 1949. Although it was worryingly close to Neil's big court case, she still decided to have a little celebratory get-together with close friends. I arrived at Thurloe Place in Knightsbridge. There was an assortment of social grandees: my old acquaintance Lucy Fox, daughter of the actor Edward Fox, and her husband, Viscount Nick Gormanston were there. I had known the Fox family from Sebastian's days at Sunningdale; their son was in Sebastian's class. I spent much of the evening chatting with Julian Fellowes, who had locked himself away for many of the previous months writing his book *Gosford Park*. He assured me it was going to be a blockbuster as he had secured a film deal to it already. Julian's wife, Emma Kitchener-Fellowes, whom I found alluringly attractive, is the granddaughter of the famous Lord Kitchener and Lady-in-Waiting to HRH Princess Michael of Kent. Christine gave a tearful and very moving little speech about the value of true friends, all of whom were in that room. Naturally Razzi and Bertie were there and have, like myself, always been totally loyal chums.

Five days later, on November 15th 1999, Neil and Christine entered the Royal Courts of Justice in their case against Mohammed al Fayed, or Fayed as Christine calls him. He added the "al" in order to ennoble himself in the Arab world. The press had gone mad. It was about to be the most media-frenzied case in English history, since my other dear chum, Margaret, Duchess of Argyle's case with the Duke. The public queued all the way round the block and down the street in the hope of getting a place in the spectators' gallery. It had become an amphitheatre, a circus of Roman proportions.

Over the previous few weeks in the build-up to the case, I had been in touch on a daily basis. In one of my e-mails to Christine I reminded her that at the beginning of the case, under no circumstances must she wear her usual flamboyant bright colours. The media may like it, but this isn't showbiz, this is the highest court in the land. I also said that I didn't think that on the first day she should march in and sit next to Neil; this was his case, not hers. There was a time for her to play the "British battleaxe", but this was not it. She heeded my advice and arrived in a beautiful dark suit, showing great respect to the court. She sat at the back until the court invited her to join her husband. I was very pleased. Neil and Christine weren't overly keen on the choice of jury, and felt that one or two of its members were insufficiently educated to fully comprehend such a complex case. In the thrust and parry of courtroom conflict, George Carmen was proving the better swordsman. Desmond, Neil's barrister, was an Etonian gentleman, who fought to the Queensberry rules. George Carmen was a Blackpool street fighter who fought to win. I raced to London to help support them in whatever way I could.

On Tuesday, November 16th I met Christine early in the morning outside their flat near Albert Bridge. She looked gaunt and tired but remained chirpy and as optimistic as was possible. The court opened at 10a.m. The queue was even bigger this day and the media had reached a point of frenzy. Dressed in my black chalk-stripe suit and sober tie, I walked confidently past the queue to the front and immediately a Court Usher escorted me to the front row of the spectators' gallery, before allowing the first forty members of the public in. They had set up a rota system whereby, as one person became bored with the proceedings, another was allowed in. An excited American tourist sat next to me. She hadn't the foggiest idea what it was all about but wanted to take part in such a big event. She said she was desperate to see Fayed so she could tell all her friends back home. I spotted Lord Longford, who was a supporter, and I was briefly interviewed by some reporter from the *Daily Express*.

Christine looked up at the gallery and acknowledged my presence with a nervous smile, but Neil had other things on his mind. At the court recess, Christine signalled me to meet her outside. We met on the stone staircase leading down to the main hall. She became weepy and hugged me; the pressure was really beginning to show. I comforted her and told her to save her tears for the courtroom. I reminded her of her friend, Mrs. Thatcher, when she told George Bush during the Gulf War, "This is no time for wobbly knees!" We walked past the throngs of gawping people to meet Neil and Desmond in the barrister's chamber, where a buffet luncheon had been laid out. Neil was the colour of Portland stone, and I could see his hands shaking as he tried to nibble on a chicken sandwich. They were engrossed in courtroom strategy and understandably he failed to acknowledge me.

The Royal Courts of Justice was specifically designed to be as intimidating a place as possible and it succeeds magnificently. The good, the bad and the great have buckled in this place. The truth is irrelevant, court is just a cockfight with wigs on.

In my belief that fortune favours the bold: again I march to the front of the queue, and again I am shown to the front of the spectators' gallery. The case continued. I was later to be with them on November 26th and at that point the case seemed to be going rather well. Neil, Christine and I went to the Café Rouge close to their London flat and managed to have an enjoyable evening, all things considered.

The following day Sebastian and I spent time together at Harrow, and in the evening I attended *Me and my Girl* at their school theatre. It was a most brilliant production and I am sure that one or two of the boys will achieve acting greatness. The actor Peter O'Toole, whose son was at Harrow, was there. He regularly helped with the directing of the school plays and guided the boys with their acting skills. Sebastian prefers to be a backroom controller rather than treading the boards himself.

In the early part of December, life at the Hall continued as usual. The Conservative Ladies held their Christmas Party of restrained merriment, and I worked on taking the two hundred handicapped children to the pantomime.

December 10th 1999. "Oh woe unto me, that I should be so plagued by this treacherous woman!" I received notice from Kelly's lawyers that I should pay her £120,000. Based on the nonsensical pretext of securing Sebastian's educational future, she wanted £70,000 paid to her immediately, and the rest over a period of time. Was this insanity ever going to end? They advised me that I should seek legal counsel without delay. I replied that I had no intention of bothering the legal profession or the judiciary.

Their response was instant, they were applying to the High Court in London. I was getting to feel rather at home in that place by this time!

They must have been wringing their hands in glee at the fact that, with no legal representation, I would be easy meat and they were going to make prime mincemeat of me. The wheels of litigation began to grind.

December 21st. Oh such tragedy! Neil has lost his fight to clear his name. Fayed has won the case and the media has gone mad, it's just terrible. My heart goes out to them.

December 22nd. Christine phoned me to say that their flat was mobbed by the press. They were trying to head back to Cheshire and hoped to be home around 8p.m. They drove to the M1 with a police escort. As they got to their house the media piranhas were waiting, en masse.

December 23rd. Neil and Christine had barricaded themselves in their house but the piranhas outside were relentless. I drove over to Alderley with a huge box containing a leg of lamb, cauliflower, sprouts, potatoes, bread, milk, tea and sugar. I knew it would be impossible for them to get near the shops.

I was now beginning to embark upon my own journey of less public courtroom drama. On Christmas Eve, 1999, in the early morning post, I received Kelly's High Court Summons. It was patently obvious that it was sent on that day to destroy the possibility of allowing me an enjoyable Christmas. I remember thinking, "Are there no depths to the level of cruelty or unkindness to which that woman would not stoop?" In the previous few weeks she had returned from a holiday in the Caribbean. This week she and Martin were taking Sebastian to Texas, and then they were all flying to Hawaii to enjoy the dawn of the new millennium. She left with the joy of thinking that I was alone and utterly miserable.

On December 30th, determined not to remain in solitude, I flew to

Nice to stay with my friends, Sue and Richard, in Cannes. We drove into Italy, and on the evening of December 31st we attended the millennium celebration in the square in Nice. It was wonderful, and it was a momentary respite from the gloom of my impending fate.

2000

More legal proceedings • My McKenzie friend • Russian relations • A friend in trouble

The world was filled with hope. President Clinton announced that he would scrap the third world debt to the United States in order to help the poor countries have a fresh start. Tony Blair promised the same. For those brief few days the world seemed united in celebration. But like Neil, I had other things on my mind.

By February, my health was failing with the lack of sleep and excessive stress. My blood pressure was at 180/120 and I was on the brink of a major stroke or heart attack. Kelly's lawyers continued to bombard me almost daily. I informed them that they were contravening the Wolff Reforms, by issuing court proceedings without a period for conciliation. They ignored my plea and continued with their ruthless pursuit. When conducting a case alone, without having a single day's training in the law, a solitary word thoughtlessly placed could lose you the case and hang you. I was informed that Kelly had secured Legal Aid on the grounds of being an impoverished single parent mum. At that time you were not permitted to have more than £8,000 in assets to qualify. I kid you not, as I wrote my response, she had flown to New York to go shopping! If I lost the case I could lose everything; if I won it, I gained nothing. An acquaintance lawyer/friend, Tony Hill, chirpily told me the famous quote: "He who represents himself in court, has a fool for a lawyer!"

Alone, I attended the first Court Directions Hearing. It was decided that the case would be heard on June 21st, 2000, Midsummer's Day.

In March, enter Neil Hamilton, barrister and chum, to the rescue!

My mother, who over the years had assisted me financially with my previous legal battles and numerous other generous acts of motherly love, had every right to protect her (loaned) investments to her son, which were now under serious threat! Neil lodged an "All Monies Charge" with the Land Registry in her favour against my assets. If the case was to go horribly wrong, my mother's charge against my properties would prevent the circling vultures from finding any meat on my carcass to pick at. "Brilliant!" I suddenly felt a lot more secure.

Romantically, I was on the hunt again. A female friend of mine arranged for me to go on a blind date. This was an entirely new experience for me, but I thought I'd give it a go. The date in question was quite a well-known actress, and at that time she was appearing on a programme called *The Bill*, but it would be terribly ungallant of me to mention her name. We were to meet in Manchester. The weather was atrocious and my ardour was further dampened by the apparition that appeared before me. As she crossed the road in the freezing driving sleet and rain, she wore a short mini skirt, bare legs and white high-heeled court shoes. I've got a thing about bare legs and court shoes. I had an instant flashback to a girl in my teens who wore an identical ensemble. I was turned off then, and I was turned off now. Perhaps her good humour, wit and sense of fun could brighten the evening, but alas that also had passed her by. I made every effort to be charming and amusing, I wined and dined her and we parted company. "We really must do this again." she said, "Oh yes," said I. Ta Ta. I don't think I'll bother with any more blind dates.

The following week, March 22nd to be precise, my dear friend and former secretary, Patricia, was getting married. She entered the Register Office at Sale as Patricia Caterina Platts-Judd, and came out as Mrs. Graham Smith. At the reception Patricia very kindly placed me next to a strikingly attractive young girl. She was blonde, bright and beautiful, and presently she was studying for her Masters Degree at University. Her name was Jeanette. She was 25 and I was 50.

She informed me she was drawn to the older man, and this older man was unashamedly drawn to all that nubile flesh. The embryo of a short-lived relationship had begun.

At the Bank Holiday my mother's family were spending a few days down at their cottage in North Wales, and my mother, who had flown over from California, had joined them. I arrived with Jeanette. My uncles, Peter and Brian Snr, remained open-mouthed and drooling for much of the day. Jeanette wore a white pleated mini tennis skirt and sneakers; she looked like an American High School Cheerleader. She and I walked hand in hand over to my old Powder House and lay in the grass there. The sun shone and it was wonderful. Litigation and all things gloomy never crossed my mind that day. Mother remained noticeably silent during the day's proceedings, and we all knew what that meant!

As time went on, Jeanette's endless conversation and comprehensive knowledge of all things football began to tell me things. I hate football: rugby yes! Football no. It was time to gently part our ways. It was fun, and I'm sure she has made a football enthusiast very happy.

In May, I was back in London at yet another Directions Hearing. The nightmare was returning. Again I entered the court alone with my briefs and a list of questions I wanted to get Court Orders for. I was confronted by a thoroughly unattractive female High Court Judge, who had a serious imbalance of hormones with an overdose of testosterone.

All of my requests were refused point-blank, despite my pleas that the information required was vital to the conduct of my case. Every request made by the plaintiff was granted. The judge systematically attempted to humiliate and destroy me in the court. I thought, "If that old cow is the High Court Judge on the day of the trial, then I'm dead in the water from the start. I'll get no justice from that bitch." It was obvious to all that she resented my audacity at entering her court without legal representation. How dare I think that I could conduct a case on an equal footing with a London barrister, within the hallowed chambers of the High Court of England! The judiciary is an exclusive club, and woe betide anyone who attempts to enter it without full membership.

Kelly, upon seeing my humiliation, laughed out loud as we left the court. I felt so desperately low that day.

Tuesday, June 20th 2000. I had every intention of going to London by train and staying in a hotel but I received a call from Christine Hamilton. She said that she and Neil were deeply worried about me. They would pick me up in Cheshire, drive me to London, and I was to stay with them in their flat. Neil said he would go through my briefs and give me pointers on how to cross-examine the witnesses. He sat up until 3.30a.m. tagging and writing little notes of instruction in my briefs. God knows, they had enough problems of their own to deal with. Their overwhelming kindness toward me when I was at my lowest ebb, and at a time when they were so reviled by almost the entire nation, shows the true calibre of their decency.

Christine said she would drive me to the court, and Neil said he would join me for the first hour as my "McKenzie friend". This is a term used in English law when a lawyer friend can sit near the defendant and pass notes of advice, but he is not allowed to speak. Neil wanted to ease the burden of my trauma of walking into that courtroom alone. I struggle to fully describe just how much of a comfort that was to me.

As he and I walked the corridor toward the courtroom, the look on the faces of Kelly's legal beagles was classic. Neil was the most famous and talked-about man in the country at that time; they couldn't believe their eyes! After the initial shock, her female barrister embarked upon furious objections: What was Mr. Hamilton doing here? There had been no application to this Court for a McKenzie friend. It was too late, the call to court was announced: Hadfield-Hyde versus Hadfield-Hyde, Court Twelve immediately! My palpitations became almost unbearable; to date I had ignored the dangerous levels of my blood pressure. I had to give the performance of my life. The only small thing in my favour was that I was used to public speaking and audiences didn't scare me.

I prayed to God that it wouldn't be that old lesbo in judgment! My prayers were answered. The judge was a kindly man with half round spectacles. Before seating himself he surveyed the court. "Oh, hello Mr. Hamilton, what are you doing here?" he said. "Are you a McKenzie friend?" "I am indeed M'Lord," said Neil. At that, Kelly's barrister launched into an attack, but the judge put her firmly in her place. "I am very aware that this gentleman has prepared this entire case by himself. If he wishes to have his friend present, then I have no objection," said His Lordship. He followed that by leaning over his bench to me. "There may be matters during today's proceedings which you may not be familiar with. If that be the case, then do not be afraid to ask me. I am here to help you!" I cannot describe the relief I felt at that moment. If nothing else, I was going to receive a Solomon-like judgment.

Neil had to leave, but promised to return before the end of the day's session. By luncheon I was unstoppable. I cross-examined Kelly, proving her economy of truth on every point. Martin stumbled and fell under my cross-examination. Despite the fact that Kelly claimed to have long separated from him, and was totally impoverished, I showed the court that within the last six months, from December 1999 to the day of the trial, they had jointly and separately travelled to the Caribbean, Texas, Hawaii, New York (three times), Italy, Spain and Greece, all separate trips. Not the lifestyle of poverty methinks!

I showed the court that she had in her possession a £27,000 diamond ring, a £10,000 necklace, a £7,000 pendant, a £2,000 set of earrings ... and the list went on. She presently was driving a 911 Turbo Porsche motor car, with her own private number plate !

I proved that Martin had given her £55,000 to start her own business, and that two days after her lawyers had received her Legal Aid Certificate, he gave her a further cheque for £10,000. Not exactly most people's interpretation of poverty, where Legal Aid and Social Security Benefits have been required, as per this case.

During my cross-examination of Martin, I hesitated in silence for two or three minutes as I glanced through my briefs. The judge became impatient with me and said, "Have you finished with your cross-examination of this witness?"

"No M'Lord, I have one last question." I replied. "Mr. Gibbins, could you tell this court whether or not you allow free access to the plaintiff to use your gold credit card, and to fraudulently impersonate your signature?" The answer was yes!

Neil had returned to join me by this time. Early in the proceedings I was aware that I was able to flaunt court protocol and get away with it in a way that Kelly's barrister could not. I took full advantage of my non-legal status and by 4p.m. I had her barrister floundering in the water like a drowning woman. Her cross-examination of me was a miserable failure, during which, and on more than one occasion, I noticed a smile on the judge's face. It was obvious to the court that Kelly's claims against me were spurious and fatuous, motivated by nothing more than her greed and a warped desire to destroy a decent man.

The judge's summing-up took an hour and three-quarters. His Order of the Court was that I should continue to support my son, until the termination of his education, as I had always done. Kelly was not entitled to a penny of her claim for £120,000 from me.

So infuriated was her high-flying barrister at losing a case to an unqualified country bumpkin such as myself, that she and her entourage packed their briefs and left the court before the judge; an unforgivable and discourteous act.

Neil and I stood to attention in front of the judge. He spoke to Neil first. With a smile, he informed him that in future he must sign the "McKenzie friend" application before the trial and not after it. Neil replied, "I promise to be on my best behaviour in future M'Lord." His

Lordship then turned to me and said, "May I thank you, Sir, for a beautifully presented case!" I was ecstatic. Neil said that in all his years as a barrister, he had never heard a High Court Judge make such a complimentary remark!

The shackles of my torment were finally broken; she could no longer hurt me. Over all those torturous years, Kelly had almost cost me my fortune, my health and my sanity. Perhaps now I could finally restart my life and move on.

From the court, Neil and I drove to attend a party at St. James's near the Palace. I can't remember the address, but it was terribly grand and filled with numerous Members of Parliament, on both left and right of the House. There we met Christine, and Neil couldn't wait to tell her of my resounding victory. Champagne was ordered, and before we left much of Her Majesty's Government were celebrating the event with us.

Again I stayed at Neil and Christine's London flat, and the following morning got the train back to their house in Cheshire, where I had left my car. Such was the removal of weight from my shoulders, it felt as if I was walking on a trampoline.

As far as I was concerned, however, the matter was not totally closed. Kelly's lawyers, Messrs Jennings Son & Ash, had flagrantly ignored Lord Wolff's directive, and I was never given the opportunity to resolve the matter by agreement, without recourse to proceedings.

On July 8th I wrote to the senior partner. I questioned the facts: At what point in the proceedings of this case did his firm realise there was an abuse of the Legal Aid system? Why did his firm fail in its duty to the Legal Services Commission? My letter was ignored and on July 27th I wrote again. I informed the senior partner, John Parr, that I was filing a formal complaint to the Office for the Supervision of Solicitors regarding the conduct of his firm. I also sent relevant documents to the Legal Services Commission. My response from them was that in view of information received, Kelly's Legal Aid Certificate was revoked. Hopefully, Jennings Son & Ash had to whistle for their money! John Parr's neglect at an early response is understandable; he was probably very busy looking for a new barrister!

In August it was Rowena McCartney's 40th birthday. Rowena is one of those women who has eaten of the fruit of eternal youth – she was gorgeous when she was twenty and she remains so. When is she going to grow old like the rest of us, I ask? Those of us fortunate enough to be invited to Mike and Rowena's house are always guaranteed a wonderful time, and this was no exception. Mike's brother, Sir Paul, was unable to come but as expected, there was a fascinating selection of interesting characters. The DJ, John Peel, was there celebrating the fact that he had just reached sixty. The saddest event of the evening was seeing my acquaintance Adrian Henri. Despite being in the advanced stage of cancer, Adrian had obviously made an enormous effort not to let Rowena down.

I first met Adrian Henri through Tom McNally. He and Tom had art studios in the Bridewell (an old Liverpool Prison) along with other famous artists and sculptors such as Stephen Broadbent. Adrian was a poet, painter and singer, and as a matter of fact was a member of a band with Mike McCartney, John Gorman and Roger McGough, before they became The Scaffold. On occasion, I would pop into Adrian's "cell" to have a cup of tea and a chat, while he painted. His art was influenced by the surrealist painters such as René Magritte and his most famous painting, "Meat Painting11", hangs in the Walker Gallery in Liverpool. For a time he was President of the Liverpool Academy of Arts, and as I write, I am honoured to say that I have recently been asked to be Trustee of the same academy.

In previous recent years, I had acquainted myself with a Russian doctor. Her name is Dr. Oksana Sigalova. I am most fortunate in the fact that I have a number, greater than one can count on one hand, of people you can rely on with unquestioning loyalty. Oksana is one of those. She has an intuitive perception of people which far exceeds the normal intuition of the average female. Her brusque, no-nonsense manner is sometimes shocking to those of us of a distinctly English, more genteel disposition. It's a cultural thing! However, most of what she has to say is invariably correct and to the point.

In her bid to match-make, she introduced me to a strikingly attractive twenty-six-year-old Russian girl called Liana. One questions the likelihood of a twenty-odd-year old impoverished Russian girl being attracted to a fifty-odd-year-old reasonably wealthy Englishman, but my over-inflated ego and vanity got the better of me, as usual. A relationship began. All was going swimmingly for quite some time until one day Oksana decided to take my blood pressure. It was 175/120. Oksana's outrage at my neglect of myself, and her furious outburst of instruction to see my own GP immediately, forced me to address the matter. I received a similar ticking-off from my own doctor in Nantwich. The result was, I was put on an instant blast of beta blockers.

The effect was indeed instant, and the side-effect was the immediate removal of my libido. From the age of fifteen I had enjoyed a stallion status. Never once in my entire sexual life had I ever failed to instantly rise to the occasion. Within two days, I went from stallion to gelding! It was absolutely disastrous – my worst nightmare had arrived.

What cruel irony was this? Was I to be doomed to a life of celibacy? Lord Lust, known to the nation as one of the great lovers, now a sexual failure! God was punishing me! I was struggling to come to terms with it, and returned to the doctor a month later. He sympathised with my dilemma and replaced my medication with statins and Amlodipine. Within another few weeks things began to return to normal but when Liana said, "James, I am vonting cheeldren!" I thought it was time to move on.

Oksana invited me to dinner one evening. The second you enter Oksana's home you are immediately aware that no English person lives there. It is cluttered to the gunnels with Eastern European artefacts and more besides. While making dinner, she challenged me to write a poem about a rather forlorn vase of plastic flowers, placed in the darkest corner of her sitting room. I was in no mood to write poetry, silly or otherwise, but persistence is her middle name and I penned the following for her.

> 'Tis a place, no sunlight bathes,
> Of fragrant scent, they have no care,
> Their lofty stems, no water craves,
> A cold transparent home they share.
>
> A noble tulip's regal coat,
> The bright carnation's papal plume,
> A passing glance is wont to note,
> Such joy in their synthetic bloom.

On September 4th I received a call from my friend and neighbour, Robert Holmes. The time was 9.55a.m. Robert was a solicitor and ran a law firm in Sandbach. I remarked that he sounded as if he were in a large empty room. His voice was quivering as if he was about to burst into tears. He explained that he was in the corridor of the courts in Mold, near Chester. His law firm was being charged with misappropriation of client funds. As the head of the firm, Robert was having to "carry the can".

"James, I won't be leaving this place a free man today; see that Margaret is OK for me," he said. I couldn't believe what I was hearing. Robert was the kindest and most gentle of men. He had helped me enormously over the years. I was deeply upset – you couldn't meet nicer people than Robert and Margaret. On the evening TV news, Robert was being led out of court in handcuffs and put into the back of a van. He got a sentence of twenty-two months. Some time later, I went with Margaret to Kirkdale Prison to visit him. Incarceration is indeed a very sobering experience, and so is visiting it. Robert had managed to secure a job in the prison post room. This is a much-sought-after job and you had to be careful of jealous inmates. He said he had started a little class, teaching some of the prisoners to read and write, which kept him busy. It was sad to realise how precious each second of Margaret's parting embrace meant to Robert. An extra five seconds were stolen after the guard's booming command for "Time up!"

There were numerous things going on at the Hall. Ann Widdecombe MP came for dinner, and also Sir Robert Atkin MEP. We filmed a programme for Sir Trevor McDonald and then there were all the usual things in the build-up for Christmas. Granada Television was holding a party and dinner, celebrating God knows how many years of *Coronation Street* at the V&A Hotel, and I was invited to escort the Queen look-a-like, Elizabeth Richards to the "Do". In November I went for a few days to France. My chum, Mike Dench, owned a Champagne House in Reims, "Champagne Granier". A handful of us went with him to tour the famous Champagne Houses and drink lots of it while we were there. It was a relief to see the back of the millennium year. It had been a roller-coaster ride from start to finish.

2001

Sebastian leaves Harrow • California and Oxford

In February 2001, I received a call from Martin to say that he believed Kelly was going bankrupt for the second time. He said she was making his life a living hell by making phone calls and writing letters to his clients and friends. Now it was his turn to have the nightmare to live with! Two weeks later he phoned to say that she had tried to commit suicide. My instant reaction was to roar with uncontrollable laughter; I knew her so well. There was no way on God's earth that she would take her own life. Her bounds of attention-seeking are limitless, and as always, I was proved right.

In March, Sebastian was attacked and beaten by a gang of Asian youths on the King's New Road in London. Thankfully they didn't stick a knife in him, which is what often happens these days. My answer to the problem would be to hang a few yobbos from lamp posts as an example to others, but you can all breathe a sigh of relief (or a feeling of regret) that I'm not running the country!

My birthday in May was certainly a lot more celebratory that year than the previous one. I hired a canal barge for the day. The weather was glorious and everyone on board took it in turn to be Captain of the ship. It was a wonderful day, chugging through the Cheshire countryside. Part way through, we stopped at a bluebell wood to picnic and celebrate.

Saturday, May 26th 2001 was Sebastian's Speech Day at Harrow. The morning starts with the ceremony of "The Bill". This is when each boy has to file past the headmaster on the steps, and tip his straw boater when his name is called. As you can imagine this is quite a lengthy process and fortunately the sun shone. The Countess von Bismark latched herself onto me and I had to entertain her with amusing anecdotes and explanations of Harrovian customs. Everyone was there including the King of Jordan, who arrived in his helicopter, but the most enjoyable part of the day is when everyone gets together for the afternoon.

We had more than enough food and Champagne for a wonderful picnic. Neil and Christine came, and Gerald arrived in his new sports car. The Bond family joined us: for reasons known only to themselves, they had called their son James! Also with us was the King of Ghana's daughter and her husband. Sebastian invited his friend, Anouska Beckworth, daughter of the infamous "It" girl, Tamara Beckworth. It was a quintessentially English sort of day, although an artistic eye, observing from the periphery, would view the scene as a Renoir, with men in straw boaters, white linen jackets, Champagne and merriment.

With the wholehearted blessing of Kelly, Sebastian decided to leave Harrow. He had achieved ten O Levels and was studying for his A Levels. He had become increasingly unhappy since the introduction of a new House Master at Bradby's and he wanted to include philosophy and photography in his A Level subjects. I was totally against the decision, but as usual, I was a dog without teeth when it came to joint decisions with his mother. His preference was a college in Knightsbridge, but a day college in central London was impractical and out of the question as far as I was concerned.

I phoned my artist friend, Philip Hathaway Jones in Oxford. His neighbour owned Cherwell Tutorial College there. This meant Sebastian would have one-to-one tuition with a Master in each subject. In addition, I had several friends in Oxford to keep an eye on him. The fees and accommodation came to just over £30,000 per annum, twice an average salary for that time, but I was prepared to accept the full burden of finance, if only to keep him out of the centre of London, and possible trouble. Harrow at that time was about £23,000.

In the summer months Sebastian and I went to California to see my sister's first born, Olivia, and as always, we had a splendid holiday.

Upon our return, he and I drove to Oxford to meet the Keoghs, his host family. The house was right in the centre of town, just near Morris's Garage where the MG motor car was born. They were a family of children, dogs and home cooking, just the sort of place he needed. I felt so much better, and visiting Oxford is to this day a great pleasure for me. We were regularly in Oxford while Sebastian was growing up, mostly to see Rosamund or Philip and occasionally we would pop in to see Twiggy and her husband, Leigh Lawson. Sebastian would play with Carly, Twiggy's daughter, who was a year or so older than him. She was a sweet little girl but she used to collect animal skulls, which I thought a little odd at the time. Twiggy and Leigh are the most lovely, down-to-earth people you could meet. I remember one time, Leigh invited Rosamund and myself to watch him in *The Merchant of Venice* playing in the West End. Leigh was the merchant and Dustin Hoffman was Shylock. The four of us had arranged to go to dinner together after the performance. I was really excited at the prospect of spending the evening with Dustin Hoffman. His performance as Shylock was faultless and his Shakespearean English was perfection. At the last minute Dustin changed his mind. There were hoards of over-excited fans all clambering to get a bit of him, and he decided to sneak back to his hotel for room service instead. It was just the three of us for dinner, but nonetheless a wonderful evening.

The latter part of 2001 was a bit of a blur and I can't find anything of any note to tell. I had completely gone to ground. So much so that in October, the *Manchester Evening News* wrote in their Diary page that they were concerned. It read that the gossip columns were missing me! But all of that was about to change!

2002

A secret shared • All is not as it seems • Art for art's sake • Goodbye to the Hall

I can't quite remember how many years I had known the society photographer, Damian McGillicuddy and his wife Christine, but it was possibly around five or six. Damian had endured a series of operations to try and rectify a twisted foot he was born with. Each operation only seemed to make the matter worse and in 1999 the unfortunate decision was made to remove his leg from the knee down. I visited Damian in hospital on numerous occasions and regularly phoned his wife for up-dates on his progress. One day I received a call from Christine; she seemed anxious and asked if she could meet me as a matter of urgency. As I drove to a pre-arranged meeting point near Damian's studio, I contemplated the possible reasons for this clandestine arrangement.

I was acutely aware that because of Damian's recent inability to work, they might be struggling for money. Christine might wish to borrow from me, without Damian's knowledge. If that had been the case, then I would have willingly helped them out.

Christine joined me in my car and seemed so melancholic and vulnerable at first. With difficulty she held back her tears, until she unfolded her shattering story. She told me that during the build-up to Damian's operation, she also had been seeing her doctor, and that she had been sneaking off to Christie's Hospital in Manchester. She had been diagnosed with leukaemia and was unaware of how long she had to live.

She put her arms around me and sobbed uncontrollably. I failed to hold back my own tears, it was just so dreadful. She said that their doctor had advised that, just for the time being, she should keep it from Damian, believing that he would be incapable of carrying the burden of any further stress. I was staggered by her bravery and totally inspired by such valour. I was determined to help in whatever way I could. A week later we met again; she had been for further tests. Christie's had been brutally honest with her and given her between six and twelve months maximum. I was devastated.

I bought her a mobile phone in order to contact me should she fall ill or need me for whatever reason – I would be there for her.

I researched a professor who had made a remarkable breakthrough in the treatment of blood cancer, and I instructed her to give his details to her GP. Surely a young married woman with a child would be high priority for treatment!

As the weeks passed, we saw more of each other. Bound by our secret, we became much closer. Such was the heightened power of emotion, and the uncertainty of the future, that we ended up making love.

It was a similar sort of passion, fuelled by uncertainty, that happened to people in the Second World War. Following intimate moments, she revealed some of the dreadful things that had happened in her life. She had been married before, when she was nineteen, to a tall, dark, handsome Irishman. He was an alcoholic, and one night in a drunken stupor, he and his brother beat her and both raped her on their sitting room floor. She was taken to hospital with liver damage. She said that years later, she found out that he had died of alcoholic poisoning and his brother was imprisoned for grievous bodily harm. She told me that, following the birth of their son, her marriage to Damian had become just a close friendship, nothing more, and she admitted having a brief liaison with Damian's brother, Christopher, as a plea for affection.

A couple of weeks had passed when she phoned with some exciting news; she had been accepted on a guinea pig course of treatment. Regularly, she would phone me with the results of her blood count. Sometimes it was up and she was elated, and sometimes it was down and things weren't so good. All of a sudden her calls stopped. As time progressed I became more concerned. If something had happened to her, there would be no reason for her family to inform me. Why should they? I didn't exist!

Consumed by worry, I drove to her home. She answered the door, and it was patently obvious she was not pleased to see me. Christopher was there and ran upstairs in order to avoid any conflict. I noticed that the large photograph taken at her wedding to Damian had been replaced with one of her and Christopher. I said, "Christine, that picture tells the whole story; I am glad you have someone to look after you, and I wish you well." I drove away and never saw her again.

Six months later, I had a call from Damian. He was filing for divorce and wanted answers to some questions. He said that Christine had confided things to his closest friend, a fellow photographer called Mr. Bebbington. Damian asked me if I had given Christine £10,000 to fly medication over from the United States for the treatment of cancer. I said, "At no point did she ever ask me for money." I asked for Mr. Bebbington's telephone number in order to find out exactly what she had revealed about our relationship.

In the end I thought I'd better come clean. Rather than confess over the phone, I would be man enough to speak to Damian face to face. That would give him the opportunity of socking me on the jaw for screwing his wife, should he choose to do so.

We met in a restaurant in Hale. He sat in total silence while I told him the truth, the whole truth, and nothing but the truth. At the end of my confession he said, "James, I have no animosity toward you whatsoever. You have been well and truly conned. She was indeed married at nineteen, but her husband died of a brain tumour. His brother has never been convicted of any crime, and she was never raped. Christine has never at any time set foot in Christie's Hospital."

As we were in conversation Damian's phone rang – it was his solicitor. We both listened to the conversation. The solicitor said that he had just received a letter from their GP. It read, "Mrs. McGillicuddy has not been, and is not, suffering from leukaemia. She is in fine health and I expect her to live a long and healthy life."

I was dumbstruck. Every word she had uttered was a lie. Every single tear shed was a sham. Every passionate moment shared was contrived.

There is a mental condition called Munchausen Syndrome, which is my unqualified layman's diagnosis of her condition, but I may be wrong.

Some weeks later, I opened the *Daily Mail* to find a full-page story, along with a big picture of me, Christine and Damian. I believe I was cited in their divorce proceedings! The *Manchester Evening News*'s concern was unfounded; I was back in the gossip columns!

After more than a decade of traumas, undulating fortune, and litigation, I was finally at liberty and in a state of mind to rekindle my long-subdued passion for art. I began by painting Colin Gurley's portrait as a gift for his sixtieth birthday. Upon its completion, Christine Hamilton saw it, and immediately gave her royal command that she wanted me to paint hers in similar style. Sebastian, who is an infinitely better artist than myself, observed that my brushwork is that of Hockney/Lucian Freud. I was to start work straight away!

To endure a number of sittings with Christine H would severely test the tolerance of even the most canonised of artists, and I settled for a series of photographs. The excuse was that her new and hectic celebrity lifestyle would preclude us from any lengthy sittings. When the painting was complete I was well pleased with my efforts. Even "Granny", Christine's very matter-of-fact, no-nonsense mother, was delighted, and said that I had captured her daughter on canvas perfectly.

I wanted to portray Christine as she really is, and not her public persona. I got her to remain in her slobbing-around-the-house clothes. I then placed her seated on a shield-back Hepplewhite chair with the sunlight streaming on her back. The mood is relaxed and slightly pensive, without inflicting a feeling of depression or hopelessness. One has to remember that this was not long after their Fayed court case, and their future was still very uncertain at that time. I transferred the bright flamboyant colours, which are so important in Christine's life, to the background wallpaper. She and Neil seemed thrilled with the end result, so much so that they went hot-foot to London to deliver it to the Royal Academy of Arts. Their hope was to get it exhibited in the Summer Exhibition. Needless to say, both they, and it, got slung out!

I started to paint and draw cartoons prolifically, and in July 2002, I held my first public art exhibition in a gallery in Alderley Edge; my feudal turf!

I had painted a spoof portrait of Her Majesty the Queen in *Coronation Street*, with her wearing a pinny with "Betty's Hot Pot" written on the front. That went down well, and was the cause of great hilarity among all the invited guests. It was an evening of fun and Champagne. The Hamiltons arrived and we unveiled Christine's portrait.

Channel 4 sent a camera crew along to film the event, and several of the press turned up. I managed to sell my first large abstract picture called "Square Up", which went for the grand sum of £2,500. Life was good again, at long last!

Along with my architect, we designed two large detached houses, to be built in a paddock in the grounds of the Hall, to be known as Hyde Court. One was "The Coach House" and the other was "The Stables". By 2001 they were up and sold. For posterity, I had asked Rosamund de Tracy-Kelly to make a mould of our Armorial Crest, which was then cast in reconstituted stone. Two were made, and placed in the side wall to the Hall and in the apex of Hyde Court. The summer of 2002 was an enjoyable one, and Sebastian spent most of it with me. We had several barbecues for friends and both of us embarked upon painting several canvases.

Sebastian had become great chums with Peter, our new neighbour, who had purchased The Stables in Hyde Court. The pair of them spent many an evening shooting much of the unwelcome wildlife in our grounds. Rabbits, squirrels, magpies and woodpigeons began to treat Willaston as a no-go area. We were particularly pleased to see the back of the American grey squirrels. They had stripped the bark from some of our two-hundred-year-old trees in order to build their nests, and the trees had started to die. Sebastian and I shot twelve of them in one day.

It was about this time that I was becoming tired of living all alone in this huge house. From the time Vanessa and I were together, I had no live-in house staff, and apart from some of my old flames, whom I could always call upon for a romp in the hay, I was basically womanless. I adored being in love, and I missed that side of my life terribly. I have never been totally happy spending life as a rogue lion, wandering the Serengeti of life.

If I have learnt one thing on life's journey, it is that there are only two things of any true value; to love, and to be loved. Nothing else really matters; "Amor Vincit Omnia".

Much of my socialising was done in Knutsford and Hale, and on occasion I would stay at a flat my mother and I owned in Brooklands, Sale, rather than drive home at night. I got to the point where I was only returning to the Hall each day to pay bills and feed the animals. Sebastian was at Oxford, and his circle of friends was mainly based in the London area. With his blessing, I decided to sell the Hall with the idea of making a new life elsewhere. The *Daily Telegraph* ran a story saying that I was selling Willaston Hall and moving to the South of France.

Before long, we found a buyer in the form of Clive Christian. Clive

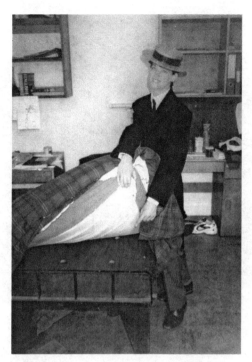

Sebastian shows the no-frills bedding at
Harrow!

Andrea and David's wedding. Left to right: me, Andrea, David, Mother and Paul.
Paul deliberately stood on a mound in order to look taller than me!

With the Maasai. There's an easier way to light a fire!

Sebastian at home with the Maasai.

Dame Barbara, the pink dame –
"James, I've dedicated my life
to love"!

My portrait of Christine, before it got
slung out of the Royal Academy.

Villa San Sebastian, Calpe, Spain. Note the roof I shot the intruder on!

Sebastian, Christine, Neil and me in the Hamiltons' new home.

Sir Tim Rice and Mike McCartney sing "Lily the Pink".

Rhys Ifans doing his "Notting Hill" pose with Davinia.

Lynda and me at Mike and Rowena McCartney's.

Lynne and me at her palace near Marbella.

Norman Rossington at a barbecue at the Hall, wearing a sandwich cover.
Beside him is John Mohin, a cousin of Sir Paul and Mike McCartney.

is an international figure, a multi-millionaire whose exclusive kitchen empire has outlets in many of the capitals of the world.

You can buy Clive Christian furnishings, kitchens, tableware, watches and remarkably, Clive Christian perfume, which sells for as much as £40,000 per bottle. There were still places in the country where you could buy low-end houses for that price. He has found a niche market for his high-status, highest-quality products, exclusively for the very rich and famous. Clive maintains a determined effort to show the world that "British" can still mean "the best".

Clive is a charismatic man with what appears to be one wardrobe: black trousers, black sweaters, black hair and black designer stubble beard. Always tanned, he reminds me of a French fashion designer. We hit it off immediately, and prior to buying the house, he would regularly call at the Hall on the pretext of discussing the purchase. Really, it was just an excuse for us to drink a couple bottles of wine and chew the cud while I sat at my easel, painting.

In preparation for our big move, Sebastian and I spent seven days just burning papers. It was a cleansing process for me; therapeutic. I took special joy in burning all those things like court papers from Barry Gray and the like. As I watched the flames lick the evidence of such heartache and pain, I felt uplifted. It was a final closure. Overall, we managed to take furnishings and paintings to no less than six auctions, keeping only the best or most sentimental of items. It was difficult to choose what to keep.

The exact chronology of events has become jumbled in my mind for those few months, mainly due to the hectic process of having to prepare for our departure. Whatever livestock we had, we sold or gave away.

At the beginning of November 2002, I decided to travel to Spain. Although I had seen a lot of this world, I had never been there before. At no time had it appeared on my radar of places to settle down in. This was mainly due to a preconceived idea that coastal Spain was full of unsavoury English people. Well, I hold my hands up and admit I was mostly wrong. I had every intention of looking for a home near Nice and Monaco where I had friends, but I think it was the influence of Lynda Sale, who was waxing lyrical about the beautiful mountain-ous area between Valencia and Alicante, which guided me. She had gone to school there as a girl. The high profile squirearchal life I'd enjoyed was about to be swapped for sun, sangria and anonymity. I resigned from most of my charitable obligations, and that Christmas I paid for my two hundred handicapped children to go to the pantomime for the last time, after doing it every year for twenty years.

On New Year's Eve of 2002, the removal men fitted the remaining of our precious objects into two large furniture lorries. Dr. Oksana came to lend a hand in packing.

All of a sudden the Hall was an empty and lifeless place. To Sebastian and me, it was as if we were witnessing the dying sigh of a much loved friend. We closed our great oak door for the very last time and posted the key through the letter box.

As we got into our Range Rover, at a funereal pace, we drove down the long driveway to the main gates. I struggled to hold back my tears, and Sebastian refused to look back.

It was a moment I would often think of over the coming years, with much sadness, and more than a little regret.

2003

Trips to Spain • Sebastian's art exhibition • Off to sunny Spain! • The Bull Run • Battle of the Tomatoes • Thieves in the night

The following few months, I mostly occupied my time by flying back and forth to Spain every couple of weeks in an attempt to familiarise myself with the place.

Lynda's description of that part of Spain was certainly not an exaggeration; it was indeed mountainous and infinitely more spectacular than the area around Nice. I was escorted by a very attractive, and very business-like lady called Jane Lewis. She and I travelled the length and breadth of the coast between Valencia and Villajoyosa, looking at villas.

The town of Calpe seemed to tick most of the right boxes for my new life of sun and sangria. Jane helped me open a bank account, and introduced me to a local English lawyer called Linda Townsend. In all walks of life it is imperative to get to know the right people. That applies whether you are just going to the tip, or to the top! Linda Townsend was not only a lawyer but also a local councillor on Calpe

Council. Her grandmother, Lady Townsend, had been Mayor of Oxford in 1935.

Linda and I spoke the same language, and we were to remain great chums from our first meeting to this day. I transferred half a million euros into my new bank account and bought an almost complete villa on the mountainside. The vista, looking down over the sea and town below, and on over to the magnificent Peñón de Ifach rock (a smaller, similar version of Gibraltar) was breathtaking. I wasn't overly inspired by the villa itself, but the view was irreplaceable, and as everyone knows, location is everything. The other thing which pleased me was that it had a larger than normal swimming pool.

I could see that I would have years of work to do in order to get the place exactly as I wanted it, but much of the pleasure was in its creation. The garden was nothing more than an expanse of mud and builders' rubble. My dream was to be able to idle my time with sculpture and painting, and punctuate my day with an occasional dip in the pool.

There, I could grow old and slip deeper into my world of dottiness and eccentricity.

In January of 2003, Sebastian was to hold his first public art exhibition in Oxford.

He was to share the exhibition with Graham, one of his Masters at Cherwell College. It was a great success and over a hundred and fifty people came to the opening show. He managed to sell his first painting there for £600, and I believe his Master didn't sell anything. I was an immensely proud father that day; after all, he was still only two weeks away from being eighteen years old.

In April, the *Manchester Evening News* wrote an article telling everyone that they'd found out that I wasn't in France as expected, but in Spain! It read, "The Diary is delighted to report that the wandering Aristo has found a new life and happiness after settling in Spain," etc., etc. Who on earth would be interested to know that? I wondered.

July 26th 2003 was the first day of our new life! Sebastian and I were up early to drive from Cheshire to Portsmouth and take the *Pride of Bilbao* to Spain. As we pulled out of port, the crowd on deck remained silent as we glided past Lord Nelson's HMS *Victory*, and moored aside her was the aircraft carrier HMS *Ark Royal*. The solemnity of the moment was broken as two armed sailors aboard her raised their arms in salute. It was impossible not to feel a welling of immense pride as we all returned a farewell wave.

The entire crossing was calm and the sun shone. The following day I managed to claim a lounge chair, and secure a vantage point on the top deck just below the funnel. I was all alone, well pleased with myself, and I blissfully slipped into a pleasant slumber. I was awakened by Sebastian: half of my shirt had fallen open and exactly half of my face and chest was the colour of a freshly boiled lobster. To add insult to injury, I was covered in soot. Although the smoke from the funnel vapour trails, the soot drops immediately below. I spent the rest of the trip portside, in a vain attempt to match the white side of my face for that all-over lobster look! I looked bloody ridiculous!

We drove diagonally across Spain, avoiding central Madrid and arrived at Calpe at 7.30p.m.

As we were now in Catholic Spain, we decided to name the villa after a saint, and what better saint than Saint Sebastian? I had it included in the deeds as "Villa San Sebastian". My son was not enamoured with the place at first, and said he was baffled as to why I had bought it. "The views are spectacular, but the house is rubbish," he said. In retrospect I had to agree with him. The original idea was to buy a French *manoir* or chateau and this was not "La Belle Demeure". The conveyance took two years, but Linda Townsend struck a deal where we could occupy the property from signing the contract to purchase. The night we arrived we swam in our swimming pool and things seemed a little better from then on.

A few days later, we were invited to the Calpe Bull Run by Carlos, the estate agent, and Pedro Jaime Crespo, a local councillor. We were told to report to the old town at 8p.m. All around us we could hear the cheers of the crowd, but for quite a while we wandered the narrow empty streets, trying to find any sign of life. Just then we looked behind us to see a herd of longhorn bulls heading straight for us at full pelt. I can't remember the last time I ran that fast, and in those tiny winding streets there is nowhere to go. We spotted Pedro Jaime shouting at us to join him in a doorway. This place was starting to look like fun!

For the bull run, the main street in the old town is blocked off and a series of large cages run the full length along either side. These are the escape routes for the people who crowd the street. The gaps between the bars are wide enough for a normal-sized person but not wide enough for the horns of the bull. In the centre of the street is placed a large metal table and as many young men as possible stand on top of it. This is their vantage point to taunt the bull. The whole thing is a romanic spectacle and the frenzied crowd become more daring as they consume more alcohol.

A lone bull would run the length of the street attacking cages, and at one point it charged the table with such force it lifted it high in the air, scattering youths in every direction. Another time the bull leapt on top of it. One boy tripped in his escape and the bull gored him several times. The crowd tried kicking and beating it, and some threw beer bottles at it in order to distract it, but the bull was having none of it. He was focused on his victim and was determined to have his revenge. A Spanish person told us that the young man had died. Most fatalities at bull runs are young drunken tourists whose testosterone gets the better of them, but not Spanish boys; they know the state of play too well.

The Calpe Bull Run is a three-night event, and the last evening Sebastian and I were back in the old town. The grand finale in this amphitheatre was the arrival in a lorry of a one-ton black bull, a truly magnificent creature. A long rope is threaded through the eye of a post in the centre of the street. At the other end of the rope are around thirty men. The lorry door is opened and the bull is tethered tightly to the post. They then proceed to clamp metal frames with Roman Candle fireworks to each horn. These are then lit and the bull is released. It is not difficult to imagine what a one-ton bull is thinking when he is surrounded by jeering crowds who are throwing food and bottles at him, and he has burning fireworks exploding from his horns. After a time he eventually became totally exhausted. He stood motionless, sweating profusely. His breathing was so heavy I thought his heart would fail. With the dying ember flames still burning and dropping from his horns, he looked a sad and sorry state indeed. I am not remotely squeamish, but the utter barbarity of this spectacle, to totally humiliate such a splendid and proud creature, and to turn him into the town's Court Jester, was beneath the dignity of man. I have no problem with bullfighting, it is a two thousand-year-old legacy which has continued in Spain from the Roman occupation. It is inherent in the very culture of the people, and you have to respect that. As for running with the bulls through the narrow streets? Now that is sport!

A day or so later, the Range Rover started to play up and I drove to an English garage in Benissa to get the problem sorted out. I returned to find Sebastian in a frantic mood. He had spent the entire morning searching for his metal suitcase from Harrow. It had been locked and contained his art books, the digital camera I had only just bought for him, his passport and a beautiful knife, given to him by his friend, Prince Mahidol of Thailand. The house seemed to be undisturbed, until I checked my secret hiding place.

My brand new laptop had gone, along with £1,300 in cash and documents relating to the purchase of the villa. Jane and her husband, Mal, came over to help immediately.

The Guardia Civil were most helpful. They said it most definitely was not Spanish people, but Romanians, Bulgarians and Albanians who were flooding into coastal Spain. They had caught dozens of them recently. We eventually found Sebastian's case and books scattered in the forest, but everything else was gone.

Wednesday, August 27th 2003. For three hundred and sixty-four days of the year, nobody goes to Buñol (pronounced bun-yol) but today 40,000 people will arrive at the tiny village from all over the globe. It is listed on the young toff's guide of things one must add to one's social calendar, along with Cowes Week and the Monaco Grand Prix. It is the Buñol Battle of Tomatoes! Buñol is a few miles inland from Valencia, and the exact date of the battle each year can easily be found if you enquire at the Spanish Tourist Office, but it is usually in August. Be prepared for the heat; it's the hottest month of the year.

Sebastian and I went with our friends Alastair and his wife, who were the people who owned the storage company where we had all our furniture. Being Buñol Battle Virgins, we were totally unaware of the format, and we arrived wearing tee shirts, shorts and sneakers.

As we entered the village, we failed to notice that everyone was bare-chested but that was soon remedied. A handful of men approached us and proceeded to remove our tee shirts and rip them into shreds, throwing the remains into the crowd. This is part of the initiation and there is a reason for it. A group of Danes arrived dressed as Vikings, wearing horned helmets, some Scots had kilts and tam-o'-shanters, and a handful of English public schoolboys arrived wearing Roman togas. These were obviously all veterans from previous year's battles. We eased our way into the little square next to the church. In the centre was placed a telephone pole which was thickly smothered with grease and lard from top to bottom. At the top of the pole, hanging by a piece of string, was a Spanish ham. By whatever means, the ham is the prize, and it all starts as an individual competition. Nobody can climb more than a few feet up the pole and it is interesting to watch humanity organise itself when there is a common cause.

A group of burly American football players linked arms around the base of the pole. Other boys climbed on top and the pyramid ascended, but the weight became too much and the whole thing collapsed. This went on for more than an hour. An eight-year-old Spanish boy was lifted up each tier of the pyramid but even he couldn't reach the ham.

In the end it was down to two young men. Mr. Nasty had consistently tried to pull people off the pole, and the crowd disliked him intensely, almost to the point of violence against him. It was down to him and another Spanish boy. As the two of them fought to climb within six feet of the prize, in an astonishing gesture, Mr. Nasty put his hand under the other boy's foot and with one arm, lifted him high enough to take the ham. The crowd went wild; Mr. Nasty had suddenly become the hero, and the two boys, plus the ham, were thrown along the heads of the crowd. Everyone was cheering in jubilant celebration!

At that point, rockets were fired into the air. This signalled the entrance of the tomatoes. Half a dozen huge lorries, laden with tomatoes, inched their way through the crowded streets, dropping tons of them evenly as they went. The streets were about a foot deep in tomato mulch. The local Spanish people had attached hoses to their upstairs taps and continuously sprayed water down on the crowds to help cool everyone.

Battle commenced!

The ripped-up remnants of people's clothing were tied in knots and used as additional soggy missiles. As the chaotic battle continued, battle lines began to form. It was Spain versus the world. Sebastian and I ended up at the forefront of the World Forces and we managed to push the Spaniards back. He and I were well battle-scarred, for not only did we have to contend with enemy fire from the front, but missiles from our own far rear guard were falling short, and landing on us! After a couple of hours, the rockets went up again to signal the end of the war. There was an uproar of cheers, and a great deal of hugging, kissing and rolling in the mush by all the participants. We were told that at the other side of the town square, two policemen foolishly arrived in their police car to observe, only to be bombarded by the crowd. They returned to their station covered in squashed tomatoes and their car was full of the stuff, but they took it in great humour.

Alistair had thoughtfully loaded the boot of his car with gallon bottles of water for us to wash as much of the tomatoes out of our hair as possible but for days afterwards, I was finding tomato seeds in my ears.

As we were leaving, fire engines arrived to wash the streets and Buñol went back to sleep until next year!

The Spanish just love to have fun, and there is hardly a month goes by that there isn't some fiesta and a reason to get dressed up and have a damned good party. I'm delighted to have shared this day with my son. These are the precious times with his father that he will always remember. Something I never had.

One day, while exploring the forest above the villa, Sebastian found a camp fire, and scattered around it were all my papers from when we were robbed. Everything I needed relating to the purchase of the villa was there. The thieves' camp had been the perfect observation point for them and they had obviously watched our comings and goings from above.

In the first week of September, Sue and Richard drove down to stay with us for a few days, which was great fun, and on September 9th Sebastian and I were packing, ready for our long drive back to Bilbao and England. All the jobs were done, and the house was clean and ship-shape. On our last evening we decided to dine down by the beach, but when we returned, we found the downstairs door open.

Our Romanian/Bulgarian/Albanians were back!

We were so incensed with rage that we armed ourselves with two cavalry sabres and made haste silently up through the forest toward their camp. I was at such a pitch of anger and hatred at the violation of our home for a second time, I could easily have decapited the perpetrators. Apparently it is a tried and tested formula among burglers worldwide, to return a week or so later. This is on the assumption that if they got essential things like laptops with their first robbery, then their victim would have replaced them within a couple of weeks. Why not return for another bite of the cherry?

Luckily for them, the "bandedos" had moved on, after discovering nothing had been replaced in our villa.

We had to phone P&O Lines, who were terribly kind and sympathetic, and we re-booked for the following week. I arranged for a highly sophisticated alarm system to be installed, and Sebastian needed written confirmation from the Guardia Civil with regard to the loss of his passport. He returned to Oxford and I continued to yoyo back and forth to Spain.

Mother had suddenly developed a deep depression and a terrible fear of leaving her house about this time. It happened almost in an instant. This was totally out of character; you couldn't meet a stronger person than my mother. After a very worrying few months, and visits to numerous doctors, my brother, Paul, got her to a leading specialist who sorted the problem out immediately. Apparently, it can be triggered as part of the growing old process, and with the right medication she was back to normal in weeks.

2004

Masquerade with the McCartneys • Poor Gerald! • Lynda tries match-making

To my astonishment, January 2004 heralded Mike McCartney's 60th birthday. It is an inconsolable fact of life that as your body slows down, time speeds up. I would have put money on it that it was only about four years since we attended his 50th.

The theme to Mike's party this time was "Masquerade", and the setting was a magnificent Elizabethan house near Heswall on the Wirral. There was an amazing assortment of Venetian masks and costumes – people had gone to a huge amount of trouble to get into the spirit of it. The music was initially provided by Mike and Paul's old chums, The Chip Shop Boys, and a little later, Mike's son Josh entertained us with his newly formed band, Trilby. The Maitre d' for the evening was the McCartneys' cousin, comedian and actor, Ted Robbins. You can always rely on Ted to provide a machine-gun volley of Scouse wit and humour for the entire evening.

As always, there was a cocktail of interesting characters: Willie Russell, who wrote *Educating Rita*, for example.

For me, the highlight of the evening was when Mike and his old pal, John Gorman, from The Scaffold, got on stage. Roger McGough had not turned up, and Sir Tim Rice stood in for him. After singing "Lily the Pink", and "Thank U very Much", Tim embarked upon an impromptu one-man show. It was the funniest thing I'd seen in ages. His impersonation of Mick Jagger easily ranked alongside the famous one done by the comedian, Freddie Starr. As always with the McCartneys it was a wonderful night.

That same year, my dear old chum, Gerald, now in his eighties, sold his magnificent estate in Norfolk and moved to the Isle of Man. The main reason was that running such an enormous house and grounds got too much for him. Sadly, Clarrie, his wife of over thirty years, died recently. I now tell this story not as a derogatory tale against my old friend, but as a warning to others. Presently, I have three friends who all find themselves in similar scenarios. As I am the only one to have experience, to a Doctorates Degree level, in Womanology, all three have come to me for counsel.

The common denominator of all three men is that they are all recently widowed after very long stable marriages, all are very vulnerable and all are very rich.

One day I received a call from Gerald, informing me he was flying over to Manchester to see his specialist for his usual check-up. He said he had received the most wonderful surprise! Clarrie's former hairdresser had flown over to see him in the Isle of Man. He was taking her back to Norfolk and could we meet up for luncheon?

We met in the hospital restaurant. I looked at her, and she looked at me. Both of us knew exactly what the other was thinking! Gerald is an 80-year-old, inexperienced, emotionally vulnerable man. "Debs" is a 40-year-old, party-loving, fake-tanned, coiffured, designer-wearing dolly bird, with three former husbands notched on her belt and two kids at boarding school!

Over luncheon Gerald said to me, "It's been the most enjoyable two days I've had in ages." With that, Debs took his hand in hers, looked lovingly and tenderly into his eyes, and with the consistency of golden syrup said, "We've laughed and laughed, haven't we Gerald?" It is impossible for the likes of Gerald, with a tear still in his eye, and his wife not cold in her grave, to resist the charms of such an experienced, pan-handling, gold-digging Klondiker, like Debs.

He fell hook, line and sinker, and accused me of being a dreadful cynic when I told him the hard cold facts. He believed that she was a brilliant businesswoman, and that he and she had so much in common. All three of her husbands had been dreadful to her!

I thought to myself, "I wonder how long it will take before she gets round to saying that she is just a teeny-weeny bit short of cash, and needs a little bit of help?" I gave it four weeks, and I was later proved to be spot-on! Debs was up to her false eyelashes in debt, credit cards, mortgage arrears, bank overdrafts, etc., etc. Gerald continued to turn Nelson's eye, despite my constant warnings to him. He was smitten; he just couldn't see it. He continued to take her to the best places and put diamonds on her fingers. All was going swimmingly, until he found out that all the time she was with him, she was shagging a young van driver in Norfolk.

In July 2004 Sebastian and I drove back for the second time by car to Calpe from England and continued to work at the villa. We started to plant bananas and palm trees but it was going to be a lengthy process before we would see any benefit. In September, Neil and Christine Hamilton came over to stay with us for a few days. That was great fun, despite the fact that we were still living in moderately primitive conditions. Neil and Sebastian, being fitness types, would go for their regular run to the town and back while Christine and I would prefer a glass or two of wine. They were still unable to avoid their celebrity status and everywhere we went people would insist on photographs and autographs. Sebastian said, "It's really great having Neil and Christine stay with us, it's like they have always lived with us." Before leaving, they surprised us by buying us two Washingtonia Robusta (fan palms, to most people). We missed their company very much after we dropped them at the airport.

In October, Sebastian flew to California He was going to do a circumnavigation of the entire United States, starting in southern California then over to New Orleans, up the eastern coast and then all across the northern part and back down to Santa Barbara. Needless to say I was worried sick, but you have to do these things when you are young. There's no point in waiting until you are rich enough and walking with a zimmer frame.

Our friends, Jeremy and Lynda Sale, had sold their Chateau in France and bought a lovely Georgian house in Frodsham, Cheshire, and also a holiday home in Finestrat, which is thirty-five minutes' drive from Calpe. We regularly saw them, but about this time we became aware that their marriage was floundering. As Lynda's youngest son, Alex, put it so eloquently, "There aren't too many sparklers left on the cake!" Lynda started to spend more time in Spain, and would join Sebastian and me a couple of days a week. She endeavoured to find me a suitable woman, but a woman's idea of suitable differs very much from that of a man's. Although we men have preferences – as "leg men", "breast men" or "bum men" – Homo sapien males are attracted to hip-to-waist ratio first and foremost. If two girls are walking down the street and one is pretty but with a straight up and down figure, and the other is less facially attractive but with an hourglass figure, men are instantly more attracted to the second. There is some tiny part of our primeval brain which tells us that she is better breeding stock, even if having children is the very last thing on our mind; we can't help ourselves. Lynda began to offer me an assortment of tree trunk shapes, pumpkin shapes, pear shapes and some so ugly they could spook the horses. Not one of her female offerings would have ever tempted me to say, "Bathe her in milk and scented oils and have her delivered to my tent!"

Lynda's visits to us increased. One day I had ordered four tons of topsoil to be delivered to the villa. The natural local soil is almost pure clay and if there was any possibility of getting something to grow, it needed a helping hand. It arrived on our driveway the morning of one of her visits, at almost the same time she did. I can honestly say that she is the least likely candidate as a manual labourer, but if it came to a digging competition, my money would be on Lynda. The soil was damp and extremely heavy but she worked relentlessly with us to shift it. As Sebastian and I had to stop for breathers, she continued to dig for England. The sun was unforgiving, and she wore a bikini top and a pair of Sebastian's shorts for the occasion. There is something enormously sexual about seeing a very attractive woman, scantily dressed, doing a filthy manual job. The vision of this joyful experience was enhanced by the fact that unbeknown to her, in her frantic digging, her breasts would reveal themselves in all their magnificence. Lynda, as the wife of my dear chum, Jeremy, had previously been out of bounds. Perhaps that was about to change?

I was unaware that in her lonely months in Finestrat she had already met an extremely handsome and much younger Spanish man, with the unlikely name of Freddie. I met Freddie, and I can quite understand why any woman of any age would fall for him.

Where have I heard this story before? Lady, middle-aged, from Liverpool, fed up with husband, meets handsome, much younger swarthy Latino type and has romance by a Mediterranean beach! I should have a word with my chum Willy Russell about this, there could be a film in it!

2005

A health scare • The Dawsons retire • Lynne and Lynda

During these months I had become increasingly concerned about my voice. It had become raspy and I had begun to sound like that old English actor, Jack Hawkins.

I visited my doctor in England who dismissed it as nothing, saying it was the sort of thing that opera singers get. I explained to him that I had never sung opera, but he sent me home anyway, saying, "Nothing to worry about."

Back in Spain, I was driving past Clinica Britannica in Calpe and thought I'd get another opinion. Immediately my Spanish doctor put an endoscope down my throat via the nose and revealed that I had a tumour on my larynx. It must be removed without delay, he said. I accepted the news with absolute calm and as much dignity as I could muster; after all it would be terribly un-British to start wailing. As I left the clinic my mobile phone went. It was Kath Smith BEM, from the Royal Manchester Children's Hospital, asking when was I returning to England. She wanted me to attend a presentation of some new operating theatre equipment we had just bought for the hospital. I told her my news. Within minutes, I received a call from Mike Rothera, a leading surgeon in the north-west, who said, "James, get a plane back as soon as possible and go straight to my house." Three days later I was being wheeled into the operating theatre at the Bupa hospital in Manchester and Mike was performing the surgery himself. I have to admit I was a little concerned as to how much all this was going to cost. I had no idea and no private medical insurance. As I was leaving, Mike turned to me and said, "James, after all that you have done for the Children's Hospital for more than twenty years, neither myself nor the theatre team will be charging you, it is the very least we can do." I was so moved by his kindness I could have cried.

Mike gave me a 60/40 chance of it being not malignant and during that week of uncertainty I became very philosophical. No man escapes his destiny, and I reflected on how blessed I had been in my life.

A week later I received a call from him with good news – the lesion was not malignant. Between God and Mike Rothera, I had been given a reprieve.

I had never known hunger or poverty. I had met many of the most interesting people in the world. I had travelled extensively and seen so many wonderful things. I have always tried my best to be magnanimous to those less fortunate than myself and I have drunk a lot, loved a lot and laughed a lot. My family motto on our Coat of Arms reads Quaere Quod Nobile Est (Seek that which is noble).

I hope I can tell my maker that I have lived up to it.

I drove to the Children's Hospital to thank everyone, and most of all Kath, for all her kindness. The *Manchester Evening News* did a story, and I asked them to include a "thank you" to their readers who had contacted me with their concern and good wishes.

Our return to Spain meant we had a procession of visitors. Mother and her sisters came to stay, followed by my cousin Anthony and his girlfriend, which was all thoroughly enjoyable.

In July 2005, Sebastian and I returned from Spain to attend the retirement party for the Dawson brothers at Sunningdale School. The Dawson twins were finally retiring after fifty years of educating so many of the world's leaders, movers and shakers.

Princes, Prime Ministers and poets have all winced at the thought of detention or being made to do six laps around the playing fields. The Dawsons are everything that is right about our great British school system. Boys who have been under their guidance have learnt that along with academic excellence, equally important is sportsmanship, fair play, good manners, honour and duty. It is far easier to keep the world in order and running more smoothly when its leaders were in the same class at school together.

At their leaving speech there was hardly a dry eye nor a stiff upper lip in the house. The great and the good turned up that day in their hundreds in order to say "thank you" and "au revoir". As expected on such an occasion in England, it rained. Irrespective, the school Highland Pipe Band played on and a Brewer's Dray gave children rides around the grounds. I had a drink and a chat with Iain Duncan Smith who had recently suffered the knives of Caesar, as leader of the Conservative Party. Iain had been most kind to Sebastian when he was at Sunningdale. On one occasion he and his family took him out for the day and Iain showed Sebastian around the House of Commons, explaining much of its history. Sunningdale school is in safe hands. Tim Dawson's son, Tom, has taken on the mantle of headmaster and even in retirement, both Tim and Nick will be at hand. The baton has been safely passed!

On the love scene, my long-standing affectionate relationship with Lynda Sale was slowly undergoing a metamorphosis from sincere friendship to the embryo of a romance. She had abandoned her "Shirley Valentine" phase and ditched Mr. Freddie Swarthy Latino. Lynda thinks in her mind that men are attracted to her because she has better than average good looks; she's totally wrong. Men are attracted to her because she has a highly charged magnetic sexuality. This is something invisible, and not too many women possess it. Jill Dando had it; Claudia Schiffer does not, even though she is astonishingly pretty. I've watched men's reactions to Lynda, even when they are in the company of a much younger woman. In the animal kingdom, males can sense a receptive female half a mile away, and Lynda is a woman who unwittingly triggers that very base instinct.

July 10th 2005 was my former love, Vanessa's, 40th birthday, and Lynda and I were invited to her party. Throughout the night Lynda endured the interrogation of several people as to whether or not she and I were an "item". Like St. Peter, before the cock crowed she denied me thrice! An additional blow to my ego came when in a throw-away remark she casually informed me that although we were the best of friends, she had never really fancied me! Dented but undeterred, over the next few weeks we continued to wine, dine and have jolly days out together.

At the same time and over the previous six months, my two friends, Justine and Ed, had tried to arrange a date for me with a friend of theirs called Lynne. For whatever reason, each time we were due to meet, it didn't happen, and I had to return to Spain. Finally, the date was fixed and we were to drive independently to Lynne's house for an afternoon together. For Lynne's sake they thought it would be easier if they were with us on our first meeting.

Lynne's home is a beautifully proportioned black and white, half-timbered Elizabethan Manor House in Cheshire. The grounds are splendid in a random way and there is no symmetrical or linear formality. At strategic points are placed an eclectic mix of very large copper/bronze modern sculptures, which agreeably mingle with the classical. This is undoubtedly a woman who has a fully comprehensive knowledge of art, I thought. I was greeted at the door by the beaming smile of an extremely attractive, slenderly built blonde. From the moment I met Lynne I felt it was as if we had known each

other for years. That day was gloriously warm and sunny, and the four
of us spent the afternoon on the terrace overlooking her lake. Her
staff had the day off and Ed was put in charge of cooking the
luncheon. After several bottles of Champagne, Ed and Justine made
their retreat as all was going so well. Lynne and I toured the house
and grounds and talked incessantly. We seemed to have everything in
common on every subject imaginable; it was magical and joyous. The
inside of the Manor House in some way reflects the exterior, with a
clever selection of dark pieces of expensive antiquity mixed with
light/white objects of modernity. A couple of days later I arrived to
take Lynne out for dinner. I had taken time in sketching a mono-
chrome pen and ink/watercolour of "Monsieur Noir et Blanc", a
fictitious one-eyed character I invented who only sees black and
white. She was thrilled to receive it and in the days that followed she
phoned to say she had arranged for it to be framed. It was to hang
next to her Andy Warhol and her Lucian Freud. Wow! I thought, my
art is going up in the world.

On the other hand there was Lynda to think about, and I have
never been good at juggling with too many women at once. She was
still with Jeremy in their marital home in Frodsham, although they
were both arranging to go their separate ways. My friendship with her
was long-standing, totally comfortable, and still heading in the
direction of romance. Lynda's insensitivity at this situation with me
was just staggering. I know she meant no malice whatsoever, but even
the most inexperienced of women knows that every man's ego and
sense of masculinity, when it comes to previous lovers, is more
delicate than a butterfly's wing. Her enthusiasm in describing graphi-
cally how utterly gorgeous Mr. Freddie Swarthy Latino was naked, was
no venial matter for me. This man was thirty years my junior! My
disadvantage appeared overwhelming, save for my vast experience
and that old Doctorates Degree in Womanology.

My empathy was suddenly with the old lion, always King of the
Harem, his face covered in scars from endless battles with young
bucks challenging his kingship. I had now come to the horrific reali-
sation I was no longer the young buck, I was him! I vowed then that
if her insensitivity continued, and our relationship was to end, before
she left I would give her the shagging of a lifetime. This is one old
scar-face who has never left a dissatisfied woman yet! And I was not
about to begin now!

A week or so later, Friday, August 12th 2005 to be precise, I arrived at the Manor House for dinner at 8p.m. David, Lynne's butler, conveyed a warm welcome, took my coat and led me into the drawing room. There, Lynne smothered me with enthusiastic affection and we sat on the settee together. Minutes later we were interrupted again by her butler who brought a bottle of Champagne, two glasses, and a bowl of tempura king prawns with sweet chilli sauce. How could her chef have known that it is my favourite starter of all time? The meal which followed can only be described as a gastronomic masterpiece, and I had to call her chef to the table to thank him. If food be the key to a man's heart, then Lynne wins hands-down for that one.

A bombshell came at the end of the meal when Lynne asked me if I would accompany her to the polo match near Tarporley. I had already got tickets for Lynda and me! In a moment of utter panic I stumbled over words telling her I was going with friends, which was the truth, and I would see her there. Lynne was unaware of Lynda at that time and the last thing I wanted was for the two of them to meet.

I telephoned my chum, Colin Gurley, who offered no advice except to sing down the phone ... "There may be trouble ahead!"

I came clean and explained my dilemma to Lynda and that I wasn't taking her to the polo after all. Understandably that went down like a lead balloon, but she still reluctantly stayed with me that night. I only managed to charm my way back into her affections in the bedroom by tap dancing in the nude while singing three verses of "I've Been a Wild Rover", at 3a.m. If ever you are in the bad books with a woman, make them laugh! It works every time!

At the polo match, the rain was incessant and the game was periodically stopped and then finally abandoned when it became too dangerous for the ponies. I arrived with Colin Gurley and several other chums. Lynne was there with her bank manager and his wife and I joined them for half an hour before sitting down for the luncheon. I had received a call from Justine, to ask me how it was all going with Lynne. In that conversation she revealed that Lynne was on the "Rich List" with a fortune of two hundred million pounds. I can honestly say, with my hand on my heart, that I would have liked her just as much if she was a Tesco checkout girl. I am most fortunate in that I have friends who are dukes and friends who are dustbin men. I have always liked people for what they are, and not what they have. The problem that people with such vast wealth face, is sorting the wheat from the chaff, and usually they end up surrounding themselves with people who are all on the payroll, as a substitute for real friends. It was that very thought which crossed my mind when I saw Lynne there with her bank manager, but I may have been wrong. Over the luncheon I decided that my affections were greater at that time for Lynda than Lynne and I left the Polo Club early to return to her and apologise.

A day later, I called again to see Lynne. I explained to her that I had someone else in my life and she took the news in a dignified, calm and ladylike way. She wished me happiness and we parted the best of friends.

The following day Lynda and I had six and a half hours of continuous and uninterrupted sex, an opening landmark for us in boudoir athletics, resulting in a celebration of ten orgasms for her, and a serious weight loss for me. Only hunger got the better of us in the end. I was determined to obliterate all traces of Mr. Freddie Swarthy Latino; he had been a thorn in my side from day one! Old scar-face was back in charge of the harem! I'm sure that Lynda will be hopping mad with me for divulging such intimacies, but you cannot write an autobiography without being totally truthful, on all matters. So, while we are on the subject I might as well get this bit over with. During our entire sex life over the next couple of years, I never allowed her to leave our bedchamber without total satisfaction. The very least was six, and on December 21st 2005, without tickertape parades or trumpet fanfares, in a three-and-a-half-hour session of animal savagery, we achieved our record of twenty-four orgasms. All discretely and accurately counted by me! Lynda, resembling a rickets sufferer, returned to her marital home in Frodsham. I am very aware that most women would be grateful for that many in a year! Let this be a lesson to all you under-achievers: anything is possible providing your man has got what it takes and knows exactly what buttons to press.

At the beginning of September 2005, I had returned alone to Spain and Lynda was arriving the following week, on the 7th. I missed her terribly; she had become a refulgent light in my life. Her plane was delayed and as I sat in the airport lounge, anxiously wishing each passing moment away, I idled my time by writing the following:

Perchance a sweet refulgent light,
Doth veil my awakening heart.
Her eyes, the rolling moon of night,
Doth drive a woeful scorn to part.

The dew I taste from her soft lip,
Doth banish love's restrain.
A chalice from my youth to sip,
From dreg to brim remain.

Her laughter is the scattered seeds,
On furrowed soil abound.
Her tears that quench love's thirsty needs,
Bond limb and leaf to ground.

Venus dare not stand aside her,
Roses hang their heads in shame.
Such beauty, God did provide her,
Mine, all mine, all mine to claim.

Toward the end of the year, I think it is usually in October, Calpe puts on the most spectacular parade at their Moors and Christians celebration. I can honestly say it was the most remarkable parade I've seen anywhere in the world. It lasts for almost five hours and includes everything from the most amazing costumes, to a platoon of Moors riding camels, and Christians on Andalusian horses. It is certainly worth flying out for a long weekend just to see it.

As I reflected over the past year it had certainly had its outrageous fortune. In April I had resigned myself to the fact that there was the possibility I might die with cancer in my larynx. Now I was as fit as when I was thirty, and I was in love again. With each passing minute of each day I loved Lynda more.

Christmas came and life was good. I bought Lynda underwear from "Agent Provocateur" and paid for Sebastian to go to Paris to visit his chum, Morgan; they were at Harrow together. Everybody was happy.

2006

Sebastian comes of age • Shots in the night
• Farewell, Aunt Mary • Mother has a health scare

January 29th 2006 was Sebastian's twenty-first birthday, and we threw a party for him in a restaurant in Hale. It wasn't quite the same, now that we didn't have the Hall to give him a grand entrance into manhood, but it was very enjoyable nonetheless. I took him to Kays Jewellers in Saint Ann's Square in order to have a signet ring made which bears our Armorial Crest.

For those unfamiliar with the tradition, men entitled to bear arms, only through a Grant from the Sovereign via the College of Arms, wear their signet on the left hand, little finger. This does not apply to people who buy a plaque with their family name on it showing a Coat of Arms. There are very strict heraldic rules governing these things and permission, subject to suitability, is granted by Garter King of Arms and his Heralds. A Coat of Arms is granted to an individual and his direct male line. In recent times it has included corporate grants such as a city, town, company or even football clubs. People are under the misconception that, just because your name may be Robinson, it entitles you to use a coat of arms from some ancient grant to a man called Robinson. Strictly speaking it is illegal to display those arms as your own. There is a famous case of the Palace Theatre in Manchester displaying the arms granted to the City of Manchester on the theatre fire screen. They were forced to remove it immediately.

Several weeks later Sebastian's ring was ready. It really is magnificent: known as the Oxford, it is beautifully cut and is more befitting a duke. Our crest is the Agnus Dei (Lamb of God) carrying the crosier of St. Patrick with shamrock intertwined, instead of the staff and banner of the cross of Christ, which the lamb normally carries.

As his father, I placed it on his finger. It signifies who he is, and what he is.

There followed a trip to the Isle of Man for Lynda and me with Gerald, and a brief journey to Spain. There Lynda and I spent most of the time decorating and making pelmets for the curtains. We were so thrilled with our efforts that we spent almost as much time admiring our work as we did doing it. The two of us returned to Calpe again in

May. We embarked upon a half-hearted effort to get fit, and several days a week we walked with a sense of great urgency from Altea to Albir and back. I estimate it would be about three to four miles in total. On the afternoon of May 20th we received an invitation to attend the opening of a new restaurant in Villajoyosa, by Lynda's friend, Shelley, and her revolting little husband. Even the most basic of social graces had completely eluded him. I've seen baboons with more congenial social skills.

For much of the evening we were standing around like two wall-flowers, not knowing a single person there, and not wanting to know most of them. We decided we would have to make an effort to be sociable and introduce ourselves to whoever looked the most interesting. Just as we were about to abandon all hope, in walked a tall, distinguished Spanish man wearing a white continental dinner jacket, accompanied by a very elegant lady. He introduced himself as Fernando and his lady friend was an English lady called Anne. Shortly after joining us at our table he gave his apology and rolled his trouser leg up to reveal a revolver and holster attached to the calf of his leg. He said the velcro gave him a rash and he had to swap it to the other leg. I know there were a number of rough English Benidormian types present, but I didn't think it would be necessary to shoot any of them. He explained that he was a Colonel in the Spanish Army and was obliged to be discretely armed at any function where there were tourists. This was in the event of a terrorist attack by the Spanish ETA group. They are a Basque nationalist separatist organisation which has been outlawed by the Spanish Government. ETA stands for "Euskadi Ta Askatasuna" which means, "Basque homeland and freedom". It soon became apparent that Fernando was very much top drawer Spanish.

He had been brought up with King Juan Carlos and his father had been the highest-ranking general under Franco. He told us that, as a young officer, his father had sent him to participate in the handing over of independence to Spanish Sahara. Anne, who was utterly charming, was a bingo caller in Benidorm, which seemed remarkable. They were an unlikely duo, but they had been together for fourteen years. Lynda and I ended up having the most enjoyable evening after all, and we have remained friends with Fernando and Anne ever since.

A week later I was obliged to visit the gun department at the Guardia Civil in order to get a renewed gun licence for my English shotguns, and Lynda came with me to overcome any language barrier.

This section of the Guardia Civil was a separate fortified building, and as we entered, we were faced with a large wall-mounted altar with a statue of Mary the Mother of Christ, decked with flowers and garlands. Behind the officer's desk on the back wall was a large crucifix. There were guns everywhere: heaped in piles on the floor, propped up against the wall, lying all over the desk. These were the most religious gun-toting people I'd ever met! It was like being on the film set of the Alamo.

The officer in charge had a cigarette hanging from his lip while we went through the formalities and every gun-carrying man that walked through the door looked like a Mexican bandit. The whole experience was totally bizarre.

My guns were always kept in a steel gun case, locked and bolted to the wall, but Lynda became increasingly concerned for our safety. The villa seemed isolated and she didn't like the fact that the Spanish coast had become a bit of a target for Eastern European "bandedos". I tried to assure her that I had as much fire-power as was used at the Somme but she quite rightly pointed out that by the time I fumbled for the keys to the gun case and loaded them, we could both be dead. My argument was that we hadn't had any problem since Sebastian and I first arrived at the villa over three years before. However, she continued to nag me to buy a handgun and you should always trust a woman's intuition! To keep her happy, I bought a 9mm revolver and a box of blank bullets. I didn't intend to kill anyone but I was assured by a friend of mine who ran a mercenary soldiers' recruitment agency that a 9mm gun, firing blanks, will send even a hardened soldier packing. They are not going to stay to find out whether it has a live round in the chamber. We also have an additional security button on our alarm system which is linked directly to the local Guardia Civil. They know the address to come to the second it goes off, so I never really thought there was ever a problem.

I have to hand it to the Guardia Civil, they are very rapid at responding and they would be there in a couple of minutes. Most of the local villas are owned by foreigners and we are the ones bringing money into the local economy, so they do look after us.

Each night as we went to bed, Lynda would ask me if I had the gun, and each night it was placed on the side cabinet next to my pillow; Lynda was happy.

At that time, about a hundred feet below the villa, there was a small road which weaved its way through the forest. I'd only had the gun for about three nights when at 3a.m. I was awakened by a flash of light at the window. In a dozed semi-conscious state I contemplated whether it was a passing car, but the more I thought about it, the more I realised that headlights wouldn't shine up that high so brightly.

Stark naked, I walked over to the window and opened the curtains. To my horror, there was a man with a torch standing down by my swimming pool. As I looked to the left of me, there was another man on the roof of the cloisters, trying to prise open the shutter to Sebastian's bedroom.

I was instantly incensed with rage and flung the window open. What came out of my mouth was a mixture of obscenities and utter gobbledygook and at the same time I reached for the gun. Bang, Bang, Bang! I fired three shots at him. The noise in the silence of the night was deafening. The man leapt from the roof to the ground down by the pool. I thought, "Nobody could jump that far without breaking his legs." Lynda, who awoke instantly to see me naked and hanging out of the window firing the gun, was more scared of me, thinking I had gone completely mad. I grabbed my dressing gown in hot pursuit, and she followed me.

As I went to go outside, she started to tell me about a film she once saw, where the man went outside to hunt the intruders and they slipped in and killed the woman. She insisted I lock her in! Outside, I continued to shout as much obscenity as I could muster and fired off another couple of shots. By this time they were hiding somewhere in the forest. In the meantime Lynda had phoned the Guardia Civil and in a few minutes Dad's Army arrived. Two of the oldest Guardia I've ever seen landed in a beaten-up police jeep with all lights flashing. Lynda explained in fluent Spanish that I'd fired my gun three times at the bandedos, and the Guardia nodded their heads with great approval. The British police would have immediately asked for my licence and charged me with disturbing the peace and the attempted murder of a poor underprivileged burglar who was forced into it by an unfair society. The Spanish have a totally realistic approach to dealing with low-life and law-breakers. The old-timers assured us that they would get them, and like the police three years before, they made a point of saying it was not Spanish people who did this. The forest goes on for miles and I thought the possibility of catching them was highly unlikely.

Three weeks later, Mr. Busybody, who is an Englishman who owns a villa down the road, and knows everything that goes on in Calpe, leaned over my wall to tell me the latest gossip. The Guardia Civil did indeed get the burglars that night. Apparently they had already robbed four villas on our mountainside by gassing the people im their beds, and they gassed their dogs. They then had a free run of their homes. It seems that the gas they use will knock you out for about eight hours. The Guardia Civil said other gang members would probably come back and mark your gate, to warn others that your house is a no-go area because there is a English lunatic living there who'll shoot you.

Mr. Busybody found out that they were two Romanian ex-special forces, who had been thrown out of the army, and decided to use their skills to come to Spain and rob people. They just picked on the wrong house that night. Thank heaven for a woman's intuition!

There was much entertaining at the villa over the next few months, including a visit from my uncle John and his wife, Michelline, from Canada, and then later, my cousin Anthony, and his girlfriend, Geraldine. On December 7th 2006 when we had returned to England, I received a long-expected call to say that my much-loved Aunt Mary was dying. For quite some time she had been in an old people's home with literally no quality of life. Mother and the rest of the sisters had been earlier in the year to see her, and Sebastian took the very last photographs of them all together. All of them had them framed and put in pride of place in each of their homes. I made regular visits to Mary but she didn't recognise me in the latter few months of her life.

Throughout my whole life, Mary was the one person who gave me unconditional love from the very beginning. Unlike the rest of the family, Mary was a simple person, deeply religious and saintly in all manner of things. I have never met anyone before, or since, with such purity of heart or kindly nature, including any of the nuns I have known.

Lynda dropped Sebastian and me at the hospital and later my Aunt Phil took Sebastian home, and I was left alone with Mary. In those silent and tender moments with her I wandered into melancholy thoughts of our days long ago. I recalled as a child, warm summer afternoons when Mary would take her two sons, John and Jim, and myself down to the banks of the river Bollin at Bowdon. There we would picnic and swim in the river. They were wonderful happy days in the 1950s. I remember 1959 was a particularly hot summer and we were often at the river that year. In my mind's eye it is as clear as if it were yesterday. I continued to sit by her bedside, gently stroking her forehead. I was 57 at this time and Mary was 84. We had shared a long journey together, and not once had she ever raised her voice in anger to me.

A few days later, on December 11th 2006, Mary slipped quietly and peacefully into death at 1a.m.

The following morning I was given the task, nay honour, of arranging Mary's funeral. The rain that day was torrential as I trudged from the registrar to collect the appropriate documents and then on to the funeral directors. Upon arrival I was shown into a small sub-lit room and most reverently greeted by a lady director. After the formalities of form-signing, she proceeded to lift what at first appeared to be a sort of wooden altar triptych onto her desk. To my amazement, when she opened it, it was a catalogue of coffins for sale. This was certainly a first for me; I'd never been shopping for coffins before. I felt I was in an Argos coffin shop.

The coffins were named after counties – The Suffolk, The Warwickshire etc. I wondered if a Gloucestershire is more prestigious than a Shropshire? I was politely informed that the one I chose was inappropriate as it was for incineration and not for burial. Apparently they are a lot thinner plywood. Yes, I did ask the inevitable question, they do burn the lot, box and all! I was also told that for incineration they need to know whether the deceased had a pacemaker or not as in the furnace they explode like a hand-grenade, causing considerable damage to the furnace and a thoroughly undignified departure for the deceased! Anyway, Mary was having a burial so it didn't matter. The sad thing is that she was being buried next to her late husband, Bill. The thought of placing her next to the man who made most of her life so damned miserable seemed to be a cruel injustice. On the other hand, Bill's tranquil slumber was about to be shattered, should he realise that Mary was arriving to spend eternity next to him! My rain-sodden journey took me on to the priest at St. Joseph's Church and my week was taken up entirely with funereal business. What hymns? What prayers? What clothes for Mary in her open coffin in the Chapel of Rest? Which photograph for the funeral card? It all sounded pretty distressing. There were other things such as the deeds to the grave which needed attending to. Dying is a complicated and expensive business for even the most humble of souls.

Days before, I had received a call from my mother who swore me to secrecy in order not to add even more trauma to the events of that week for the rest of the family. She had five cancerous skin growths on one of her legs and some of them were malignant!

The morning of December 22nd arrived, and Lynda drove from Heswall, having spent the night with her friend, Claudia Philips, daughter of the actor Leslie Philips. Sebastian had his ponytail cut off by Mary's son, cousin Jim. He said he wanted to look his best for his great-aunt Mary. At the funeral, my cousin Anthony read the Liturgy of the Word, and I spoke a Farewell and Commendation as follows:

> John and Jim have asked me to thank you all for coming to yet another one of Mary's funerals. Over the years, Mary had a great deal of fun by telling everyone how much she thoroughly enjoyed her first funeral. For those who are unfamiliar with the tale, Mary's sister-in-law was also called Mary Flatley. She had lived almost all of her life in London, but when she died her funeral was held at St. Joseph's in Sale. On the day of the service the church was packed, much to the bewilderment of the family, who had received dozens of condolences. It was highly unlikely that no more than three people in the North of England knew that particular Mary Flatley! There was a tumultuous gasp of horror from the entire congregation as Mary filed past what was believed to be her coffin, having just received Holy Communion. I'd wished I had a video camera, it would have made great television.
>
> Mary was a role-model of Christianity. She lived her life as Christian people should live their lives. Without envy, without greed, and without malice. She had an unquestioning faith, and a total belief in the power of prayer. She was the kindest and most selfless person I have ever known. During the course of Mary's life, if everyone who was ever a recipient of her kindness were to bring a single flower to her graveside, Mary would lie beneath a mountain of flowers. I have no doubt that the Gates of Heaven will be flung open for Mary, with full trumpet fanfares blowing, but this world, our world, is very much a poorer place this day.

On the other side of the Atlantic, Mother had radium treatment for her skin cancer and was given the all-clear, although it has caused her to have a slight disability in walking as it tightened the tendons in her leg by burning the good live tissue. She says she can live with that. She just has to be extra careful when walking, for fear of falling over.

2007

Time at Neil and Christine's manor • Farewell, Uncle Den
• Flood! • Lynda and I go our separate ways

My relationship with Lynda continued as a linked chain of sexual marathons and travelling to and fro from Spain. However one day completely out of the blue, she phoned me from her marital home in Frodsham to say the relationship with me was not going in the direction that she wanted, and it was over. I was dumbstruck, but I thought I'd call her bluff. It all blew over in a couple of days, but I did wonder whether she was on one of her agendas.

In February 2007, Lynda and I went to the cinema one evening. This was to mark yet another landmark in my life. She enquired as to whether it was cheaper for OAPs. Can you honestly credit it! The girl behind the desk didn't hesitate in issuing me with an old-age pensioner's cinema ticket, with a £1.50 reduction. In two hundred-odd pages of this book, I'm already an OAP. This life story is going to be shorter than the book of Twentieth-Century Italian War Victories!

February 26th 2007. Sebastian and I decided to call and see my father. He seemed chirpier than our last visit, but Sebastian insisted on having photographs of the three generations, for fear there might not be another opportunity for the three of us to be together at the same time. We had barely left my father's company when he phoned Sebastian's mobile. My uncle Tredennis had just died. Sebastian and I were deeply upset, but my father was cool and utterly philosophical about losing his only brother. He just said, "Ah well, Den and I have had a good innings. Most of Den's friends died at twenty years of age in Lancaster bombers; he was 85, so he had much to be thankful for."

Two days later, after a sleepless night of wine and sex, Lynda and I drove down to Wiltshire to visit Neil and Christine at their splendid new home. They had risen from the ashes. Fayed, the infamous camel dealer and London shop owner, had failed to destroy them, with all his money and power. Their newly acquired beautiful Manor House, built in local stone, started its life in the Middle Ages. The banquet room has a selection of late-thirteenth-century geometric bar tracery windows. The rest of the house consists of leaded mullions and later additions. This wonderful old home would sit equally comfortably in

Normandy or the Cotswolds. To my great joy we were greeted at the door by Christine's friend Razzi, who had come especially to see me. Neil and Christine seemed thrilled that the prodigal son had returned as I'd not seen them in ages. As always with the Hamiltons, fizz (Champagne) is the first order of the day, and lots of it. Luncheon was a gastronomic orgasm of locally killed venison. Christine is the most amazing cook and Neil is forever the perfect host. Luncheon continued throughout the entire afternoon, and my next surprise was the arrival of Sheila, Christine's other chum. It was so lovely to see her again and we all had a thoroughly enjoyable evening.

Everyone liked Lynda very much, but Christine confided later that all three ladies agreed that I wouldn't be spending the rest of my life with her. At the time I was inwardly a little upset and I was hoping they were wrong. Naturally we were given a grand tour de la maison, which as expected is impeccably furnished and filled with objects of intrigue, curiosity and antiquity. Lynda and I retired to the most beautiful bedroom. The end of a gloriously enjoyable day.

Shortly after dawn, the morning mist allowed an opaque stream of sunlight through those great mullion windows in our room. I decided to rise and capture the tranquillity of the house and grounds by photograph, allowing Lynda to continue to luxuriate in bed and baronial splendour.

Like me, Neil is an early riser and he is forever busying himself with jobs around the house. The kitchen table was already set for breakfast, meticulous to the last detail, even down to the little vase of narcissus picked at dawn from the garden. We left by mid morning. Our host and hostess couldn't have been more accommodating.

Back in Manchester, my Aunt Andolores had treated herself to a new Mini and was offloading her BMW. I was busy in the kitchen making one of my now famous "Cow Pies" when she called. After a brief bit of horse trading, I swapped the pie for the BMW. One of my better deals! Within days, Sebastian and I were driving to the Cotswolds, to the home of my late Uncle Tredennis, Aunt Alice, and some of my cousins. Neil and Christine had kindly offered to put us up for the night. By the time we reached Staffordshire we had a puncture and the police had to close much of the motorway. We explained we were on our way to my uncle's funeral and the police changed the tyre for us, which was remarkable and much appreciated. That night, I was back in that sumptuous bed in Wiltshire which I'd shared with Lynda the week before.

The following afternoon Sebastian and I arrived at the crematorium in ample time to meet up with family. I hadn't seen many of my cousins in years. The Curran girls were always renowned for their beauty, but they are now all in their fifties and sixties and there is a whole new generation of beauteous offspring which has followed.

The funeral of my Uncle Tredennis was one of the most moving I can remember. My cousin Val's husband, Howard, took charge of the proceedings and presented a most heartfelt eulogy. He had gone to a great deal of trouble and managed to get Uncle Den's war citation from the RAF. It read … "His cool and calm manner, while under heavy fire from the enemy, and his overwhelming sense of duty and determination to bring his men back safely, was inspirational." He had successfully completed twenty-four raids on Germany and was awarded the Distinguished Flying Medal.

Sebastian and I sat with tears of pride and sadness streaming down our faces. He was a humble and modest man, and all of us today owe him and his comrades so much. Howard finished his eulogy by simply saying, "Chocks away, Den." I couldn't have thought of anything more fitting.

April 6th 2007. I was back in the Isle of Man with Gerald and we decided to call on my long-standing chum of nearly forty years, Don Plaster, who lives in Castletown. The plan was that we would go to the Flying Club, of which we are both members, before calling on Don. There we were informed that Don had got a new girlfriend. I was genuinely delighted for him. When I enquired what she was like, the answer was, "distinctly ropey", which I thought a little unkind at the time. As we drove down the road, we could see Don's Rolls-Royce approaching. He was shocked to see me standing there flagging him down. His woman, Denise, was the current Northern Ireland Gurning Champion, and if she wasn't, she should have been. We all returned to Don's house by the Castletown Quay and had a thoroughly enjoyable afternoon of whisky and cigars, while the Gurning Champion sunbathed herself outside by the pavement. The following week I phoned Don. He'd ditched the Celtic Gurner and got himself a new one. When I asked him what this one looked like, he said, "A Toby Jug." Don has great fun dating women from the internet; it's one of his latest hobbies.

On my own love scene, by early September of that year, things were beginning to show hairline cracks and one morning Lynda said "I think we should both find new relationships." Immediately, my portcullis began to drop and my drawbridge started to crank up.

Lynda was used to being with Jeremy who is the most passive, laid-back man I know. Any of her vitriolic cannon fire sailed completely over his head and he had the most brilliant way of removing the wind from her sails. I've witnessed it on more than one occasion. If she was verbally attacking him, he would say something like, "Is that a new dress you're wearing today darling? You look beautiful, it really suits you." Knowing Lynda's insatiable appetite for flattery, it worked every time. I, on the other hand, won't let her get away with it. The more you allow people to get their own way all the time, the more the boundaries of precedent expand and it gets worse. The minute we set foot in Spain, she would be totally different and life would be blissful.

September 19th 2007, and Lynda and I were back at the villa. At 3a.m. we were suddenly startled awake to the most deafening sound, the like of Niagara Falls. As I opened the master bedroom door, there was a cascade of water pouring over the landing and a torrent coming down the stairs. The water was so deep you couldn't see the defini-tion of the steps and within seconds the downstairs rooms were being flooded several inches high. At first we were confused, but battled our way upstairs to the main door. Although pitch dark, we could see a river torrent bursting down through the forest just above us. Because the villa is on the side of the mountain, the main gates are slightly higher than the house with the driveway sloping toward it. The living area is upstairs and the sleeping area is below. We tried to wade against the flow up to the gates, where I had only recently had several railway sleepers delivered as part of some landscaping. Our thinking was, if we could lodge them up against the gates it would divert some of the force away from the house. It washed them away as if they were matchsticks. The noise of the flood was almost deafening and forked lightning crashed all around us. Although Lynda was very frightened she fought on like a trooper and I was really proud of her. The two of us could quite easily have been washed away down to the valley below. The flood carries with it boulders, trees, mud, and everything in its path; we were living a disaster movie.

The following morning revealed the true devastation. The residue of mud throughout the house was several inches thick. My collection of eighteenth-century books from our library at the Hall was beyond redemption and eventually had to be thrown in a skip. My insurers arrived and although it was impossible to replace or value the books, I received six thousand euros as compensation for them. Lynda and I spent the next three weeks cleaning. We started by having to wash the entire house out with the garden hose. When all was complete and the villa was back to being ship-shape, we prepared to return to England: I hasten to add, not before securing the railway sleepers to the electric gates, just in case. Lynda said, "I'll say one thing, living with you is never boring!"

As we were about to leave for the airport, all seemed well, save for a rather odd telephone call from Lynda's father whose garbled message upset her. She said, "There's something terribly wrong at home and I can't quite get to the bottom of it. My father wasn't making any sense!"

The following day we were back in England and I drove her to her parents' house. All of her concern and worry was confirmed. As we entered their home, her son Daniel was slouched on the settee, grim and ashen-faced. Her elderly father was trying to be his usual humorous self, but appeared confused.

Their home had been subjected to a raid by the Serious Crime Squad, a full-blown and terrifying raid by ten black-clad officers who entered by smashing their front door. Lynda's forty-eight-year-old brother, Dave, was arrested for possession of narcotics with a possible charge of low-level dealing. Her other brother and her son were also arrested but released after thirty-six hours of interrogation. It is a tragedy in the most vivid sense of the word. I know Dave and he is an extremely kind and intelligent man but as everyone knows, addiction necessitates funding. All three of Lynda's brothers are handsome, witty, funny, and from a wealthy background; Lynda is the only girl. Their father is a highly respected and successful business-man and they are a stable loving family, but drug addiction has no social barriers. The family were distraught, confused, ashamed and angry at what he was putting them through. As I write, the parents are both eighty, and the fear was that the trauma might kill Lynda's father. Her mother said she worried that she might not live to see her son again. Before any of us start wagging our righteous fingers in the air, think carefully; in modern Britain this could happen to any family.

In Georgian and Victorian England, drug addiction was reserved mainly for the rich; the poor just got drunk. Opium was freely available from any chemist for medicinal purposes, and many of the greatest pieces of English literature, poetry and music were created under its influence. If they were alive, you could ask Shelley, Keats, Byron, Scott and Wordsworth what they thought about it; I think you might be shocked.

Mid-October, and still in England, I received a panic-stricken call from Sebastian, who was staying with his mother at her house in Rome. He said, "Dad, quickly, turn the news on, Calpe is being hit by the worst storms in recorded history!" Minutes later I received another similar call from my old girlfriend, Sue, who lives near Toulouse in France.

I packed and jumped on a plane, praying all the time that we wouldn't have a repeat of only a few weeks before. I arrived at the villa and to my utter elation, my railway sleeper barricade had worked perfectly. There was not a blade of grass out of place.

I drove down to the town, which could only be described as a war zone. There were one thousand five hundred cars submerged under water. At the bottom of the main shopping street, the Gabriel de Miro, three cars had ended up inside someone's restaurant. Any vehicles parked at the top of the hill were all washed down into a mangled heap at the bottom. The sea walls and lovely walkways were broken and scattered all over the beach. The carnage was devastating. I have to admire the Spanish; immediately the Government Minister in charge arrived from Madrid and the army moved in en masse. They brought pumps and every kind of equipment needed. Within three days the town was as good as new. The beach was spotless and the palm trees were all replaced. Around the same time in England, York and Sheffield suffered a similar fate. People from there were still living in makeshift caravans two years later.

The Spanish are not so good at drainage, and because it rarely rains they often think they don't need it. Along with my Brummie chum, Lee, we immediately set about putting in a proper drainage system at the villa. I am pleased to report it has worked brilliantly since.

In November Lynda and I discussed the demise of our relationship. There were cumulative reasons, but really nothing that couldn't have been resolved with a little more open and honest discussion. Communication is the secret to success but if one person has their own agenda then it's not going to work. We had a lifestyle that the vast majority of people only dream about. We had little or no baggage of young children, mortgages, or commitments to worry about, and we were free to enjoy our homes abroad whenever we wanted. 98% of the time, we thoroughly enjoyed each other's company, but on December 1st we parted. There wasn't any wailing or gnashing of teeth; just a simple farewell. I was deeply saddened. The one thing I wasn't going to do was to pine over it for years as I had done with Vanessa. I was becoming very aware of my own mortality, and these days I go to a lot more funerals than weddings. Many of my friends seem to be popping their clogs, with increased regularity. Sad though it was, I had to move on with my life; my time is shortening.

Gerald had undergone a serious operation at the Alexandra Hospital in Manchester and I said I would help him and escort him back to the Isle of Man. On the plane I bumped into another old acquaintance of mine, a Liverpool comedian called Stan Boardman. I'd not seen Stan in years; the last time was at an exhibition of Mike McCartney's photographs in Liverpool, when Mike, Rowena, Stan, Lord David Putnam and myself went out to dinner together. When we arrived at Douglas Airport, Stan joined Gerald and me as we waited for our respective drivers to pick us up. He was going to visit Sir Norman Wisdom, who was now in an old people's home on the island. Stan gave us a twenty-minute non-stop private comedy show. He said he was trying out some of his new topical material on us; it was hilarious. I was worried Gerald would split his stitches; anyway it certainly cheered him up after the trauma of his operation.

Christmas came and went and as always at my Aunt Phil's house there was much wassailing and merriment. Sebastian had gone to see his mother in Rome over Christmas. I always miss him and in honesty I missed Lynda, but I wasn't going to wallow in solitude and I was determined that 2008 was going to be an interesting and exciting year.

2008

Back with Lynne • A Rolls at last! • From Santa Barbara to the Sierra Nevada • Neil and Christine's Silver Wedding • Another Spanish summer • The *QE2*

I telephoned Lynne. I was unsure as to the reception I would get; after all, it was two years since I had last spoken to her. She could have got married in that time, or she might have said, "Sorry old chap, you had your chance, push off!" To my great delight, she was pleased to hear from me and we arranged to meet.

Saturday, January 5th 2008. I arrived early at the Manor House. Lynne and I had decided we were going to take a drive in the country, heading south into Staffordshire.

What better place to stop for luncheon than the Rambler's Retreat at Alton, one of my favourite little hideaways. Inevitably we wandered into the forest in order that I might introduce her to one of my dearest old friends, "The Druid's Oak". Modern guidebooks just refer to it as "the chained oak" – perhaps no one alive is old enough to remember its proper name. When I was at school it was reputed to be two thousand years old. Its enormous limbs are supported by great chains as thick as a ship's anchor chain. They were put there in 1830 by the then Earl of Shrewsbury. The story goes that the Earl was stopped by a beggar woman who asked if he could spare her a few coppers. He refused, and she cursed him and his family (the Talbots), saying that every time a limb broke on the great oak tree, a Talbot would die. Taking her seriously, the Earl had his blacksmith chain all the limbs together and they remain so to this day. I have loved that tree nearly all of my life, and I always have a little chat with it whenever I visit. When I was eleven years old, I climbed to the very top, and we have had a special bond with each other ever since. As Lynne and I approached, I was heartbroken to see a major branch had recently snapped, and some of the chains were strewn on the ground. The present Earl should be feeling a little queasy by now!

Lynne and I started to see each other on a regular basis. Sebastian finally met her and charmed her as he does with everyone. Lynne, rather flatteringly thinks "the apple didn't fall far from the tree"! A day later, he and I drove to Whalley Bridge to look at a Rolls-Royce that I'd had my eye on for several weeks. From the first day I opened the Chuckwagon all those years ago, when Jim Parry allowed me to drive his, I always said, "One day I'll treat myself to a Rolls-Royce." Nearly forty years have slipped by since then. Whenever there was a time when I could possibly have afforded one, my practical brain would always kick into gear and I avoided the actions of folly. But now, as I rapidly headed toward sixty years of age, and before I started to nosedive into senility, I thought I'd cast care to the wind and fulfil a dream.

February 1st 2008, Yippie! I bought the Rolls! Driving a Rolls-Royce is a completely different driving experience. Sebastian adjusted the

CD player for me, and what a joy it was to float along the highway accompanied by the dulcet tones of Sir Edward Elgar and Mozart.

The Spirit of Ecstasy gently rose and sank as if she were the figure-head on a great galleon ship gliding through near calm waters. I captained this grand land vessel in a state of absolute euphoria. I can highly recommend it to those car lovers yet to enjoy the experience. An acquaintance of mine had similarly just treated himself to a Bentley. I joined him for tea and scones one afternoon, during which, I penned this rather silly poem for him ...

My one and only Bentley

There is a lady, n'er to betray me,
She does not saunter or delay me.

She has no need of sexy glances,
Bulging muscles or men's advances.

Her gaze is always straight ahead,
Men cannot woo her to their bed.

Yet I would miss her cushioned embrace,
Her sparkling eyes, her gleaming face.

As any lady, I treat her gently,
She is my one and only Bentley.

In February I found myself back in Calpe and as I wandered into the town, my leisurely perambulation was interrupted by a ridiculous parade of Germans. Never have I seen such a motley array of individuals, utterly ludicrous. I couldn't quite fathom out what it was all in aid of, but I was told that Germans had travelled far and wide to be there. Those dressed in eighteenth-century ensemble attempted to look dignified, and they were obviously thoroughly pleased with themselves. Their costumes looked straight out of a pantomine to me. I struggled to conceal my mirth as the surrounding German spectators were taking it all very seriously indeed. Perhaps as an Englishman I was missing the point and it had something to do with German humour! (A possible oxymoron?) At 5.30p.m. there was yet another parade of them, only this time there were a lot more. I decided, "when in Rome", and I ended up at a German restaurant with a whole crowd of leather-shorts-wearing, knee-and-shoe-slapping, Stein-clinking "sour krauts". It was a great night, but I never did find out what it was all about.

The day after, on the Sunday, I was in the Antiques Bar at El Cisne with our mutual friends, Michael and Eileen, when Lynda and her friend Shelley walked in. She had flown over to find tenants for her house and was staying at Finestrat. It was a tears and laughter sort of afternoon! Lynda came and sat with me, kissing and hugging me and telling me what a dreadful cad I was, while at the same time telling me she had a new boyfriend. Apparently she went to school with him in Liverpool, although he was older. They had only been reacquainted a week before, and she said he had already asked her to marry him. "I'm seriously considering it," she said. I would call that ricochet rather than rebound. He didn't sound right in the head to me. I thought, "I wonder how long it will be before she discovers all the hidden baggage he probably has?" It won't last! And I was right!

Back in England, Lynne and I were at the Manor House when Davinia, Lynne's strikingly beautiful actress daughter, arrived. She had been at the 34th birthday party of her best friend, Kate Moss. Kate had moved in with Davinia, in the house Lynne bought for her near the Abbey Road, while she was having renovations done to her own home close by. Davinia's husband, David Gardner, a former footballer, had gone to Africa with David Beckham, who was the best man at Davinia and David's wedding. Davinia had recently given birth to the most gorgeous baby boy called Grey, but was suffering from post-natal depression among other things. When you are young, beautiful, staggeringly rich, and you are a major player in the celebrity "Primrose Hill Set" with Kate Moss as your best friend – well, it will give you some idea of the lifestyle she led. You can also imagine, as the loving mother of a single child, the many tormented sleepless nights of worry Lynne must have had to endure.

Things with Lynne and I were going along splendidly, and before I left for Spain she told me she was in the process of buying a flat in London as a little love-nest just for the two of us. She said we were going to have such fun picking all the things to go in it. We could fly to Rome, Paris and New York to the best antiques shops and get anything we fancied. I said that one of my favourite places was the Souk in Paris, and it was decided that that would be our first port of call. I was thrilled and was so looking forward to it. Lynne and I have identical expensive eclectic tastes, and the chances of us arguing over things was almost nil. At the Manor House, Lynne had dismissed her former butler and chef, whom I met two years previously, and replaced them with two other gay fellows.

I often wondered where the connection between the true dictionary definition of the word "gay" (mirthful/light-hearted) and homosexuality lay, and I only recently found out it stands for "Good As You!"

These two weren't exactly employed on contract; they enjoyed a more employee/friend relationship. I had observed that they had skilfully manoeuvred themselves into a position of almost indispensability. They served Lynne a daily diet of fussy little favours of servitude, while being quite bossy to her in a mincing gay kind of way. I shan't satisfy them by putting their names in print, so let's just call them Pinky and Perky Puff.

The minute I returned to England I received an excited call from Lynne saying that she couldn't wait for me to see our little nest. I said I would get the train to London the following day. The flat was in the best part of Hampstead near the village, and I'm sure you could buy a row of houses in most parts of the country for the same price. When I got there, it was indeed magnificent as one would expect, but the place was fully furnished and kitted out. I can't even begin to describe how hurt and disappointed I felt at that moment. To add insult to injury, while I was away, she had taken Pinky Puff to Paris to help choose the furnishings and objets d'art. As I was given a tour of the flat, low and behold I was shown Pinky and Perky Puff's bedroom. This little love nest had two bloody cuckoos in it!

I did everything to conceal the pain I felt. In my mind I gave her the benefit of the doubt that she was possibly so enthusiastic to get it ready for us that she must have forgotten. My disappointment was overruled by the fact that I so thoroughly enjoyed every minute of Lynne's company, and there was never a moment of silence or breathtaking to punctuate our endless conversation and laughter.

It was an early rise for us the following day, as we were due to be at Davinia's house in St. John's Wood. Her home is very stylish, detached and slightly Gothic in appearance.

Davinia has obviously inherited her mother's impeccable eclectic taste but with a little more arty, expensive chic. Her husband, David, comes across as a shy and pleasant Mancunian who hails originally from the Worsley area of Salford. We all drove out to somewhere near Burford in Oxfordshire to inspect a house Davinia had almost persuaded her father to buy her as their new family country home.

We arrived at a very splendid-looking Cotswold stone mansion set in 50 acres of parkland and I immediately started looking for leaks in the roof. Having been brought up in property, and knowing full well the insatiable appetite very large houses have for repair, I made it my business to look for the practical pitfalls. To start with, a bad roof is a bad house. In the meantime Lynne and Davinia had already decided on what the curtains were going to look like. After I had given my professional opinion we ended up at a charming country pub for a luncheon of fish and chips. Guess what? The mansion was just down the road from Kate Moss's country farmhouse! *Quelle surprise*!

In February my Aunt Phil and I decided we would go again to California to surprise Mother on her birthday in March. As usual the plot was hatched with my sister, Andrea, and we secretly stayed at her home in Los Angeles. As a way of saying "thank you" Phil and I wandered to the shops the day after we arrived. Phil bought Andrea an enormous yellow Dendrobium (orchid) and knowing that my sister has a number of wine snobs among her stockbroker friends, I bought her an extremely fine bottle of Gevery-Chambertin. Even the greatest connoisseurs of French wines wouldn't turn their noses up at that. After all, Chambertin was the favourite wine tipple of Napoleon himself. He used to dilute it with a little water in order to keep a clear head. Who knows – the course of history might have been altered had he drunk it neat!

Mother couldn't have been more surprised or thrilled at our arrival. Even though I have been going there for much of my life, one forgets just how beautiful Santa Barbara is. Mother made a wise descision in moving directly in front of the old Mission after the bush-fire razed our other home to the ground. There are twenty-one early Catholic missions all along the California coast, but Santa Barbara is known as the finest (the Queen of Missions). Built in the eighteenth century by Father Serra of the Franciscan Order, over the centuries it has enjoyed visits from everyone who is anyone, including Her Majesty the Queen. The Franciscans still occupy it to this day, and although I confess to being a lapsed Catholic, I never miss Mass and Holy Communion when I'm there (followed by a free coffee and doughnuts in the cloisters, gratuity optional!).

Santa Barbara is a town of old money and old movie stars, and you never know who you are going to bump into in the supermarket. I bumped into Bette Davis one day, although not in the supermarket. Residents of Santa Barbara have included everyone from Michael

Jackson, Oprah Winfrey and Kirk and Michael Douglas, to John Cleese, Bo Derek and President Ronald Reagan. There are certain old haunts of mine which are not on the tourist trail but are a prerequisite for any locals. If you are looking for real American cooking in an all-American atmosphere, there is nowhere better than Harry's Plaza Café. I've been eating there since Harry first opened it nearly forty years ago. The walls of the place are covered with sepia photographs of the town's history, and signed pictures of the famous residents who dine there. The back room is the headquarters of an exclusive club of rich Santa Barbara ranchers and businessmen called "The Rancheros". President Ronald Reagan was a member and a regular diner at Harry's. Another place you will find me in is the Montecito Inn. It was owned by Charlie Chaplin and because of my grandfather's close friendship with Charlie, in a funny old way I feel a spiritual kinship with the place. The food is good and a valet will park your car for you even if you're only going in for a chicken sandwich.

Mother's birthday was a thoroughly enjoyable one and I treated everyone to dinner at the Biltmore Hotel. A couple of days later I got tickets for us all to go to the re-opening of the Granada Theatre on State Street; Natalie Cole was performing that night. I spoke to Sebastian to check all was well on the home front, and Lynne sent me a text message with a photo of herself: she wrote, "Just in case you start to forget what I look like!" which I thought was very sweet.

Mother was still having to visit the hospital each week because of the cancer on her leg, and there were all the usual property and business things to attend to. On March 17th 2008, St. Patrick's Day, Mother, Phil and I drove to "Amber Gardens" which was another one of Mother's houses. We had gone there primarily to see whether the men had replaced the motor to the electric garage doors. During a conversation between my mother and Phil I heard my mother say that I was an American millionaire. I was quick to contradict her by saying, "I have no money or investments in America!" Mother turned to me and said, "Well you do now, I've just given you this house, you should easily get a million for it!" It took me a few minutes to recover. Previously, I thought I was doing rather well by swapping a cow pie for a BMW with my other aunt, Andolores!

Phil and I made our parting with Mother easier this time by taking lots of photographs just as we were leaving. Mother is not good when it comes to saying goodbye – she gets very upset. My brother, Paul, dropped us at Santa Barbara Airport and returned to her as quickly as possible.

We returned to England with Heathrow Airport in turmoil because the new terminal was not fully functioning, and they managed to misplace the baggage of twenty thousand passengers. Fortunately we were not among them, but there was no connecting flight and we ended up having to get a train back to Manchester. We arrived at Stockport just after nightfall; it was dank, dirty, dark and drizzling. The yellow-tinged street lights gave a Dickensian ambience to the place. The walls were covered in graffiti and everyone seemed to look emaciated and be wearing black. After the bright, clean, sunny affluence of Santa Barbara this place looked like my idea of hell.

Sebastian managed to pass his driving test with a 100% pass rate, and not long afterwards I gave him the cow pie BMW as a present. He promptly drove all the way to Rome in it with his girlfriend, Lydia, to visit his mother there. It was very much against my better judgement, I might add.

Upon his return, he and I drove over to see our dearest of friends, Brian and Wendy Dalley at Cliffe Park Hall by Rudyard Lake in Staffordshire. The view from their Hall is spectacular and looks out toward the Pennines and Wildboarclough (reputed to be the last place in England where wild boar were hunted and killed). Brian and Wendy are a quintessential English couple, charmingly eccentric, and that's why we love them so much. Brian, who is an expert on arms and armour, is in his seventies and has for some time been sporting pink hair, including his moustache. This was not intentional, it's just that he could never quite get the hair dye mix right! For a time Wendy also had pink hair but she returned to normality when she started to go back to the hairdressers. Rudyard Lake, which stretches out below them, is now a magnet for walkers, boating and railway enthusiasts. John Lockwood Kipling and his wife, Alice, adored the place so much that they named their son after it; Rudyard Kipling. Brian and Wendy had been kindly storing some of our paintings and furnishings from when we sold Willaston, and Lynne suggested I could bring them over to her place, which is what we did.

In early May 2008, I returned to the villa in Spain alone. I was to be joined by my love, Lynne, a few days later. Much to my panic-stricken horror, she arrived two hours early having got her flight times wrong. After a much-needed stiff vodka and tonic at the villa, I took her to another one of my favourite eateries, Dels Artistes, in the old town at

Altea. The next couple of days were blissfully enjoyable. I showed her all the local tourist highlights including the spectacular mountain village of Guadalest, which is only thirty minutes' drive inland from Calpe. A few days later we decided to go on a little adventure trip, and drive all across the southern coast of Spain to spend some time at her home near Marbella.

For our journey, Lynne kindly insisted on hiring a top of the range BMW. There were two reasons why she did this; firstly, because of her thoughtfulness in that I was doing all the driving, and secondly that her comfort threshold is considerably higher than my own. Part way through our journey we decided it would be foolish to miss a visit to the magnificent Alhambra Palace at Granada. It is the most splendidly preserved Moorish Palace still remaining on mainland Spain. After getting completely lost in the maze of one-way streets in the town of Granada, which I can only describe as similar to Manchester's industrial estate, Trafford Park, only with palm trees, we finally got to the Alhambra. Our next obstacle to overcome was accommodation. We came across a pleasant-looking hotel, but the sight of the arrival of a Saga Holidays bus with zimmer-frame holidaymakers clambering out of it dampened our enthusiasm. Finally we spotted the Alhambra Palace Hotel in all its magnificence and Islamic architectural opulence. The hotel was built in 1910 by the Duke of San Pedro de Galatino and inaugurated by King Alfonso XIII. "This is more our cup of tea," said Lynne. Lynne has very exacting views when it comes to accommodation! For her it is either "5 star" or "No star" and nothing in between will do. My sentiments exactly! Only my pecuniary disadvantage allows me to be more flexible.

The queue of visitors waiting to tour the Alhambra starts at 6a.m. and the gates don't open until 8a.m. When we arrived the following morning at 7.15a.m., there were already several hundred people in line. If it wasn't for two lovely Chinese girls near the front who offered me their two extra tickets (much to the annoyance of the people behind) goodness knows what time we would have got in. It was truly magnificent and by luncheon we were seriously fatigued and I still had a long drive ahead.

Our eventual arrival at Marbella, following only minimal misguides by my navigator, was a considerable relief for me. We had foolishly chosen to travel the scenic route over the Sierra Nevada and its snow-capped mountains. For much of the way we travelled along narrow sheer cliff-edge roads in double-thick fog.

Lynne's own stunning beachside home is the former Royal Household of a Middle Eastern Sultan. You enter via a magnificent circular white marble colonnaded courtyard: a harem, containing nine individual apartments, one for each of the Sultan's wives. Lynne is far too modest a person to ever refer to it as a palace, but officially that is exactly what it is. I shall refer to it as such merely as a point of definition and not for the sake of sounding grandiose.

As we arrived in the walled enclosure, Warwick, the butler, came rushing out to greet us and gather our cases. Cook had already prepared a magnificent meal for us.

Lynne's meticulous eye for furnishings, art, sculpture and colour combinations is unsurpassable. The Palace contains the best that money can buy, but only the most talented have the ability to put it all together so magically.

No sooner had I left my old leather case in what I was informed was my dressing room, than upon my return, I found the case empty and all my shirts starched, ironed and hanging neatly in the wardrobe; not so much as an hour had passed. This was a far cry from the service of my own former butler and cook, Mr. and Mrs. B.

Much of the following day was spent luxuriating in the sunlight and having every desire catered for by the servants. In the evening we were invited to dinner at Stuart Webb's home further down the beach. Stuart was a multi-millionaire and former Chairman of Derby Football Club. His home is another terribly grand palatial place but the interior décor and furnishings are exactly what you would expect a football club owner and his wife to possess – nouveau riche. There was an interesting mix of guests, most of whom were on the "Times Rich List" and all in all it was a thoroughly enjoyable evening. Stuart confided in me that although he had known Lynne for some years he had never seen her so relaxed or happy. Lynne let her hair down that night and by the end of the evening she made a dignified exit with my arm for assistance. Warwick was waiting with the car door open to drive us the two hundred yards back home.

In what I can only presume was additional grounds to the Palace is another very splendid home which is only accessed via Lynne's main gates. It is the Spanish home of the actor Antonio Banderas and his wife Melanie Griffith. Antonio was born and brought up in Malaga and regularly visits to be with family and maintain his roots there. The day after Lynne bought the place she was sunbathing by her pool when she was suddenly startled by the sight of a man climbing over her eight-foot wall. In a fit of panic and thinking he was an intruder, she screamed at him and summoned Warwick to throw him out immediately. The man, dark, tanned and handsome, made profuse apologies, explaining that one of the children had kicked a ball over and he had been unaware she was there. The following morning Melanie knocked on the door to give additional apologies. She said she had never known a time before when her husband was chased away by a woman! Up to that point, Lynne had no idea who he was but they have been good friends ever since.

The next couple of days were equally indulgent and enjoyable and on May 12th in the evening Warwick drove us to the airport to pick Sebastian up. He was flying in to attend my birthday. Sebastian was thrilled to learn that he was staying in the harem suite which is always reserved for Kate Moss and he can truly say he has slept in Kate's bed!

The following day I awoke a year older. It was a truly wonderful and memorable birthday. Lynne bought me a solid gold Hunter fob watch, made in 1949, the year of my birth. She also had a thick gold fob chain made for it; I was so thrilled!

In the evening she had booked a table at a restaurant in Marbella called "Bandedos", just for the three of us.

When we arrived back, the staff had filled the harem courtyard with hundreds of lit candles for me. I was deeply touched at the amount of thought that Lynne had put into celebrating my birthday. Warwick brought us drinks at midnight on the Palace roof, Cook had baked me a cake and Sebastian took photographs. It was the end of a lovely day.

A couple of days later and by the time we were up, Warwick had polished the car and filled it with petrol ready for us to drive to Gibraltar. I was delighted, because neither Lynne nor Sebastian had been to the top of the rock before. As always, the traffic was congested at the entrance to Gib and after luncheon I managed to find a tour guide to take us round and give us the full history lesson. Later in the day, while we were sitting at the pub across from the Governor's House, we witnessed him leaving to attend a function in a manner that only the British do so well. The black Jaguar arrived accompanied by four police outriders, and the car number plate had been replaced by the Sovereign Crown. Other police scurried around to redirect traffic. You could see there was tension and apprehension for the players in this mini drama. The moment arrived and the Governor and his Lieutenant appeared resplendent in their military uniforms, with sashes, braid, medals, spurs and cavalry sabres glinting in the afternoon sun. The motorcade sped off leaving everyone in no doubt as to how terribly important they were. It is a last gasping breath of an empire that gave the world so much.

By Friday it was time for Sebastian to return to England and on the way to the airport he told me he would be moving to London. I would miss him terribly as we had become more than father and son; we had become the best of friends. Before leaving we were served a gastronomic masterpiece out by the pool, and Cook had very kindly made sandwiches for Sebastian to take with him for when he arrived home.

Lynne and I were happy doing nothing save for being appallingly pampered and worshipping the sun. I happened to casually mention that I had a little bit of backache. No sooner had the words left my lips when a masseuse was summoned to come from Marbella. I was ushered into the massage room in the Palace where I was stripped, rubbed with scented oils, elbowed in the back, thumped, slapped and beaten into submission. Just when I thought the coast was clear I had to suffer the excruciating pain of reflexology.

I managed to hobble into the cinema room where the staff brought us dinner on trays and we settled down to an evening of films. There was certainly no "amore" that night. I was in agony for the next two days.

Sunday was a sad day as I had to return to Calpe. Lynne didn't want me to go but I couldn't abandon my villa before returning to England. There are always things to attend to with houses. Warwick booked my flight, and I was chauffeured to the airport alone; like my Mother, Lynne hates airport goodbyes.

Upon my arrival at Alicante, I discovered, to my great horror, that my driver, Frank, was ill and he had sent his ridiculous wife, Rita, to pick me up. I knew for a fact that Rita did not possess a driving licence! Frank had told me previously how she had considerable difficulty in understanding even the most basic rudiments of road procedure. To add to my initial horror, she arrived in a miniature Smart Car instead of the normal vehicle. I had to scream at her on the motorway as she veered off the road toward the barrier because she was busy looking under the dashboard for the heat control. I needed a double dose of blood pressure tablets when I got home; that woman is a bloody maniac!

By the first week in June 2008, Lynne and I were back at the Manor House with Pinky and Perky Puff. We decided to drive to London in a new Range Rover she had just treated herself to and spend a few enjoyable days alone at the flat in Hampstead.

Sunday, June 8th was Neil and Christine Hamilton's 25th Wedding Anniversary celebration and Lynne and I were invited.

We were met in Neil and Christine's field (which was the car park for the day), by Sebastian and his chum, Morgan, who attended Harrow with him. Sebastian looked great in a white suit and panama hat. (The jacket was mine, kept by me in perfect condition since 1971.) As we approached the Manor, we were then greeted with jubilant salutations by Sir James Holman (Christine Hamilton's brother) and his wife, Lady Fiona. Neil and Christine made a big fuss of Lynne with which I was delighted – I really wanted her to feel at home with my friends. Everything was perfect for them on their special day. The sun shone, the jazz band played and there was a plethora of eccentric nobility and showbiz personalities there to amuse and entertain us. I introduced Lynne to Lady Fiona's nephew, a super young fellow called Bear Grylls. Bear was in Special Forces and is now making a successful career doing a survival television programme. His real name is Edward, but as a child he was called Teddy Bear by the family. It got abbreviated to "Bear" and he has been stuck with it ever since. It's not done him any harm; it sounds great as a television name and you are not likely to forget it.

A huge marquee had been erected in the grounds for a sit-down dinner and I was anxious to take note of the place-settings. Christine had informed me that I was on the eccentrics' table. "I know you will feel right at home there James," she said. Horror of horrors, poor Lynne was placed next to Alexander (the Marquis of Bath) who is as deaf as a post and utterly potty. She spent the entire afternoon staring at a bit of quail's egg and a piece of stilton cheese which were lodged in his beard. They remained there long after dinner. Other guests at our table included Chris (Viscount Monkton) and a lovely couple named Ian and Barbara Pollard, whom I'd not met before. Sebastian did rather well for himself by bagging Miss Great Britain, a little Northern Irish girl. He arranged to take her out for dinner the following Tuesday. Lynne shrugged her shoulders and said, "He's a chip off the old block!" We drove back to London after having the most wonderful day. Lynne said she thoroughly enjoyed meeting my chums and they were all exactly what she expected – great fun and quite dotty.

A few days later I turned the television on to see a programme about

my two most recent pals, Ian and Barbara Pollard. They live in a magnificent Elizabethan mansion, Abbey House in Wiltshire, which has
extensive grounds and is open to the public. There was Ian, pruning
his roses and chatting to a group of little old ladies with their twin-sets
and pearls and he was stark bollock naked. Barbara was bending over
digging, wearing nothing but a pair of wellies! They are naturists. They
open their house to the public and you get those two thrown in for
nothing. What value! English eccentricity at its very best!

A week later I was meeting Lynne's friends, only this time it was in
Cornwall at one of their anniversaries. They were all delightful and
friendly, save for bombastic, boring, booming, Bob. That's the name I
privately gave him. He was a very large and overbearing unattractive
man with a Lancashire accent you could cut with a knife. The minute
we were introduced he attempted to assume a dominant demeanour
over me, which I'm sure he does with everyone. I can imagine many
people would be very intimidated by him, but it quickly became
apparent that he was out of his league and he wisely retreated from
my company. Lynne's closest friends, Cathy and Virginia, were both
great fun and corpulently well-upholstered. As Lynne stood between
the two of them chatting, they resembled a piece of prime ham in a
ciabatta sandwich. We all celebrated at Jamie Oliver's restaurant by
the beach and I seem to remember the bill for our little group came
to well over a thousand pounds. The food was good, but not that
good!

A couple of days later we drove back to Cheshire but not before
stopping off for luncheon, again with Neil and Christine. When we got
back home we found Pinky Puff in panic mode and feigning illness for
the following couple of days. While we were away he had foolishly
texted Lynne to tell her that he had been stopped by the police for
driving her Mercedes sports car at 104 miles per hour. She was
naturally furious. Inwardly it made my blood boil that she should
allow them carte blanche access to cars and money. I continually had
to bite my tongue as they were her darling boys and her court jesters.
I don't think I have ever met two more successful blatant freeloaders.

Saturday, June 28th 2008, I arrived at the Manor for 1p.m. It was
Lynne's little grandson Grey's 1st birthday party. I was greeted in the
kitchen by a charming and most hospitable young man by the name
of Darren Ferguson. He was chalk and cheese different to his father,
Sir Alex Ferguson. I find it impossible to understand a single word
that man has to say. On the rare occasion when I have been in his

company the only word I could ever decipher from his conversation is "foootbol". Kate Moss's nanny and her husband arrived with Kate's little five-year-old daughter, Lila Grace, as Kate had a photo engagement that day. Lila is a stunningly pretty child, a cloned miniature of her world famous super-model mother. Talking to this child is like talking to an adult one minute and a child the next, and minutes after our initial acquaintance she insisted that she and I should play hide and seek, with her doing all the hiding. There was a large gathering of family and friends and the guest of honour was undoubtedly Lynne's mother. She was a matriarchal and no- nonsense sort of lady with just the slightest hint of a Liverpool accent. Grey, the birthday boy, enjoyed all the attention and I captured the entire day in photographs for his future approval. Perky Puff entertained us with his wonderful singing voice, which for me is his only redeeming quality. After a thoroughly enjoyable day Lynne was flagging, and by late evening I escorted her up to bed for her to have an early night. I was later informed in no uncertain terms by Perky Puff that it was his job to escort Lynne, and not mine! I was beginning to get to the end of my tether with Pinky and Perky by this time.

In early July, Lynne and I were planning to return to the Palace in Spain. Davinia telephoned from London to ask Lynne if she and Kate Moss could come and join us for a few days. "Absolutely not!" said Lynne. "James and I are going there for some peace and quiet, just the two of us." When the girls are there, sunbathing by the pool and out of sight of the prying eyes of the press, Davinia and Kate are prone to wearing nothing but the tiniest thongs to achieve that all-over tan. Heaven forbid that I should end up lying by the swimming pool with Kate Moss and Davinia Taylor lying next to me and them wearing little more than the suits they were born in!

July 15th 2008, and Lynne and I arrived at the airport at Marbella. Warwick was already parked at the front entrance with the rear car door open, awaiting our arrival. It is remarkable how quickly one adapts and accepts a VIP lifestyle as the norm. It must be terribly difficult for the likes of politicians and movie stars who reach the stratospheric heights of wealth and celebrity and then end up having to get the bus like the rest of us when it all goes horribly wrong. I have a more chameleon approach to life; enjoy it while it's there, "Que sera, sera!" After all, an undulation of one's fortune can make life more interesting and challenging. On second thoughts, no, I was happier when I was rich!

July 24th. This last couple of days Lynne had been feeling decidedly unwell and the doctor confined her to her bed. Despite her earlier protests that we were to be left alone in Spain, Davinia flew in with baby Grey and the nanny. All that was required to alleviate Lynne's symptoms were two of Grey's chuckles and all of her illness seemed to disappear, which was lovely.

The following day by about luncheon time, David, Davinia's husband, arrived accompanied by a vivacious "rock chick" by the name of Francesca, who I believe is in some way related to Ronnie Wood of the Rolling Stones, and the movie star Rhys Ifans. The most notable of Rhys's films which comes to mind is *Notting Hill* with Julia Roberts and Hugh Grant. He played the part of Hugh Grant's unsavoury Welsh flat-mate, Spike. I greeted Rhys in Welsh which made an instant hit and from then on we were chums. He is equally funny off the big screen as he is on it. The rest of the afternoon was spent sunbathing, cooing over Grey, whom Rhys always referred to as "The Baby Jesus", and being thoroughly entertained by Rhys and his anecdotes.

Evening time, and Davinia, David, Fran and Rhys went off to meet up with Liam Gallagher whom they bumped into at Malaga Airport. He was staying at the Marbella Club Hotel. Davinia suggested I should join them but there was no way I would leave Lynne – let's be honest, my constitution has far expired its capability of a night of partying with the likes of Rhys Ifans and Liam Gallagher. They all arrived home at 3.30a.m. but none of them could remember exactly how. They did vaguely remember being chased down the road by the Marbella Club Hotel manager as they all drove homeward-bound in one of the hotel golf carts.

July 26th. I arose early as usual to find Rhys wandering the grounds. He doesn't sleep but cat-naps, regardless of his alcohol intake. I greeted him with, "Behold, Laza-Rhys has arisen!" As expected the morning was a subdued affair with the four of them nursing their heads, and in the afternoon Rhys and I sat quietly by the beach talking films and books and putting the world to rights. Lynne continued to put a brave face on things but her illness had not eased. That evening, with their batteries recharged, the gang of four planned a quiet meal together in Puerto Banus.

July 27th. They all surfaced in time for luncheon and were keen to tell us of their quiet night out in Puerto Banus. They'd mistakenly wandered into a Gentleman's Club and it was only when they noticed the hookers and the pole dancing starting that they realised where they were. As none of them are shy or retiring sorts, before long Rhys had swapped clothes with one of the hookers and proceeded to give his version of pole dancing. The mind boggles at the mental vision of it. Customers filed up to him to say how much they enjoyed his films, but he informed them that things were a bit slack at the moment on the film scene and so he'd got this job as a transvestite pole dancer! Some weren't quite sure whether to believe him or not. Before long the management became keen to get rid of them and offered them transport home. An enormous stretched Hummer limousine arrived and as they got in a couple of Russian girls of dubious employment insisted on a lift. As the journey progressed the Russians demanded that they wanted "pee pee" but the driver refused to stop. Rhys, forever the Welsh gentleman, handed them a Champagne bucket and when the bucket was full they were ordered to throw the contents out of the window. It was at that very moment, while speeding along the Marbella Coast Road, that an unfortunate man on a moped along side of them got the contents full in the face. All in all it was a quiet night out for our gang of four. "How did your night go?" enquired Rhys.

David and Rhys were driven to the airport to return to London, leaving the girls and "baby Jesus" to remain for another few days. I had also planned to return to Calpe only this time I thought I'd drive rather than fly. Lynne had recovered from her illness and had the joy of her family around her.

July 30th. I hired a car, said my sad goodbyes and left Marbella in the morning. At a leisurely pace I drove the length of southern Spain and arrived home at around 6p.m. It had been two months since I last set foot in the house and as I opened the door the ghost of Lynda permeated the place. Many of her belongings were still scattered around. Her wardrobe still contained her clothes and her bathroom toiletries remained untouched. As I opened the kitchen door, there was the vision of her and me dancing over by the cooker, as we did on so many mornings. We attempted to master "Le Rock", which is a French version of jive, or to simply dance in each other's arms to "Il Divo". It was all so vivid. Suddenly, I found myself being plunged into an emotional darkness. I missed that tenderness, that passion, that romance. The fridge was bare and I was tired and couldn't be bothered to make my way into town to dine. I settled for a very large Bombay Sapphire and tonic and an old tin of tuna which I found in the bottom of the cupboard.

The following Sunday I arrived early at El Cisne Market, but somehow it had lost its charm and I wandered over the road to the Antiques Bar. You may recall how much Lynda and I used to enjoy it there, sitting under the palm trees in the heat of the day, listening to live music, sometimes classical, sometimes Sinatra. Today, it was a 50-year-old transvestite, dressed as Shirley Bassey and miming to her songs while holding a large realistic phallus as a microphone. At the end of this nonsensical performance he expected a rapturous applause as if he had achieved something. Another part of his act was when he had a costume change and returned with his dress up and the phallus placed between his legs. This was undoubtedly his greatest theatrical achievement as it got the loudest audience response. It is well documented that I am no prude, but it was patently obvious that the proletariat had moved in, so it was time for me to move out.

Thankfully, they got rid of him shortly afterwards and they returned to their original formula as the attendances had dropped like a stone.

In August, I was back at the Manor with Lynne but all was not well. Davinia's inability to deal with life, her periodic breakdowns and alcohol dependency had become more acute recently. Naturally, as a mother, it was becoming an all-consuming responsibility for Lynne, and I started to see that there was little room in her life for a man and the pursuit of a normal loving relationship. Lynne flew Pinky and Perky out to the Palace in Spain for a few days at this time. "The poor boys are exhausted and need a little break!" she said. I had to agree with her. Being a twenty-four-hour, seven-days-a-week freeloader can be a thoroughly exhausting business!

Lynne's birthday was approaching in mid-September and what do you buy for one of the richest women in the country who already owns everything in triplicate? Enter my dear ex-girlfriend and now chum, Sue, to the rescue! She had a large collection of perfect condition, early original cinema posters. I settled for the 1951 original French poster of *American in Paris*, starring Gene Kelly and Leslie Caron.

I found out that Leslie Caron, now 80 years old, ran a restaurant/hotel called Auberge La Lucarne aux Chouettes (The Owl's Nest) seventy miles south of Paris. My birthday plan was for us to fly out there to meet her, stay in her hotel and get her to sign her original poster! Later events prevented this from happening.

The same day, September 16th, Davinia and David decided to go to

Los Angeles and stay with David and Victoria Beckham; Lynne and I were thrilled. We thought it would be good for Davinia to get away and spend a little time there in a totally sane family environment. David and Victoria are very clean-living people: they don't drink, smoke or take drugs. Kate and Rhys are not the influence you need if you are trying to get your act together. The following night at around 3a.m. we received a frantic call from David: Davinia had suffered a major breakdown at David and Victoria's. It is desperately sad. People have little sympathy for any kind of mental disorder, in particular those caused by depression or addiction. If you have a broken leg everybody sympathises, but there is a tendency to steer clear when a person has unpredictable behaviour. In panic mode, David telephoned friends around the world to seek counsel. He had been advised to fly her to a clinic in Arizona. Lynne was deeply upset and wavering with indecision at this point. I insisted that too many opinions only confuse and cloud sound judgement – stick to plan A. Get her back home as fast as possible where Lynne could be in full control of the situation; she eventually agreed.

September 19th. I arose early at the Manor House and brought Lynne tea in bed. Davinia and David were due to arrive at 11a.m. but I could see the panic in Lynne's eyes that I might still be there when they arrived. In Davinia's present predicament she could only cope with the company of her mother and husband, and I understood that, though naturally I couldn't help feeling a little pushed out. Even Pinky and Perky kept their heads down, although I was sure that it wouldn't be too long before they came mincing in with their two-pence worth of advice. Before their arrival, Lynne and I discussed our own situation, and she said that if I'd had enough and wanted to move on, she would understand. I put that remark down to the trauma of the moment, but in my heart I could see the writing on the wall. I thought, by the time Davinia fully recovers, if ever, I will long have faded from memory; my name would be written in the running waters of a babbling brook. Few people want to grow old alone without a partner to share their life with, but Lynne had more than enough to occupy herself with at that time, and a man didn't really fit into the equation. A couple of days later I decided to fly back home to Spain with my tail between my legs. Messages from Lynne no longer contained "my darling" and there was now a formality to them; the flame was flickering. We would just have to settle for being good friends.

September 24th. How exciting! A train crashed into Calpe railway station. The driver had approached the station far too fast and mounted the platform. Thankfully, nobody was hurt. That should look good on his curriculum vitae!

Later in the evening, I was invited to a Biker's Café by my chum, Mal Lewis. Mal is a local celebrity with a terrific gravelly singing voice, similar to Morrissey. I believe he played with his fellow Brummie, Ozzy Osbourne, in their younger days. The place was heaving with rockers, some as old as myself. Most of them were covered in tattoos, and some with both noserings and earrings. There was much screeching and screaming with both guitar and voice. Outside, rows of Harley Davidsons waited patiently for the return of their masters and I noticed that some had Nazi helmets hanging from the handle-bars. Many a person would be thoroughly intimidated by such tribalism, but I found this grizzly bunch to be extremely courteous, charming, well-mannered and kind. A thoroughly enjoyable evening was had by all, not least by me.

October 7th. Gerald phoned. The *QE2* was going on her very last cruise around the Mediterranean before being taken into dry-dock in Dubai. She was then going to be turned into a hotel just as the *Queen Mary* is in Los Angeles. If she has to be decommissioned, take her out into the Atlantic and scuttle her where she may rest in peace with her sisters, I say. "Why don't we go on it, and I'm paying," Gerald said. Who would turn down an offer like that? Lynne and I had parted company and I had no pressing engagements, why not?

October 11th. I received a text message from Lynda, saying she was flying over to Spain and could she collect some of her things from the villa. In truth, I admit, I craved her company, her passion, her womanly body. It was her womanly brain I had the problem with.

October 16th. I received a call from Sebastian saying he was down on the Thames riverbank alone at 4a.m. taking photographs of Parliament in full moonlight. He got some great shots. I worry myself sick when he tells me these things.

October 18th. I picked Lynda up from her house in Finestrat. It was so lovely to see her again, it felt so comfortable and we talked and talked as if we had never been apart. It was a glorious day and although I managed to convince her to stay at the villa, she slept in the master room and I was confined to the French room; damn! She continued to stay for the next few days and finally on October 21st as we retired to our respective bedrooms, five minutes later she succumbed and joined me in the French room. Amore, Amore. Amore, I just loved sleeping with that woman!

The following day we were both returning to England, albeit to different airports.

October 26th and Gerald and I drove down to stay the night in the New Forest in preparation for our early boarding of the ship the following morning at Southampton.

October 27th. The journey from the hotel was brief, the sun shone and I am pleased to say that Gerald announced that he was in "holiday mode". We were the first to board with priority boarding and after we had settled into our berth, or staterooms as they are called on the *QE2*, we made our way up onto the upper outer decks. Daylight was slipping away on this cold, crisp, cloudless evening. England was in no doubt that the queen of ships was on her way, her last journey before being dry-docked in an alien Arab land. The engines stirred and the foghorn blasted thrice. Over the loudspeaker in great volume, Elgar was played – it was as if we were at the last night of the Proms – followed by "Land of Hope and Glory", "The Hornpipe", Sir Charles Hubert Parry's "Jerusalem" and finally, all six of the verses of "God save the Queen". Gerald and I scowled at two people who dared to move before its conclusion. One couldn't help being moved by the occasion and we felt honoured to share another tiny punctuation mark in England's history.

The following day we were at sea, but on the Wednesday, October 29th we arose early to find that we had already docked in Lisbon, Portugal. There had been some turbulence at around 4a.m. when things went bump in the night in the Bay of Biscay but nothing too disturbing. We were taken ashore and Gerald and I decided to take a boat trip around the city, stroll down the Praca do Comercio to take luncheon at a pavement restaurant, and wander the city sights. It was a short but invigorating visit to Portugal's beautiful capital. We were back on board just in time to dress for dinner. The food was a gastronomic delight and an attack by calorie tailors is inevitable. They are those dreadful little creatures who live in your wardrobe and continually reduce the waistband of your trousers. As requested, Gerald and I were given a table on our own in the best spot by the window. We didn't really want to be on a group table of ten and be saddled for the entire trip with people we couldn't stand. There is constant entertainment on board ship to suit all tastes, from classical singers and harpists to comedians, dancers and Beatles impersonators. Karl, the young chap who impersonated Paul McCartney, became great pals with Gerald and me. It was through him that I was later to be introduced to his mother, June Lornie, who is director of the Liverpool Academy of Arts. Eventually, she was to invite me to be a Trustee of the Academy.

Thursday, October 30th. Having been lulled to sleep by contentment and easy living, I awoke refreshed and a hearty breakfast beckoned. Today was going to be a sunbathing sort of day, and my first mission was to capture a sun-lounger. I needn't have worried, there were no Germans on this vessel. The English on board were so utterly polite and genteel that one could thrust and parry in debate for ages as to why the other person should most definitely have the sun-lounger. Opposite me, two homosexual men, impeccably dressed and both wearing crewneck sweaters, white shirts with cravats and identical Panama hats, attended to their petite-point needlework contained within little wooden frames. By 5p.m. Gerald and I were busy getting changed into black ties. As we had now entered the Mediterranean I had exchanged my black dinner jacket for my white one. Black jackets are more appropriate for more northerly climes I always think. 5.45p.m. We were greeted by the Captain in order to attend his cocktail party. He was a small man, lacking in charisma, and it was obvious he felt ill-at-ease with people; no ambassadorial skills. I believe he was the *QE2*'s youngest captain.

October 31st. We arrived in Sardinia to a dull and overcast day. Two tug-boats gently manoeuvred us into the harbour of Cagliari and again Gerald and I went off on our own. I'm not one for organised tourist group trails, never was. Instead we chummed up with a charming American couple and took luncheon on the Via Baylle. In torrential rain we reluctantly trudged the streets. Gerald laboured his way with me up to the Bastione St. Remy. We were totally inappropriately dressed in cream linen suits and panamas, but we sauntered on regardless, as if oblivious of the monsoon downpour.

Although I was anxious to visit the Cathedral and the Viceregio Palace, the elements got the better of us and we were forced to return on board, just in time for afternoon tea.

Tea, cucumber sandwiches and cakes were served in the Queen's Room, where the waiters wore white gloves, short white jackets with gilded epaulets and braid. This is where the civility of 1930s England comes into play, and I fear that this glorious Empire tradition going back to the Raj may possibly die with this ship.

November 1st and we slipped silently into Naples at 6a.m. The weather had made no improvement. The Queen moored directly below the foreboding Castle of Naples. The last time I was there, some 40 years earlier, some people were still living in the bombed buildings of the Second World War. They have replaced those buildings with ones with no architectural merit and generally I find Naples to be shabby and industrial. It has one saving grace as far as I'm concerned ... the women! I saw at least a dozen Catherine Zeta-Jones look-a-likes along one stretch of colonnaded trattorias, and that was in the pouring rain when they shouldn't be looking their best. The inclement weather forced us to return to the ship and our own little world of Bertie Wooster.

Sunday, November 2nd. At last, dawn greeted us with the warmth of a refulgent sunlight over Sicily. Most passengers had booked a bus tour of the island. Gerald and I, being forever mavericks, hired a local taxi driver for the day. The first stop, some 45 minutes' drive away, was the splendid mountain town of Taormina with its magnificent Greek theatre, later modified by the Romans. The town is charming and unspoilt since the eighteenth century, save for ghastly tourists such as ourselves.

The local tipple there is a delicious almond wine, and I would wager anyone it is impossible not to order a second glass. Our driver showed us the sights of Sicily and eventually returned us to Messina, leaving us in the magnificent square in front of the Cathedral. This astonishing building, festooned in gilded statuary and built to the glory of God is breathtaking in its beauty. Even the most cold-hearted pagan couldn't fail to be inspired.

Before long, we were on our way again. It is remarkable that even though the ship has thousands of passengers and crew, there are occasions when on the upper outer decks it is possible to find yourself totally alone. On that same evening Gerald and I decided to take some fresh air on the upper bow deck. Below us, at the very sharpest end of the ship and out of bounds to the passengers, was a pretty young girl, a member of the entertainment crew. Believing she was completely alone, she performed a truly wonderful ten minute solo ballet. She then paused for a couple of minutes, scanning around to see that no one was looking. I could see exactly what was going through her mind. If she didn't do it now, she would never get the opportunity again for the rest of her life! We watched her as she climbed up onto the railing by the forward flag and for several minutes 'flew' as Kate Winslet did in the film *Titanic*. She'll be able to tell her grandchildren about it one day!

The air was too cold for Gerald and I was given a few solitary moments. For the strangest of reasons a veil of sadness came over me and I couldn't understand why, until I suddenly realised that we were sailing directly past Bari Harbour at the heel of Italy, the exact place my mother's brother, James, the man I was named after, was killed in December of 1943. No member of the family had ever been here up until this moment. I retired to the library to write letters on *QE2* writing paper. They would be among the last to be sent from this wonderful queen of ships.

Monday, November 3rd. George Bernard Shaw once said that if you wanted to find paradise on earth you need look no further than Dubrovnik, and I have to agree, it is very special. No longer Yugoslavia but Croatia, this magnificent fortified city with its wealth of culture has almost fully recovered from its recent civil war. There are still bullet holes in some of the buildings but much of its Roman and medieval architecture has been preserved and restored to perfection. It was not possible to dock the *QE2* in the shallow harbour waters, and so we anchored offshore and journeyed to the city via a small tender. After walking the city ramparts, visiting the Maritime Museum and wandering the streets and churches, we took luncheon at a restaurant at the steps of the city's glorious baroque Cathedral. Many passengers were expecting a grand send-off with pipe bands and fireworks when we left Dubrovnik for the very last time that evening. Instead we silently slipped our moorings and skulked off. Some passengers were heard to comment that it exemplified exactly what had happened to "Britain" now that the "Great" had been removed during the course of their lifetime.

November 4th. We had now entered the Greek Islands and were moored off the island of Zakynthos. Mentioned in the Iliad and Odyssey by Homer, it spent much of its time under Venetian protection against Ottoman domination until it eventually became another piece of our Great British Empire, after we took it in 1809. In an act of sheer philanthropy we gave it back to the Greeks in 1864: whoever said that we didn't have a heart!

Each evening there was a continuum of entertainment and that evening there was a young woman who sang with a voice equal to that of Céline Dion. Rather unnervingly she chose as her finale the theme tune to *Titanic*.

Gerald retired to bed early, as the following day he was going on a bus tour without me. I, on the other hand, intended to fulfil a dream of my own by climbing up to the Parthenon.

Wednesday, November 5th. It was a long-awaited day for me. Ever since I first saw a picture of the Caryatids in my Greek history book at boarding school I had longed to see them, and today was the day, more than 50 years later. Early morning, and we were moored in the densely busy Port of Piraeus in Athens. There is an unpleasant pollutant haze which hangs over this city, similar to Los Angeles. The city fathers were wise enough to prevent high-rise buildings which might detract from the importance and majesty of the Parthenon, but I doubt if the founders of Athens who created western civilisation before Christ would be proud of it today. Most of it is a huge sprawling mish-mash of low-rise characterless box apartments of 1960s style. Having said that, just to walk on the same ground as Plato, Aristotle and Pythagoras is privilege enough for me!

As I stood on the very spot just below the Parthenon where democracy began, an American lady standing next to me received a call on her mobile phone. Obama had just been voted in as the first mixed race President of the United States of America.

The founders of this ancient city who were first to give their people a right to vote by placing a white stone in a jar for "Yes" and a black stone for "No" must have been smiling with contentment at that very moment. I left this land of Spartans and boyhood dreams and arrived back on board just in time for tea and cucumber sandwiches. A wonderful day!

Thursday, November 6th. We left Athens and had two days with no ports of call until we reached Gibraltar. Gerald and I received a notice in our stateroom that at 10.30a.m. we were to meet with the ship's Commodore in order to be presented with the QE2 Medal. I couldn't for the life of me think why I should deserve such an honour, unless it was a Gastronomic Overindulgence Medal. I could visibly see that there would be more of me leaving this ship than when I got on it.

The ship's Commodore was suitably bearded and seafaring in his appearance but it was patently obvious that pinning medals on people's chests was a chore to him. Not however, his gushing over-friendly Chinese/American wife, Kim, who revelled in her part of the ceremony as First Lady. This was the first overcast day since we had arrrived in Sardinia and there was a general feeling of boredom on board, although there was certainly no shortage of things with which to occupy people. Eating and drinking plays a major part of life on board ship.

November 7th. The weather had improved little, but one remained hopeful. I was joined at my breakfast table by the Commodore and our Beatles chums. Today was a big day for Gerald as he had his book signing. It had been announced in the ship's daily newspaper and a large poster had been placed outside the library. The book, which is really a booklet, is about the life of Sir Richard Sutton and Lynford Hall. A table and chairs were placed in the corridor and his booklets were neatly stacked awaiting the arrival of the author. I took photographs of eager customers standing around Gerald awaiting his signature and any pearls of wisdom which might drop from his lips.

November 8th. We arose to find that we had already docked in Gibraltar. I suddenly found that my mobile phone was working again and picked up messages from Christine Hamilton, Sebastian and Lynda who couldn't get through while we were at sea. This was very much a flying stop and we were instructed to return to the ship by 1.30p.m. We jumped in a taxi to Main Street where Gerald wanted to get estate agents' details of property for sale. He had a mind to move there. We took luncheon in Macintosh Square and to our delight the Band of the Royal Marines, resplendent in their red tunics and helmets, were playing there. I strolled over to chat to the Commanding Officer to ask if they were going to play at our sail-away; alas, no. The HMS *Ark Royal* was in port and they were going to be busy playing for the tourists visiting the aircraft carrier. Most passengers were bitterly disappointed by the fact that we hadn't had a send-off from any of the ports we called at. These ports will never see the most famous ship in the world again, and over the past forty years this iconic vessel has brought a considerable amount of much-welcomed cash with her every time she has docked.

Sunday, November 9th. The Red Ensign fluttered aft against a backcloth of a dark and foreboding sky. It was Remembrance Sunday on board the *QE2*. After a brief service of prayer by the Captain in the theatre, we all moved to the three tier decks at the stern. I stood in the centre of the upper deck, directly in line with the ensign and the Captain. Beside me, and immediately to my left, stood the bugler. It was a deeply moving occasion, and many of us wiped our moistened eyes as the Last Post resounded out. The Captain and crew remained in salute as the Red Ensign was slowly lowered. All our thoughts and prayers mingled in the boiling froth of the wake left behind us. Ever mindful of those who surrendered their lives, we stood there in liberty because of them.

By the afternoon we had arrived in Vigo, in northern Spain. I think because of the brevity of our visit it was to do little more than refuel. We slipped our moorings early evening and my gratitude goes out to the Spanish people there. They lined the docks in their hundreds to see the ship and to wave us all goodbye! They were the only ones to do so on the entire voyage.

Dinner that evening was festive. The dining room was decked with multi-national flags and there followed what is known as "The Baked Alaska Parade". This is in honour of the United States union adding Alaska as an additional state. The lights were lowered and the Maitre d' and his staff, including all the chefs, cooks and waiters paraded through carrying burning Roman Candles. It was a wonderful event although I couldn't quite see the full significance, save for humouring the American passengers.

November 10th. It was a rough ride the previous night and the ship's metal moaned and groaned as she fought her way through the Bay of Biscay and homeward bound. It was Gerald's birthday and I had arranged a couple of surprises with the crew. As we dined, the entire staff surrounded our table. Tara, our waitress, brought out the most beautiful birthday cake and the crew and passengers sang Happy Birthday. We moved on to be entertained by a Liverpool comedian called John, who included several jokes about Gerald in his act. By 10.30p.m. "The Beatles Experience" were entertaining everyone at the farewell party and they included songs for Gerald. Even the Captain gave him a card. Gerald enjoyed his on-board celebrity as everyone stopped to congratulate him on his book and his birthday.

November 11th. I was wide awake at 5.30a.m. and decided to take some air on the quarter deck at the stern. It was still pitch dark and there was only one other passenger there besides myself. Everyone else was still sound asleep. As I leaned on the rail, I noticed that we were extremely low in the water and we were going nowhere! I could see the lights of two tug boats approaching. I turned to my fellow passenger and said, "Oh my God, I think we've run aground!" and the two of us just burst out laughing. This old queen was making her final defiant gesture; she wasn't going to sit the rest of her life in a dusty, desert dry-dock. The two tugs had to be joined by a further three. I sent a text message to Sebastian saying he was probably the first civilian onshore to learn that the *QE2* had just run aground! I went to wake Gerald and turn on the television. My fellow passenger had just phoned the BBC and it came on television that a passenger on the *QE2* was reporting that she had grounded herself on the straits between the Isle of Wight and the mainland. After more than an hour of pushing and shoving, with an almighty shudder the old girl reluctantly freed herself.

By 10a.m. we were disembarking the ship and as we were about to collect our luggage we were informed that the two-minute silence was about to begin. As the hour struck, a First World War biplane flew over us and a million poppies rained down. Minutes later, we were deafened by the sound of a Harrier jet. She thundered down from the skies and hovered perfectly still just a few yards from the side of the ship. She then tipped her nose in a farewell salute and roared almost vertically back up into the sky. It was a most fitting closer to a wonderful journey.

I escorted Gerald back to the Isle of Man and a week or so later Lynda and I were back at the villa in Spain.

2009

My bus pass arrives • Norman Rossington • Strange days in Cyprus

January 29th 2009 was Sebastian's 24th birthday and for the first time we decided to incorporate his photographic exhibition with his party. It was a great success: all sorts of people turned up including the McCartneys, Clive Christian, actors from *Coronation Street* including Michael LeVell and Nigel Pivaro and our super-model relative, Alex Leigh. It was a wonderful evening. As I later viewed the photgraphs taken of us on the evening, I was horror-struck. An old man with an Orson Wellesian physique stared back at me! I couldn't believe it was really me. Lynda and I were now back in a full-time relationship and spent much of it yoyoing back and forth to Spain. In March I flew alone to California to attend my mother's birthday but spent most of my time there in excruciating agony, having pulled my back out. The walking stick I originally bought for my mother came in jolly handy.

May 13th. It may have been May, but this was the first day of the

autumn of my life, or was it the winter? 60 years old! The grand celebration I had envisaged years ago didn't happen. Lynda arrived at
luncheon and that cheered me up, and in the post my OAP conces-
sionary bus pass arrived. In the evening, Lynda, Sebastian and I drove
in the Rolls to a restaurant in Hale for a quiet celebration. I was greatly
surprised and delighted when a crowd was already there waiting for
us.

In June, Lynda and I were busy looking at investment properties
and we bought a three-bedroom house to rent out. I thought that if
we acquired maybe half a dozen houses together, it would give us a
common joint interest and help bond our relationship long term. Not
long afterwards Lynda would embark upon an agenda of her own
which sadly would ultimately lead to the end of our relationship. She
had moved into a luxury apartment on Duke Street, Liverpool, which
had been given to her by her father.

My own new life of sun and sangria had become more settled and
although I had planned to do a lot more painting and sculpture, there
was little time for it. The villa required considerable changes to the
grounds and house and most of my time there was preoccupied with
manual labour. Nonetheless there were a number of chums in Calpe
who owned yachts down at the Royal Yacht Club Nautica and I was at
liberty to go sailing with them any time. I have to add that I am not
the greatest sailor. Being a Taurean, and one who is also born in the
Chinese year of the Bull, makes me a creature who likes to keep his
feet firmly on terra firma. I have thoroughly enjoyed my days sailing
with my friends, Craig and Wendy, on their yacht and also my chum,
Eugenio, on his. However, I have always adhered to the fact that it is
better to be a boat owner's friend rather than a boat owner. While I
have this thought in mind, I shall write a poem to suit:

> Beware, the raging Neptune's swell,
> Beware, the reaper's mournful bell,
>
> Take heed, the crystal prism's light,
> Take heed, the guiding starry night,
>
> Fear well, where mate 'n' bosun sleep,
> Fear well, tooth and scale of fathoms deep,
>
> Be not wooed, the Siren's murmur,
> A Taurean's place is terra firma.

I spent little time frequenting places down in the main tourist beach area, but preferred to chew the cud with characters and chums up in the old town. As in Santa Barbara, California, I have places I go to where I can walk in and people will say "Where've you been?" In Calpe, the haunts worth going to in the old town, where you will always be made welcome, are, Barbara and Thomas's at "La Llar de Barbara" and Ervin's Bar. If it's quality cuisine you are looking for, then you can't do better than visiting my friend, Eugenio, who owns Le Petit Café de Paris. His Chateaubriand is as good as any I have eaten in the finest restaurants around the world, and his sauce is to die for. Tell him James sent you!

One of the problems with getting old is that funerals become a more frequent part of your social calendar. I wouldn't dream of boring the reader by listing off the amount of them I've attended over the past two years, but it is a lot. In addition to that depressing thought, the passage of time rapidly gathers momentum the minute you get the bus pass. I was rummaging in some drawers this morning, only to find a memorial card dated 1999 for my dear old chum, Norman Rossington. If questioned, I would have said he died four years ago, not ten.

Norman was an actor who was never out of work from when he first started his career in 1957 until just before he died. He could never play the swashbuckling hero parts because he was far too small for that. I remember when I was very young, I first saw Norman play Private Cupcake in *The Army Game* on our black and white television. He was in the very first "Carry on" film, *Carry on Sergeant* and he appeared alongside many of the biggest names in Hollywood. To name but a few, Rock Hudson and George Peppard in *Tobruk*, Peter O'Toole in *Lawrence of Arabia* and the list goes on. Norman was the only actor in the world to appear in films with both Elvis Presley (*Double Trouble*) and The Beatles (*Hard Day's Night*).

When we lived at the Hall he was a regular visitor and he would never refuse an invitation to a barbecue or a party. I always felt that he was a lonely man, and if on occasion he made an impromptu visit, knowing he lived alone, my housekeeper would never let him go without giving him something to take home for his evening meal. One day, completely out of the blue, Norman phoned me to tell me he was getting married. I was both shocked and thrilled for him. In all the years we had been friends, I had never known him to have a girl-friend. A week later, I telephoned Norman to ask him to come to dinner at the Hall, in order for us to meet his fiancée. He said, "James old chap, I don't think I'll be able to make it. I'm going into hospital soon, I'm dying!" I was devastated.

His long-standing friend, Cindy Barnes, had been good to him over many years. He married her on his deathbed. I think it was in order to thank her for all her kindness, and so that it would be easier for her to inherit his money. He just hated the thought of the government getting it.

I visited him every day during the last four weeks of his life in a hospice in Bowdon, Altrincham. A reporter asked him what his epitaph would be. Instantly, he replied, "Came here, thoroughly enjoyed it, gosh, didn't it go quick."

If ever we had a large dinner party and there was a lull in conversation, you could always rely on Norman. Usually we would insist that he recite "Albert and the Lion" which was written by Marriott Edgar and made famous by Stanley Holloway.

When Norman died, I remember thinking how sad that we would never hear him doing "Albert and the Lion" again. As a tribute to Norman, I made a concerted effort to learn it off by heart; all eighteen verses!

Norman's closest friend was Albert Finney; they met in London in the late 1950s. I first met Albert Finney with Norman when Albert was appearing in a play called *Reflected Glory* in Manchester. Over dinner one night, Albert told me that when he and Norman were doing drama in the early days, they were the only two northerners. Albert was a Salford boy but moved to Urmston, and Norman was from Liverpool. Theatre and film was dominated by terribly grand people like Ralph Richardson and Johnny Mills in those days. Previous to that, Albert worked in Massey Ferguson at Trafford Park with my Father, and was later to be joined there by Ian McShane, also an Urmston boy. Albert worked in the "goods inwards" department, but cut short his time there when he drove a stacker truck into the shelving containing millions of different sized nuts and bolts. The impact caused a "Mexican wave", spilling the entire contents all over the floor. I don't think he hung around to collect his wages that week. Albert always remained totally true to his roots: he refused a CBE and later a knighthood, believing that honours only perpetuated snobbery. Amusingly, whenever he met me, he would bow with a great sweeping theatrical gesture and declare in a loud voice ... "My Lord!", particularly when we were in a restaurant like Coco2, where there was an appreciative audience.

I couldn't help think that there was an irony with my father and his own father. Albert Finney and Ian McShane followed their dream, which my father could easily have done with his amazing musical talent. Equally, my grandfather could have gone to America with Charlie Chaplin and Stan Laurel when he had the chance, but he didn't. The precedent ends there, as I have no particular talent in any direction.

In November of 2009, Lynda and I were still very much an item and I continued to plan, and pay towards, our future together. At the beginning of this month, Gerald asked us to fly to Cyprus to celebrate his 83rd birthday there. Instead of Gibraltar, which was his original plan, he ended up being talked into investing ridiculous amounts of money in Cyprus. Gerald wanted to introduce us to the new love of his life, and all of his recently acquired friends.

I was delighted that our mutual chum, Susie Hodge and her husband, Paddy, were also flying out there. At least we knew that we were in for a few laughs. Although Susie and I had spoken several times on the phone, we'd not seen each other for years and it would be good to catch up on all the gossip. Susie played the part of Mimi la Bonque, the naughty little waitress in the television series *Allo Allo*, which for ten years was all filmed at Gerald's old estate, Lynford Hall, in Norfolk.

We were met at Paphos Airport by Gerald and his 40-year-old Filipino housekeeper/maid/nurse/carer and new love of his life. Ron, his 80-year-old chauffeur, also had a Filipino wife less than half his age. We were driven to a hotel to meet up with Susie and Paddy. There, we were introduced to a brotherhood of wealthy 80- and 90-year-old northern European men who were all married to 20- to 40-year-old Filipino women. It was like being in the Galactic Bar in a *Star Wars* movie. To see a 30-year-old woman kissing a 90-year-old man and saying things like, "I lub you daling, I lub you," left me not only shell-shocked but slightly nauseous at the absurdity of it. These old buggers, on the cliff edge of senility, believed every word these women said.

Lynda and I couldn't wait to return to England but we were forced to endure Cyprus for another four days. We tried to make the best of it by seeing the sights of antiquity and travelling around the island, but the flight home was the most enjoyable part. The following week we were back at the villa in Spain but I began to notice cracks appearing in the relationship. I couldn't quite put my finger on it, but I started to think she had lost interest. There were never arguments, no cannon fire: on the contrary our time together was filled with laughter and incessant conversation as usual. Perhaps we had inadvertently sailed too close to the Doldrums and the wind was leaving the sails. I was dolorously aware that she might have another agenda in mind.

Nonetheless, Christmas was approaching and Lynda and I were busy fighting our way through the crowds of shoppers in central Manchester. We happened to be in the HMV shop when I bumped into Jason Orange. I had known Jason from the very earliest days of his pop group's success. On this day he was incognito and heavily disguised and although the shop was packed, not one other person recognised him, even though a film of him was showing on a huge screen in the shop as we spoke. I introduced him to Lynda and he very kindly said to her, "James and I are old friends," which wasn't exactly true. Over the years, he and I have been little more than acquaintances, but it was very nice of him to say it. When we left the shop, Lynda said, "He's a handsome young man, what does he do?" I said, "Oh, he's in a pop group called Take That."

2010-12

Farewell, Aunt Betty • Sebastian and Lydia move on • A bizarre funeral • Closing thoughts

After cold winter with heavy snows over Christmas, in February we were to learn the sad news that my Aunt Betty was desperately ill, and there was little chance of recovery. Mother flew over from California immediately. Much of the time over the next two months was spent visiting my aunt with Mother. On April 15th my mother and her sister, Andolores, drove to the hospice to be with Betty in her final moments. Mother's eventual return journey had to be postponed due to Icelandic volcanic ash fallout over Britain and Europe.

The day before Betty's funeral on April 27th I bought myself a beautiful Jaguar XK8 sports car. I presently own a Range Rover, a Rolls-Royce, and now a Jaguar Sports, which amplifies my overwhelming sense of patriotism to buy British. When I think of it, I've had seven Range Rovers, a Morgan, two Morris Minors, a 1965 Jaguar 420, a 1938

Austin, and several others. No one could ever accuse me of not putting the British economy first! Although I have a passion for classic Big Boys' Toys, I am almost ignorant of their mechanics and how they actually work.

I was required to fly to the Isle of Man in May, not only to attend to my own financial affairs but also to offer assistance to Gerald. My long-suffering accountant on the island, Keith Kermeen, despairs at my cavalier approach to book-keeping. Although I spend time in America, Spain, England and God knows where else, I'm based in the Isle of Man. I actually love the place and I would spend a lot more of these retirement years there if the weather wasn't so bloody awful. When the sun shines, you would struggle to find a more picturesque place or a more friendly people. The island has many similarities to England in the 1950s with very little traffic on the roads and more courteous and civilised behaviour from the people, plus a much slower pace of life. While I was there, I received a text message from Lynda saying she needed space; now we all know what that means, don't we? When a woman says she needs space, get your hat and coat on, it's time to go! The text was followed by a telephone call of profuse apologies and upon my return to the mainland we jointly agreed on a period of sabbatical. She said she wasn't going to accompany me back to the villa this time. I was at Ervin's Bar in the old town as usual when Spain won the World Cup which all the ex-pat Brits were thrilled about.

The minute the final whistle was blown, fireworks erupted in every town in Spain and all the church bells rang out. It was amazing. The Spanish just love a party, and everyone gets kissed, no matter who you are. England hasn't seen that degree of celebration or let its hair down to that level since VE day!

It was at this time that I was thinking of selling my Rolls-Royce, and I left it at Cliffe Park Hall with my chum Brian Dalley. He said he would write an advert to sell it for me while I was away, but I didn't hold out much hope. Nobody wants a Rolls-Royce in these days of recession and "green" consciousness. I stopped at the traffic lights one day and a chap shouted at me, saying, "You're destroying the planet by driving that bloody thing!" I shouted back, "Tell that to the bus driver in front, and the lorry driver behind, you silly bugger!"

Three days later, I received a call from Brian saying a fellow had called him from Norway: he wanted the Rolls. How small the world is now that we have the internet! The damnedest thing is, I was really sad that the

Rolls wouldn't be waiting for me when I returned; I really loved that old girl.

In August, Sebastian had moved to London with his girlfriend, Lydia, and they rented a flat in Southgate, North London. It was a struggle for them as Sebastian was not getting sufficient income from his photography, and so in addition they got themselves a stall on Camden Market. Lydia's little car was continually playing up, and in a moment of madness I bought them a Land Rover Freelander in order for him to be able to carry his lights and photographic equipment. I spent considerable money on it to make sure it was in top running order and they were genuinely thrilled to receive it.

September 8th. I had an 8a.m. flight to Heathrow and a noon flight to Los Angeles. As I boarded the LA flight, Sebastian called to tell me he had got a job as a wine broker; the brokerage was owned by an old friend of ours. "Fantastic," said I. "It's in Singapore and I start next week, Dad," said he. I was dumbfounded. "How long for, son?" "Indefinitely," was his reply. The selfish side of me didn't want him to go: I would miss him terribly, but it would be an adventure for him and Lydia which mustn't be missed. If you don't do these things when you are young, then you never will. "Anyone want to buy a Land Rover Freelander?"

October 7th and I was back in England. My California trip had been mostly to see what I could do to be of assistance to Mother. Back in Sale, the following morning I walked into the town to have breakfast with my friend of forty years, Bob Greaves, the long-retired TV broadcaster from Granada Television, along with Mike Healing, his friend, and Peter Reece, a journalist. Bob told me that he had recently been diagnosed with stomach cancer and things weren't looking too good. Bob Greaves, until his last breath, would never be a wilting flower; he could be a prickly pear at times, but I can honestly say that in forty years he and I never had a cross word with each other. I enjoyed his wit, his intelligence, his anecdotes and his company. We finally laid him to rest on April 1st 2011, at a star-studded and much televised send-off.

Later on that day I drove to Liverpool to take Lynda out to dinner. She told me that she was in a relationship with someone else and had been since my last trip to Spain. Not the best of days I thought, but it didn't surprise me. However, my understanding of a sabbatical is that it is a time of contemplation and reflection, not a time for rushing off in a new direction with another man.

I did promise the reader that I wouldn't start to refer too much to funerals, but there is one funeral I went to recently which has got to be recorded for posterity.

I received a call from another former girlfriend, Carole Davies, for whom you may recall I wrote the "camp fire in a damp woodland" poem. She told me that my old adversary, Philip Jay, had died. In our early days of frequenting the Hale Wine Bar, Philip and I counted about nine women who were joint conquests of ours. Philip was the Robert Redford of the town at that time, and he was never seen without a flashy motor car or a selection of great-looking girls on his arm. I hadn't seen Philip for about six or seven years when Carole told me of his sad demise. He had lost all his money, sunk lower, and depended more on alcohol than food. As a consequence he ended up losing his teeth, walking with a stick, and living alone in a bedsit, with only a bottle of booze for company. Carole said he was to have a pauper's funeral which saddened me deeply. Only one of his many former women still cared enough to drop in on him to see if he was all right. He had been dead for a week when she found him.

Fearing that no one would be at his funeral Carole asked if I would escort her, which I was more than happy to do. We arrived at Altrincham Crematorium on a warm and sunny morning. To our pleasant surprise, there were about fifty to sixty people there, many of whom we both knew from the old days.

These funerals are like a conveyer belt, one in, one out, and as we all stood around outside, waiting for things to get under way and catching up with old friends, a car arrived. Out stepped a black woman and a white one. It became instantly apparent that the white woman was already drunk, despite the fact that it was only 10a.m. Carole held my arm tightly, saying that the drunk one was an alcoholic ex of Philip's who assisted in his rapid descent. Worryingly, she staggered in my direction and declared, "What are all these fucking people doing here?" then proceeded to burst into tears, shouting, "I loved that bastard!"

Carole and I were desperate to ensure we were going to get as far away from her as possible. In the chapel, we managed to get seated third row from the front on the right of the aisle. The drunk and her black friend were seated nine rows back on the left.

The girl that had found Philip's body had gone to a great deal of trouble and written a very moving eulogy all about Philip's life, which was beautifully read by the lady vicar. The reverend lady got to the point where she said, "... and Philip brought laughter into all of your lives!" From the ninth row came a very loud, slurred, inebriated voice ... "No he fucking didn't, he was a fucking bastard, he used to beat me up and he broke my arm!" The black woman tried to gag her with her hand, shouting, "Will you shut up!" She then thumped her in the face. An almighty cat-fight ensued in the pews with lots of hitting, scratching and pulling of hair. We had always believed that Philip had no living relatives, but two nieces both leapt to their feet, climbed over the pews and joined in, beating the hell out of the white woman! In the meantime the reverend lady nervously continued with the eulogy. Just then, three seats to my right, a man's mobile phone started ringing. I said in a loud voice, "Oh, that'll be Philip!"

The two nieces and the black woman managed to physically drag the drunk one kicking and screaming out of the church and into a taxi. From inside the chapel we heard her parting words, "I'm glad he's dead, the fucking bastard!"

Philip would have loved every minute of it. It was a comedy sketch-writer's dream. If you saw it on television you would never imagine it really happened, but it did! So that's the last funeral I'm going to tell you about!

I have been most fortunate in my life in that I have been able to enjoy the acquaintance of some of Britain's truly great contemporary artists. Stephen Broadbent, the sculptor who was apprentice to Arthur Dooley, Sir Peter Blake who needs no introduction, Alex Corina who painted the famous "Mona Lennon" picture of John Lennon as the Mona Lisa, and the list goes on and on. In my younger days my taste was strictly limited to the classical. At all English boarding schools, in my day, we were only ever exposed to Renaissance, Pre-Raphaelite and Impressionists; Turner being the father of impressionism, irrespective of what the French may say! An enormous copy of "The Fighting Temeraire" hung in our art class at school as a constant reminder of the fact. It wasn't until I was in my twenties that I started to understand and appreciate the joy of good modern art. My most recent acquaintance in the world of art is for me the most accomplished, innovative modern British artist of our time, Geoffrey Key. His works hang in the best galleries and private collections from Hong Kong to New York and although remarkably he still isn't a general household name, I assure you, he will be. Keen-eye collectors from around the world don't allow his paintings to linger in his studio. Since our first meeting he has most generously showered me with gifts of books of his amazing paintings. He has fired me up to get back to the villa as quickly as possible to my own brush and paints!

I suppose this is as good a time as any to finish my story. To the hundred or so women who have shared my bed along the way, and are delighted and relieved not to be included in this book, I say "Thank you", it was fun. To those who are furious that I didn't include them, sorry, but thanks anyway. Do I have any dreams and aspirations for the future? My immediate plans are to travel throughout the Far East with my son and possibly get involved in a new exciting business project out there; to visit Papua New Guinea and find the people who provided my school friend at Alton with that shrunken head; to fulfil a promise to my father and see the sun rise high in the Himalayas in the tiny mountain village where he first experienced it. Most of all, I shall never cease in my quest to find that most elusive of creatures, "the perfect woman".

I hope that I have many more adventures to experience before my journey's end, but if not, then I leave you with my final poem ...

Mourn not for me when I have passed,
No furrowed brow or moistened eye,
But jest and laughter will to last,
When thoughts of me are nigh.

For I have savoured every fruit
Loved, lost and loved again
A life enriched, a privileged pursuit
That petal's fragrance I retain

For I shall nourish every bloom,
Above my place of rest,
Then I shall dwell in many a room,
In flowers, God has blessed.

Sebastian leaving for Singapore.

Lightning Source UK Ltd.
Milton Keynes UK
UKOW031345020812

196964UK00002B/1/P